To _____

From _____

Joy for the
Journey

Joy for the Journey

morning and evening
devotions

Contents

January

Oh come, let us sing to the Lord!
Let us shout joyfully
to the Rock of our salvation.

PSALM 95:1

Morning

. . . .

Soak in the Moment

I want so desperately to freeze this moment. To drink in every sound, every sight, every delightful evidence of life. So many things to be thankful for. I've had thousands of these everyday life minutes, but tonight is different. I remembered to pause. To acknowledge what I've been blessed with. . . . I sat and soaked in the moment. And with every tear that spilled out, I felt more and more full.

Maybe this is the true secret to being fulfilled and content. Living in the moment with God, defined by His truth, and with no unrealistic expectations for others or things to fill me up. Not reaching back for what was lost in my yesterdays. And not reaching for what I hope will be in my tomorrow. But living fully with what is right in front of me. And truly seeing the gift of this moment.

LYSA TERKEURST

Becoming More Than a Good Bible Study Girl

Evening

• • • • • • • • • •

I will greatly rejoice in the LORD,
My soul shall be joyful in my God;
For He has clothed me with the garments of salvation,
He has covered me with the robe of righteousness.

ISAIAH 61:10

"I have come that they may have life, and that they
may have it more abundantly. I am the good shepherd.
The good shepherd gives His life for the sheep."

JOHN 10:10—11

Every good gift and every perfect gift is from above.

JAMES 1:17

Live Fully Alive!

Laugh whenever you can. . . .

Find a cause bigger than yourself.

Pray for the impossible.

Dust off that Schwinn.

Get to know someone with a piercing.

Spread the good news of God's love with boldness. . . .

Nap, but not while driving.

Stay curious.

Take a college course.

Learn something new.

Live. . . .

The glory of God is man fully alive: striving in the midst of all odds. Never satisfied with the status quo. Seeking excellence in every area of life. Because Jesus can raise the dead and because He Himself was raised from the dead, then no matter what my situation, I can know the power of His resurrection to live my life fully alive.

KEN DAVIS

Fully Alive

Blessed be the God and Father of our Lord Jesus
Christ, who according to His abundant mercy
has begotten us again to a living hope through
the resurrection of Jesus Christ from the dead.

1 PETER 1:3

I can do all things through Christ
who strengthens me.

PHILIPPIANS 4:13

A wise man will hear and increase learning,
And a man of understanding
will attain wise counsel.

PROVERBS 1:5

JANUARY 3

Childlike Joy

Don't you love being around children who are wiggling, squirming, jumping up and down, and shouting for you? I do! I believe God does too.

In fact, I believe God wants us to exhibit that same childlike joy as we worship and enjoy Him. I'm not talking about "feel-good" emotionalism that fluctuates with circumstances. I'm talking about deep-down joy that bubbles up out of a grateful heart that knows and loves Jesus. That is the kind of heart that is instructed to rejoice in the Lord.

Happiness depends on *something*. Joy depends on *Someone*.

SARA TROLLINGER
Women of Faith Devotional Bible

Evening

· · · · · · · ·

Be glad in the LORD and rejoice, you righteous;
And shout for joy, all you upright in heart!

PSALM 32:11

Rejoice always.

1 THESSALONIANS 5:16

I will greatly rejoice in the LORD,
My soul shall be joyful in my God;
For He has clothed me with the garments of salvation,
He has covered me with the robe of righteousness.

ISAIAH 61:10

This is the day the LORD has made;
We will rejoice and be glad in it.

PSALM 118:24

A Journey of Prayer and Praise

It's been said that faith may move mountains, but prayer moves God. Amazing, isn't it, that our prayers, whether grand and glorious or feeble and faint, can move the very heart of God who created the universe? To walk with God we must make it a practice to talk with God. . . .

Prayer moves God, and when God moves in your life, things get exciting! Years ago I never dreamed that God would move in my life the way He has. Even after my accident, when I signed up at the University of Maryland for art and English classes, I never realized how God would use diverse elements in my life to mold me to His will. But I sensed God was preparing me for something, and He started me out on a spiritual journey of prayer and praise that has not yet ended. You, too, have a journey through life ahead. Why not make it a journey of prayer and praise?

JONI EARECKSON TADA

Seeking God

Evening

· · · · · · · · ·

Now this is the confidence that we have in
Him, that if we ask anything according to His
will, He hears us. And if we know that He hears
us, whatever we ask, we know that we have
the petitions that we have asked of Him.

1 JOHN 5:14—15

If I regard iniquity in my heart,
The Lord will not hear.
But certainly God has heard me;
He has attended to the voice of my prayer.
Blessed be God,
Who has not turned away my prayer,
Nor His mercy from me!

PSALM 66:18—20

JANUARY 4

9

The Beginning of Joy

While I may have read in my Bible that we are in a spiritual war, that truth had not fully adjusted my expectations of this life. To accept that life is supposed to be hard is the beginning of joy.

There is freedom in understanding that heaven is coming and we are not there yet. We're called to live, instead, aware that we are at war with a ruthless enemy who is trying to destroy us if we are living surrendered to Jesus. . . .

Something about war makes us better. We live more thankful, less numb. We aren't quite so spoiled. . . . [God] allows us to suffer because we change through suffering. We hurt with others better. We become humble. We want Him more. . . . Honestly, we grow up through suffering. And most of us need to grow up. I've learned to quit wishing away the hard stuff. Because I don't want to miss all the good stuff that goes with it.

JENNIE ALLEN

Anything

We do not wrestle against flesh and blood, but
against principalities, against powers, against
the rulers of the darkness of this age, against
spiritual hosts of wickedness in the heavenly places.
Therefore take up the whole armor of God.

EPHESIANS 6:12—13

"In the world you will have tribulation; but be
of good cheer, I have overcome the world."

JOHN 16:33

In this you greatly rejoice, though now for a little
while, if need be, you have been grieved by various
trials, that the genuineness of your faith, being much
more precious than gold that perishes, though it
is tested by fire, may be found to praise, honor,
and glory at the revelation of Jesus Christ.

1 PETER 1:6—7

Turn Up Your Light

When you first gave your heart to God, He did a remarkable thing. He filled you with His light. He turned on the switch of His Spirit so that you would be able to recognize Him anytime you stepped out into the dark world. You are His beacon, His sunbeam. Now and then you may wonder if the light is still on or if you've allowed so much of the world to get into your heart and head that you have somehow closed the door on it. That may just mean it's time to get a jolt of direct current from the Source of all the light in the world.

You're God's moon reflecting His Son's light wherever you are. What an amazing thought! You never have to worry about whether God wants you to shine your light. You simply have to be willing to do so, and a beam will go out from you to anyone who is seeking it. You're a beacon on a hill and a welcome sight to those who wander yet in the darkness. What joy that brings!

Your Promises From God Today

Evening

· · · · · · · · ·

You are the light of the world. A city that is set on
a hill cannot be hidden. Nor do they light a lamp
and put it under a basket, but on a lampstand, and
it gives light to all who are in the house. Let your
light so shine before men, that they may see your
good works and glorify your Father in heaven.

MATTHEW 5:14–16

In Him was life, and the life was the light of men.

JOHN 1:4

Light is sown for the righteous,
And gladness for the upright in heart.

PSALM 97:11

Praise the LORD, call upon His name;
Declare His deeds among the peoples,
Make mention that His name is exalted.

ISAIAH 12:4

13

Neighbors

Some of us grew up in neighborhoods. We knew most of the people who lived on our street or in the houses surrounding ours. As neighbors, we knew we could count on each other when times were tough and that we all had a lot in common.

It's not quite so easy to define neighbors today. Sure, neighborhoods still exist, but the advent of the internet has changed our definition of "neighbor" in a way that nothing before it has done. Now we realize that we have neighbors who live in other states and need our help when hurricanes and tornadoes level their homes. We see that there are children starving in countries around the globe, and there's a strong realization that we're part of a huge global family and we each have a part in that family as well. Seeds of hope need to be planted in the hearts and homes of people close to us, but at other times, our neighbors are far away.

When God reminded us to "love our neighbors," He had a wide net. Love your neighbor, offer hope to those in need, and your life will forever be rooted in joy.

Little Seeds of Hope

Evening

· · · · · · · · ·

Behold, how good and how pleasant it is
For brethren to dwell together in unity!

PSALM 133:1

"Love your neighbor as yourself."

MATTHEW 19:19

"For I was hungry and you gave Me food; I was thirsty
and you gave Me drink; I was a stranger and you took
Me in; I was naked and you clothed Me; I was sick and
you visited Me; I was in prison and you came to Me."

MATTHEW 25:35—36

Character
That Holds

When storms begin to blow, the integrity of a building is revealed—the strength of its foundation, the practicality of its design, and the quality of its building materials. Will it stand or will it fall?

The same holds true for your own integrity. When the pressure is on, weak spots in your faith or character readily come to light. If this happens, take note. Your integrity matures over time. If you've made unsound choices in the past, make better choices today. Make sure your foundation rests solely on what God says is true, not on what your emotions or contemporary culture says is right and fair. Then turn your face toward the wind with confidence. You and your integrity are built to last.

Living God's Way

Evening

· · · · · · · · ·

Keep my soul, and deliver me;
Let me not be ashamed, for I put my trust in You.
Let integrity and uprightness preserve me,
For I wait for You.

PSALM 25:20—21

"The Helper, the Holy Spirit, whom the Father will
send in My name, He will teach you all things, and
bring to your remembrance all things that I said
to you. Peace I leave with you, My peace I give to
you; not as the world gives do I give to you. Let not
your heart be troubled, neither let it be afraid."

JOHN 14:26—27

He who walks with integrity walks securely,
But he who perverts his ways will become known.

PROVERBS 10:9

JANUARY 9

Let God Take the Credit

As you anticipate an exciting new chapter in your life, remember: The coming chapter, like every other, begins and ends with God and with His Son.

God will touch your heart and guide your steps—if you let Him. So dedicate this day to God's purpose and give thanks for His grace. Take a minute to write a note of thanks to God, celebrating the good things about your life right now and in the future, and expressing your gratitude. Tuck the note in your Bible or journal so you can look back at it often.

This is the day the Lord has created—give thanks to the One who created it, and use it to the glory of His kingdom.

Living God's Way

Evening

· · · · · · · · ·

For the Lord God is a sun and shield;
The Lord will give grace and glory;
No good thing will He withhold
From those who walk uprightly.

PSALM 84:11

He who did not spare His own Son, but
delivered Him up for us all, how shall He not
with Him also freely give us all things?

ROMANS 8:32

Whatever you do in word or deed, do all in
the name of the Lord Jesus, giving thanks
to God the Father through Him.

COLOSSIANS 3:17

Say Yes to God

I think God sometimes uses the completely inexplicable events in our lives to point us toward Him. We get to decide each time whether we will lean in toward what is unfolding and say yes or back away. . . .

[When] God chooses Moses to lead, Moses puts up a fight, saying nobody will follow him. God gives him three miracles to perform to establish confidence with his audience, but Moses protests again, saying he . . . can't speak and asks God to please choose somebody else. When Moses protests yet again, God gets a little angry and instructs Moses to take Aaron with him. . . .

The last thing I want to do is miss an opportunity or make God mad, so I just keep saying yes. Maybe God is doing some inexplicable things in your life. Each of us gets to decide every time whether to lean in or step back—to say yes, ignore it, or tell God why He has the wrong person.

So the next time God asks you to do something that is completely inexplicable . . . say yes.

BOB GOFF

Love Does

Evening

Then Moses called Joshua and said to him in
the sight of all Israel, "Be strong and of good
courage, for you must go with this people to the
land which the LORD has sworn to their fathers to
give them, and you shall cause them to inherit
it. And the LORD, He is the One who goes before
you. He will be with you, He will not leave you
nor forsake you; do not fear nor be dismayed."

DEUTERONOMY 31:7—8

"I have chosen you and have not cast you away:
Fear not, for I am with you;
Be not dismayed, for I am your God.
I will strengthen you,
Yes, I will help you,
I will uphold you with My righteous right hand."

ISAIAH 41:9—10

Unplug

I'm thinking that God didn't rest after Creation because it really tuckered Him out. He merely spoke and things came to be. No, God knew that if He didn't model rest for us, we wouldn't get it. So He did. He worked, and then He rested.

For many of us, resting does not come easily. We feel unworthy if we are not pulling our weight. But any farmer worth his salt knows that you can't plow with the same oxen more than six hours at a time. The beasts need rest. The farmer also knows that if you continue to plant a field season after season and never allow it to go fallow and replenish its nutrients, the harvest will be weak. . . .

It is difficult for us to admit that we need it, but a once-a-week "unplugging" from the frenetic pace that is now our norm can be one of the most spiritually liberating experiences for us and for our family.

ANITA RENFROE
The Purse-Driven Life

Evening

· · · · · · · · ·

"Work shall be done for six days, but the seventh
is the Sabbath of rest, holy to the LORD."

EXODUS 31:15

Rest in the LORD, and wait patiently for Him.

PSALM 37:7

"This Book of the Law shall not depart from your
mouth, but you shall meditate in it day and night,
that you may observe to do according to all that
is written in it. For then you will make your way
prosperous, and then you will have good success."

JOSHUA 1:8

God Is in Control

One morning my computer simply would not obey me. What a nuisance. I had my work laid out, my timing figured, my mind all set. My work was delayed, my timing thrown off, my thinking interrupted. Then I remembered. It was not for nothing. This was part of the Plan (not mine, His). "Lord, You have assigned me my portion and my cup."

Now if the interruption had been a human being instead of an infuriating mechanism, it would not have been so hard to see it as the most important part of the work of the day. But all is under my Father's control: yes, recalcitrant computers, faulty transmissions, drawbridges which happen to be up when one is in a hurry. My portion. My cup. My lot is secure. My heart can be at peace. My Father is in charge. How simple!

ELISABETH ELLIOT
Keep a Quiet Heart

Evening

. . . .

Be anxious for nothing, but in everything by prayer
and supplication, with thanksgiving, let your
requests be made known to God; and the peace of
God, which surpasses all understanding, will guard
your hearts and minds through Christ Jesus.

PHILIPPIANS 4:6—7

Whom have I in heaven but You?
And there is none upon earth that I desire besides You.
My flesh and my heart fail;
But God is the strength of my heart and my portion forever.

PSALM 73:25—26

Rejoice always, pray without ceasing, in
everything give thanks; for this is the
will of God in Christ Jesus for you.

1 THESSALONIANS 5:16—18

Morning

· · · · · · · ·

A Toxin Cleanse for the Soul

Little did I know how very spiritual the fast [my "toxin cleanse" of twenty-one days] would become. . . . Without the distraction of frappuccinos and French fries, I quickly realized there were more toxins clogging my *soul* than there were triglycerides clogging my arteries. The extra weight I was carrying in my spirit was much more dangerous than the fluff I was carrying around my hips and waist. . . .

For the moment my heart feels significantly lighter. It's not weighed down by emotional fatty deposits like, *Why do I always have to be the one who says "I'm sorry" first? . . .* Or *If God isn't going to give me a husband and children, why doesn't He at least bless me with a best-selling book and a high metabolism?* Today—well, at least this morning—those kinds of toxic thoughts that sometimes clog my soul are gone. I am fasting from whiny narcissism and a sense of entitlement. Right now I'm content just being a sturdy, mistake-prone girl who is absolutely adored by a perfect Redeemer!

LISA HARPER

Stumbling into Grace

Evening

· · · · · · · · ·

Who can discern their own errors?
Forgive my hidden faults.
Keep your servant also from willful sins;
may they not rule over me.
Then I will be blameless,
innocent of great transgression.

PSALM 19:12–13 NIV

The good that I will to do, I do not do; but
the evil I will not to do, that I practice.

ROMANS 7:19

Whatever things are true, whatever things are noble,
whatever things are just, whatever things are pure,
whatever things are lovely, whatever things are of
good report, if there is any virtue and if there
is anything praiseworthy—meditate on these things.

PHILIPPIANS 4:8

God's Song in Me

I've heard that creative scientists have learned how to take a person's DNA structure and make music out of it. . . . I love knowing that my DNA, which is like no other DNA in the whole wide world, is also a song like no one else's.

God not only created me, He wrote a song in me. And I believe He sings that song to me every day of my life. Zephaniah 3:17 says, "The LORD your God is with you, he is mighty to save. He will take great delight in you, he will quiet you with his love, he will rejoice over you with singing."

Did you get that? God, the Creator of the universe, *sings* to me.

And to you. . . .

Girlfriend, peel back the layers, listen for God's voice singing your song into your life, and rediscover the original, marvelous *you* He created you to be.

SANDI PATTY

Layers

Evening

· · · · · · · · · ·

It is good to give thanks to the LORD,
And to sing praises to Your name, O Most High;
To declare Your lovingkindness in the morning,
And Your faithfulness every night,
On an instrument of ten strings,
On the lute,
And on the harp,
With harmonious sound.

PSALM 92:1—3

Be filled with the Spirit, speaking to one another
in psalms and hymns and spiritual songs, singing
and making melody in your heart to the Lord,
giving thanks always for all things to God the
Father in the name of our Lord Jesus Christ.

EPHESIANS 5:18—20

While I live I will praise the LORD;
I will sing praises to my God while I have my being.

PSALM 146:2

Hugging *the* Book

I haven't always been a reader; in fact, I didn't become one until I was an adult. . . . Once I discovered the joy of hugging a book, I've been knee-deep in volumes of reading material ever since. And the one Book that I return to again and again has been the Bible. It is the most important book in my library. . . .

I would have to say my favorite book in the Bible is Genesis. Perhaps because I love beginnings and hearing how God established the world. . . .

But then again I also love Proverbs for its in-your-face practicality, and Philippians for its joy-filled encouragement regardless of life's vicissitudes, and Isaiah for its holy imagery, and the Psalms for their divine music, and John for its tender accounts of Christ, and, and, and . . . Okay, okay, I like the whole Book because it helps me become a whole person and gives me hope for future generations.

PATSY CLAIRMONT

Contagious Joy

Evening

· · · · · · · ·

How sweet are Your words to my taste,
Sweeter than honey to my mouth!

PSALM 119:103

The law of the LORD is perfect,
converting the soul;
The testimony of the LORD is sure,
making wise the simple;
The statutes of the LORD are right,
rejoicing the heart;
The commandment of the LORD is pure,
enlightening the eyes. . . .
More to be desired are they than gold,
Yea, than much fine gold,
Sweeter also than honey and the honeycomb.

PSALM 19:7–8, 10

JANUARY 16

"Happy in God"

Day by day, morning by morning, begin your walk with God in the calm trust that He is at work in everything. George Mueller used to say, "It is my first business every morning to make sure that my heart is happy in God." He was right! It is your personal business, as a discipline of your heart, to learn to be peaceful and safe in God in every situation.

Some of my mornings I read this, written in my notebook:

> The light of God surrounds me;
> The love of God enfolds me;
> The power of God protects me;
> The presence of God watches over me;
> Wherever I am, God is.

Remember, friend, where your real living is going on. In your thinking, in your reacting, in your heart of hearts—here is where your walk with God begins and continues. So when you start to move into trusting Him, stay there. Don't wander out again into worry and doubt!

ANNE ORTLUND

Disciplines of the Heart

I will both lie down in peace, and sleep;
for You alone, O LORD, make me dwell in safety.

PSALM 4:8

"I will dwell in them
And walk among them.
I will be their God,
And they shall be My people."

2 CORINTHIANS 6:16

The LORD our God is He who brought us and our fathers up out
of the land of Egypt, from the house of bondage, who did those
great signs in our sight, and preserved us in all the way that
we went and among all the people through whom we passed.

JOSHUA 24:17

The Daily Routine Redeemed

Anne Morrow Lindbergh observed somewhere in her timeless little book *Gift from the Sea* that most of us don't really mind pouring our lives out for a reason. What we do resent is the feeling that it is being dribbled away in small, meaningless drops for no good reason.

For me, one of the greatest frustrations of walking through the "dailiness" of my life as a Christian is that I don't always get to see how the bits and pieces of who I am fit into the big picture of God's plan. It's tempting at times to see my life as a meal here, a meeting there, a carpool, a phone call, a sack of groceries—all disjointed fragments of nothing in particular.

And yet I know I am called, as God's child, to believe by faith that they do add up. That in some way every single scrap of my life, every step and every struggle, is in the process of being fitted together into God's huge and perfect pattern for good.

CLAIRE CLONINGER
When God Shines Through

We are His workmanship, created in Christ
Jesus for good works, which God prepared
beforehand that we should walk in them.

EPHESIANS 2:10

"Whoever desires to become great among you
shall be your servant. And whoever of you
desires to be first shall be slave of all."

MARK 10:43—44

Who can find a virtuous wife?
For her worth is far above rubies. . . .
She opens her mouth with wisdom,
And on her tongue is the law of kindness.
She watches over the ways of her household,
And does not eat the bread of idleness. . . .
A woman who fears the LORD, she shall be praised.

PROVERBS 31:10, 26—27, 30

Small Surrenders

I found out a great thing about God. He doesn't require that we become *completely* willing. He doesn't wait until our faith or our motives are absolutely pure and perfect. If He did, He'd wait forever, and while He has the time to do so, we don't. He took my small surrenders, my little steps of willingness, and began to do little miracles with them.

It's like the story of the boy in the New Testament who suffered from epilepsy (Mark 9:17–24 NIV). . . . "If you can do anything, take pity on us and help us."

"'If you can'?" Jesus repeated. "Everything is possible for one who believes." . . .

Was Jesus saying that his son's healing depended on how much faith he had? . . .

"I do believe; help me overcome my unbelief!"

Jesus healed his son. . . .

I love that story because of the father's raw honesty, and Jesus' response to it. . . . It was healing to realize that I didn't have to have perfect faith! I could admit my insufficiency and ask God for what I needed.

DENISE JACKSON

It's All About Him

With God nothing will be impossible.

LUKE 1:37

"Ask, and it will be given to you; seek, and you
will find; knock, and it will be opened to you. For
everyone who asks receives, and he who seeks
finds, and to him who knocks it will be opened."

MATTHEW 7:7—8

"For assuredly, I say to you, if you have faith as
a mustard seed, you will say to this mountain,
'Move from here to there,' and it will move;
and nothing will be impossible for you."

MATTHEW 17:20

A Blessed Perspective

It's so easy for us to be focused on the negatives and forget all about the positives. Recently a good bit of my jewelry was stolen from a hotel room. Obviously that didn't make me happy, and I was doing everything possible to try to find it. The local police came to take my report, and the hotel security people were doing all they knew to help me. They kept apologizing to me, but I said to them, "Well, it's just jewelry. I haven't been notified that any of my family is sick or has a problem; I still have good health. This won't change my life in any significant way. I have so much to be thankful for that I refuse to let this unfortunate incident get to me."

Have you learned to stop and count your blessings in the middle of a bad day? It is such a good way to get your perspective back.

MARY WHELCHEL
How to Thrive from 9 to 5

Evening

• • • • • • • •

Blessed be the God and Father of our Lord Jesus
Christ, who has blessed us with every spiritual
blessing in the heavenly places in Christ.

EPHESIANS 1:3

You meant evil against me; but God meant it for good.

GENESIS 50:20

The LORD gave, and the LORD has taken away;
Blessed be the name of the LORD.

JOB 1:21

Resting in God's Peace

Soon after the Vietnam War ended, the American Art Institute opened a contest asking people to send their artistic rendition of the meaning of peace. The institute received hundreds of paintings, most of them the kinds of things that typically depict calmness and tranquility. . . .

However, in the painting the American Art Institute chose, the artist had captured a raging storm so vividly that, looking at it, you could almost hear the thunder. In the center of the picture was an open field, and there, nearly lost in the darkness of the clouds, the artist had painted a tree bowing to the strong winds. And in that tree was a nest where a mother bird hovered over her young. The one-word caption was simply: Peace.

That is the peace that "passes all understanding." It is peace in the midst of the storm, peace that comes with the cry, "Thy will, not mine, be done." Peace born of the assurance that we are not alone.

VERDELL DAVIS

Riches Stored in Secret Places

"Peace I leave with you, My peace I give to you;
not as the world gives do I give to you. Let not
your heart be troubled, neither let it be afraid."

JOHN 14:27

[Jesus] arose and rebuked the wind and the raging
of the water. And they ceased, and there was a calm.
But He said to [His disciples], "Where is your faith?"
And they were afraid, and marveled, saying to one
another, "Who can this be? For He commands
even the winds and water, and they obey Him!"

LUKE 8:24—25

Be anxious for nothing, but in everything by prayer
and supplication, with thanksgiving, let your
requests be made known to God; and the peace of
God, which surpasses all understanding, will guard
your hearts and minds through Christ Jesus.

PHILIPPIANS 4:6—7

Solitude and Silence

The ancient Desert Fathers used to commit themselves to a disciplinary creed: silence, solitude, and inner peace (*fuge, tace, et quiesce*). Only after adequate amounts of time listening, did they consider themselves ready to speak. . . .

Among many Christian women today, there is a strange sort of logic that suggests that spiritual resource and renewal are found in constantly seeking new voices, attending more meetings, listening to incessant music, and gathering to exchange half thought-out opinions. How often do we fall into the trap of believing that God is most pleased when we have maximized our information, our schedules, our relationships? . . .

Disengagement means silence before God, first of all. It is a time of heavenly discussion during which we listen more than we speak. And silence demands solitude.

GAIL MACDONALD

High Call, High Privilege

Evening

. . . .

A great and strong wind tore into the
mountains and broke the rocks in pieces before
the LORD, but the LORD was not in the wind; and
after the wind an earthquake, but the LORD was not
in the earthquake; and after the earthquake
a fire, but the LORD was not in the fire;
and after the fire a still small voice.

1 KINGS 19:11—12

Now in the morning, having risen a long while
before daylight, [Jesus] went out and departed
to a solitary place; and there He prayed.

MARK 1:35

Hear instruction and be wise,
And do not disdain it.
Blessed is the man who listens to me,
Watching daily at my gates,
Waiting at the posts of my doors.
For whoever finds me finds life,
And obtains favor from the LORD.

PROVERBS 8:33—35

Morning

· · · · · · · · ·

Walking in Bunny Slippers

It's healthy to be willing to laugh at yourself and make light of your shortcomings. We all have our quirks, so we shouldn't take ourselves too seriously. One of the best solutions I know for that is to take the "bunny slipper approach," a philosophy of life we all need to practice.

A friend sent me a pair of bunny slippers, and every now and then I put them on, especially when I'm tempted to start thinking I'm important or "nearly famous." There's something about bunny slippers that keeps my perspective where it belongs, but in addition to that, my bunny slippers remind me that whatever happens doesn't have to get me down. I can still be a little silly and laugh and enjoy life. Pain dissolves, frustrations vanish, and burdens roll away when I have on my bunny slippers.

BARBARA JOHNSON
Mama, Get the Hammer!

Evening

· · · · · · · · · ·

A merry heart does good, like medicine,
But a broken spirit dries the bones.

PROVERBS 17:22

As a father pities his children,
So the LORD pities those who fear Him.
For He knows our frame;
He remembers that we are dust.
As for man, his days are like grass;
As a flower of the field, so he flourishes.

PSALM 103:13—15

"Heaven and earth will pass away, but My
words will by no means pass away."

MARK 13:31

Your Passion and Your Purpose

You are here for a reason. There is nothing accidental about you. There is a specific purpose, assignment, and mission on earth that only you can fulfill. Never doubt your specialness. Even on days when you can't see an end in sight and the light at the end of the tunnel seems more like a faint spark, press on through the dark. Trust in your destiny. It is calling you, beckoning you, waiting for you . . . even when you can't yet see it.

Your identity was decided long before you were ever born by a God who is daily placing new desires and hopes and dreams into your heart. Your heart is the foundation of everything that makes you *you* and is the clearest signal you'll ever receive about your destiny, your purpose, your calling. To identify who you are, you must first identify what you love. . . .

When you step back and gaze upon where your passion and your personality intersect, therein lies your purpose.

MANDY HALE
The Single Woman

Evening

. . . .

My frame was not hidden from You,
When I was made in secret,
And skillfully wrought in the lowest parts of the earth.
Your eyes saw my substance, being yet unformed.
And in Your book they all were written,
The days fashioned for me,
When as yet there were none of them.

PSALM 139:15—16

I heard the voice of the Lord, saying:
"Whom shall I send,
And who will go for Us?"
Then I said, "Here am I! Send me."

ISAIAH 6:8

Take great joy in the Eternal!
His gifts are coming, and they are all your heart desires!

PSALM 37:4 THE VOICE

Know God!

The entire quest of theology can be summarized in these two words: "Know God!" Our primary source for doing that is the Bible with all its narratives of God's work in the world and its names for God and descriptions of God's character. The biblical illiteracy in contemporary U.S. culture has resulted in a terribly narrow picture of God. Some of the biblical pictures we would rather not face— and some of them we overemphasize. . . . For example, our culture likes the coziness of a loving God, but skips over His wrath. We want to feel comfortable with God, but we bypass "the fear of the Lord," which is "the beginning of wisdom." We need all of the Scriptures to reveal to us all that God wants to tell us about Himself.

MARVA DAWN

Morning by Morning

Evening

· · · · · · · · ·

The fear of the LORD is the beginning of wisdom;
A good understanding have all those
who do His commandments.
His praise endures forever.

PSALM 111:10

All Scripture is given by inspiration of God,
and is profitable for doctrine, for reproof, for
correction, for instruction in righteousness,
that the man of God may be complete,
thoroughly equipped for every good work.

2 TIMOTHY 3:16—17

I will meditate on Your precepts,
And contemplate Your ways.
I will delight myself in Your statutes;
I will not forget Your word.

PSALM 119:15—16

JANUARY 24

49

Receiving God's Hard Lessons

Each time God gives us a hard lesson, He desires also to give us Himself. If we open our hands to receive the lesson we open our hearts to receive Him, and with Himself His vision to see the glory in the surrender, whether of small things like self-esteem and reputation, or bigger things like a career and a home. He has been over the trail first, for He surrendered His glory, His equality with the Father, His omnipotence, His omnipresence, His all, when He came into our world. He stands ready today to supply us with His wisdom to understand what He wants to teach, and His strength to carry through, for He never allows us to undergo anything for which He has not promised the strength to endure. His commands are always accompanied by power to obey.

ELISABETH ELLIOT
A Path Through Suffering

Evening

· · · · · · · · ·

Scarcely for a righteous man will one die; yet perhaps
for a good man someone would even dare to die. But
God demonstrates His own love toward us, in that
while we were still sinners, Christ died for us.

ROMANS 5:7—8

"Be strong and of good courage; do not be
afraid, nor be dismayed, for the LORD your
God is with you wherever you go."

JOSHUA 1:9

Hear my cry, O God;
Attend to my prayer.
From the end of the earth I will cry to You,
When my heart is overwhelmed;
Lead me to the rock that is higher than I.

PSALM 61:1—2

· · · · · · · · ·

Trusting God

We ask God to provide for us, but do we trust Him to decide what and how much we really need? In a day where we celebrate "no limits," dare we invite God to establish limits in our lives?

Frankly, if we have risked trusting ourselves, it should be easy to trust God. He has a much better record of faithfulness than we do. God has never overcommitted or under-delivered. He has never been motivated by selfish ambition or greed. He is just and generous; wise and patient.

God knows the future and understands our past. In every moment, He fully comprehends what is best for us.

ALICIA BRITT CHOLE

Sitting in God's Sunshine

Evening

· · · · · · · · ·

"It shall come to pass
That before they call, I will answer;
And while they are still speaking, I will hear."

ISAIAH 65:24

You will keep him in perfect peace,
Whose mind is stayed on You,
Because he trusts in You.
Trust in the LORD forever,
For in YAH, the LORD, is everlasting strength.

ISAIAH 26:3—4

Behold, God is my salvation,
I will trust and not be afraid;
"For YAH, the LORD, is my strength and song;
He also has become my salvation."

ISAIAH 12:2

JANUARY 27

Seeking
Shelter in God

Some Christians treat God as a kind of insurance agent. In hard times, they expect Him to issue a claim check to restore what they've lost. While waiting for Him to change their circumstances for the better, they withhold fellowship from Him. Life's "squeeze" reveals their lack of submission and stubborn attitudes.

It is the heaven-born instinct of a child of God to seek shelter beneath the wings of the Almighty. The tendency to complain or to assert that God owes us something is not spiritual.

The godly instinct of a child of God is to say with Job, "Oh, that I might find Him."

JONI EARECKSON TADA

Seeking God

Evening

. . . .

Keep me as the apple of Your eye;
Hide me under the shadow of Your wings.

PSALM 17:8

You have been a shelter for me,
A strong tower from the enemy.
I will abide in Your tabernacle forever;
I will trust in the shelter of Your wings.

PSALM 61:3—4

Deliver me, O LORD, from my enemies;
In You I take shelter.
Teach me to do Your will,
For You are my God.

PSALM 143:9—10

A Joyful and Rugged Life

My longtime friend and the chaplain for Women of Faith, Lana Bateman, often reminds me, "The sign of true maturity in a life is when joy and sorrow walk hand in hand." . . .

Lana also says, "Sovereignty is the salvation of regret." What a relief to know that God's established plans from the beginning of time cannot be interfered with by my mistakes. His holy purposes are not hampered by our failures. He will accomplish and complete His work. The Lord longs to give us a full life with an array of emotions that enhance our faith. . . . He will give us definition, He will guide us toward resolution, and He provides us the hope of a divine destination. But it's a process, so don't be discouraged. It's an Emmaus Road of ongoing revelation.

Expect life to be joyful and rugged. Let's be wise enough to lean into what comes our way. If God has allowed it, it comes with purposes we may not understand . . . yet. . . .

Follow the narrow road; it leads to the widest joy.

PATSY CLAIRMONT
I Second That Emotion

A man's heart plans his way,
But the LORD directs his steps.

PROVERBS 16:9

Oh, bless our God, you peoples!
And make the voice of His praise to be heard,
Who keeps our soul among the living,
And does not allow our feet to be moved.
For You, O God, have tested us;
You have refined us as silver is refined.

PSALM 66:8—10

Sing praise to the LORD, you saints of His,
And give thanks at the remembrance of His holy name.
For His anger is but for a moment,
His favor is for life;
Weeping may endure for a night,
But joy comes in the morning.

PSALM 30:4—5

Morning

· · · · · · · · ·

Waiting with Hope

There are so many periods of "waiting" in life that make time seem long, while the rest of life flies! There is waiting to finish school, waiting for exam results, waiting for the wedding day to arrive, and waiting for the baby to take nine months to grow; there is waiting for a long illness to "break" and signs of recovery to be real; there is the waiting for that event all Christians most urgently desire (at least in most periods of their lives)—for Christ to return and restore the fallen world, giving us our new bodies to be His Bride, with only glory ahead and no waiting left.

That will be a fulfillment with no shadow of disappointment.

EDITH SCHAEFFER

The Tapestry

Evening

· · · · · · · · ·

Those who wait on the LORD
Shall renew their strength;
They shall mount up with wings like eagles,
They shall run and not be weary,
They shall walk and not faint.

ISAIAH 40:31

We desire that each one of you show the same
diligence to the full assurance of hope until the end,
that you do not become sluggish, but imitate those
who through faith and patience inherit the promises.

HEBREWS 6:11–12

Wait on the LORD;
Be of good courage,
And He shall strengthen your heart;
Wait, I say, on the LORD!

PSALM 27:14

59

One Choice Away

We're all one choice away from heading in the right direction. One choice away from falling from the course that is good and true. One choice away from hardening our layers of harshness, anger, disappointment, sorrow, false happiness, withdrawal, food, addiction. . . . The list is endless. We're also one choice away from removing those layers bit by bit and easing their tight hold on us.

We decide our direction, one choice at a time.

Think about it: at any point in your life's journey, you're one choice away from heading in the right direction. Throughout our day we're offered choices—look for them; they *are* there. And every time we choose, we can decide to head the right direction, peeling back one of those layers a little bit more to reveal our real selves. Or we can decide to recede into the layers and shield ourselves away from authentic relationships with our loved ones and, most importantly, with God. . . .

[We're] one choice away from heading in the right direction.

SANDI PATTY

Layers

Evening

· · · · · · · · ·

Choose for yourselves this day whom
you will serve. . . . But as for me and my
house, we will serve the LORD.

JOSHUA 24:15

Trust in the LORD with all your heart,
And lean not on your own understanding;
In all your ways acknowledge Him,
And He shall direct your paths.

PROVERBS 3:5—6

The steps of a good man are ordered by the LORD,
And He delights in his way.

PSALM 37:23

JANUARY 30

Need a Rest?

Do you ever just get tired of trying? It feels like you've prayed and you've tried a lot of things, but nothing seems to change. You start to wonder if you have some kind of black cloud that just hangs over your head. Maybe you're just tired. Maybe it's time to give yourself a break and take a little rest. After all, even Jesus enjoyed a good nap now and then.

Put your head on God's shoulder and relax a bit. Some days all you need is a chance to stop the noise and the chaos of all that is going on around you and simply rest. God invites you in. He knows you need a break and is happy to spend some quiet time just with you.

Your Promises from God Today

"Come to Me, all you who labor and are heavy
laden, and I will give you rest. Take My yoke upon
you and learn from Me, for I am gentle and lowly
in heart, and you will find rest for your souls."

MATTHEW 11:28–29

Be anxious for nothing, but in everything by prayer
and supplication, with thanksgiving, let your
requests be made known to God; and the peace of
God, which surpasses all understanding, will guard
your hearts and minds through Christ Jesus.

PHILIPPIANS 4:6–7

He gives power to the weak,
And to those who have no might He increases strength.
Even the youths shall faint and be weary,
And the young men shall utterly fall.

ISAIAH 40:29–30

February

The joy of the Lord is your strength.

NEHEMIAH 8:10

Looking for Beauty

There is so much beauty around us, if we will only take the time to notice it. You can make a conscious effort to look for the essence and therefore develop an appreciation for the beautiful things in life. Your days will seem a lot less harried, I promise you. Beauty has a way of totally capturing our senses, making us forget the fact that the car stalled on the way to work this morning, that the kids spilled chocolate milk on the carpet, that the workload keeps piling up. For a few brief shining moments, nothing else seems to matter. And the wonderful thing about beauty is that we can store it in our minds to be played over and over again.

LUCI SWINDOLL

You Bring the Confetti

Evening

· · · · · · · · · ·

Whatever things are true, whatever things are noble,
whatever things are just, whatever things are pure,
whatever things are lovely, whatever things are of
good report, if there is any virtue and if there
is anything praiseworthy—meditate on these things.

PHILIPPIANS 4:8

Let the words of my mouth and the meditation of my heart
Be acceptable in Your sight,
O LORD, my strength and my Redeemer.

PSALM 19:14

Be filled with the Spirit, speaking to one another
in psalms and hymns and spiritual songs,
singing and making melody in your heart to the
Lord, giving thanks always for all things to God
the Father in the name of our Lord Jesus Christ.

EPHESIANS 5:18—20

The heavens declare the glory of God;
And the firmament shows His handiwork.

PSALM 19:1

FEBRUARY 2

Focusing on God

Prayer is not merely going to God with a shopping list of things we want Him to do for us and for our families. Rather, it is being in relationship with Him, listening to Him, and sharing our hearts with Him. . . .

We must remember who it is that we are talking with—the Almighty God. I have found it helpful to begin and end my prayers by focusing on His character traits. He is the Almighty God. He is the God who heals. He is the God of peace. He is the God who forgives. He is the God who provides, and He is the God who is in control. He knows everything that is happening. He is not caught off guard. His love is perfect.

As I consider who He is instead of focusing on myself or another person or my situation, I am better able to pray with faith.

SUSAN ALEXANDER YATES
A House Full of Friends

"In returning and rest you shall be saved;
In quietness and confidence shall be your strength."

ISAIAH 30:15

The works of the LORD are great,
Studied by all who have pleasure in them.
His work is honorable and glorious,
And His righteousness endures forever.
He has made His wonderful works
to be remembered;
The LORD is gracious and full of compassion.

PSALM 111:2—4

So we are always confident, knowing that while
we are at home in the body we are absent from
the Lord. For we walk by faith, not by sight.

2 CORINTHIANS 5:6—7

Hearts Refreshed

Joy catches us off guard. It is a response that wells up in our hearts from love. We can't control it, and we can't bring it about. We don't find joy; it finds us, often surprising us when it arrives, making us smile for no apparent reason, break into a tune when no one is around to hear it, or trust peacefully when things are falling down around our ears. Joy is never tied to wealth or circumstances or conditions, only love. A person who has every material possession might never experience joy, while someone who has nothing the world considers valuable may have joy like a rushing river. If you know love, you'll be surprised by joy.

NICOLE JOHNSON
Women of Faith Devotional Bible

Evening

· · · · · · · · ·

We have great joy and consolation in
your love, because the hearts of the
saints have been refreshed by you.

PHILEMON V. 7

The joy of the LORD is your strength.

NEHEMIAH 8:10

Though the fig tree may not blossom,
Nor fruit be on the vines;
Though the labor of the olive may fail,
And the fields yield no food;
Though the flock may be cut off from the fold,
And there be no herd in the stalls—
Yet I will rejoice in the LORD,
I will joy in the God of my salvation.

HABAKKUK 3:17—18

FEBRUARY 3

71

The Secret of Joy

What secret do believers filled with joy know? They practice the presence of God. Remember the euphoria you had as a new believer? How amazed you were to discover that the God who made the universe loved you and might intervene personally in your day? You were on the right track then, but so often as time passes we lose that sense of anticipation. We lose the glow.

Run after God the way you did when you first fell in love. Wake up talking to Him, thanking Him for the hot shower, the fragrance of coffee. Ask Him for direction for your day. Expect Him to speak to you from His Word. Watch for Him in the people who cross your path—yes, even in the interruptions. Talk with Him in the night. Set the Lord always before you, and He will fill you with joy and with pleasures forevermore.

DEE BRESTIN

Women of Faith Devotional Bible

You will show me the path of life;
In Your presence is fullness of joy;
At Your right hand are pleasures forevermore.

PSALM 16:11

"Are not two sparrows sold for a copper coin?
And not one of them falls to the ground apart
from your Father's will. But the very hairs of your
head are all numbered. Do not fear therefore;
you are of more value than many sparrows."

MATTHEW 10:29—31

Your words were found, and I ate them,
And Your word was to me the joy and rejoicing of my heart.

JEREMIAH 15:16

Your God Knows

Just imagine how heaven grew silent and God's heart swelled with joy when—"Whaaaaaa!"—you arrived on earth to become, to be, to live! Another baby girl, created by Him was born! God is crazy about you! From the moment of your conception, He hovered over every week of your growth in the womb as you came to resemble more and more the person He designed you to be. He watched intently as you made your way into the world, screaming, writhing, and adjusting to earth's air. His complex little girl had been launched on her journey, which already was recorded in His book.

He knew your beginning.

He knew the family that would shape you.

And yes, He even knew the struggles you would have along the way.

He knew them then and He knows them now.

JAN SILVIOUS

Big Girls Don't Whine

Evening

· · · · · · · · ·

Your eyes saw my substance, being yet unformed.
And in Your book they all were written,
The days fashioned for me,
When as yet there were none of them.
PSALM 139:16

You will show me the path of life;
In Your presence is fullness of joy;
At Your right hand are pleasures forevermore.
PSALM 16:11

Cause me to know the way in which I should walk,
For I lift up my soul to You.
PSALM 143:8

Think YES!

When we get up in the morning, we have just so much energy. We can spend that energy creatively, seeking positive solutions, or we can spend it dragging ourselves down with negative thinking. Either way, we may still be tired at the end of the day. But in the first instance, we will have accomplished something and made progress. In the other we will have plodded along and managed to make ourselves not only tired, but depressed as well!

Half the battle in solving problems is our attitude. We are not just pumping ourselves full of sunshine when we say, "Think YES!" How we think about a situation usually dictates the course we will take. And sometimes, when we get bogged down in all the tangle of detail, we need a friend who will help us think clearly about all aspects of the situation, refocusing our attention from the obstacles to the possibilities in striving for proper choices and desired goals.

GLORIA GAITHER
Decisions

The LORD is for me among those who help me. . . .
It is better to trust in the LORD
Than to put confidence in man.
It is better to trust in the LORD
Than to put confidence in princes.

PSALM 118:7—9

Listen to counsel and receive instruction,
That you may be wise in your latter days.

PROVERBS 19:20

The righteous and the wise and their
works are in the hand of God.

ECCLESIASTES 9:1

Morning

· · · · · · · · ·

Choose Joy, Find Strength

I remember, years ago when we lived in England, putting my children to bed one night. My husband was in Australia—literally on the other side of the world. He wasn't coming home for three long, hard months. My father had been diagnosed with cancer, my daughter had fallen and broken her arm the day my husband left, and my hands were more than full, running a preschool during the day and programs for dozens of needy teenagers in the evenings. (During this time it didn't help to catch mumps from my kids either!) Yet as I sat by the crackling fire in our tiny home, a huge sense of well-being invaded every corner of my life. . . . My heart was singing, and my soul was dancing. . . .

I have learned to accept what God allows and to change what He empowers me to change; and that's usually my own attitude.

JILL BRISCOE

Heartstrings

Evening

. . . .

Do not sorrow, for the joy of the
LORD is your strength.

NEHEMIAH 8:10

"Come to Me, all you who labor and are heavy
laden, and I will give you rest. Take My yoke upon
you and learn from Me, for I am gentle and lowly
in heart, and you will find rest for your souls.
For My yoke is easy and My burden is light."

MATTHEW 11:28—30

A man's heart plans his way,
But the LORD directs his steps.

PROVERBS 16:9

Morning

. . . .

Emotions Under Control

Emotions accompany all the events of our lives. If you have a broken relationship, chances are you'll feel sad or rejected. If your spouse dies, you'll likely feel lonely. If you're unjustly accused, you'll probably feel angry. The more importance you assign to the event, the more intensely you'll feel the emotion. . . .

What we hold in high esteem will eventually govern us, but what we hold in low esteem, we will govern. Yes, we need to acknowledge our feelings, but we should never regard them more highly than God's Word. Don't ever bow to your feelings because you hold them in such high regard. Instead, make them bow to your God.

JENNIFER ROTHSCHILD

Lessons I Learned in the Dark

Evening

· · · · · · · · ·

Add to your faith virtue, to virtue knowledge, to
knowledge self-control, to self-control perseverance,
to perseverance godliness, to godliness brotherly
kindness, and to brotherly kindness love.

2 Peter 1:5—7

I have been crucified with Christ; it is no longer I
who live, but Christ lives in me; and the life which
I now live in the flesh I live by faith in the Son of
God, who loved me and gave Himself for me.

Galatians 2:20

His divine power has given to us all things that
pertain to life and godliness, through the knowledge
of Him who called us by glory and virtue.

2 Peter 1:3

Singing God's Praises

As a little girl, I would sing all the time in the privacy of my great-grandparents' little back alley apartment. I would sing old hymns and choruses like "Nearer My God to Thee," "What a Friend We Have in Jesus," and "Jesus Loves Me, This I Know." I'd sing those songs and feel something swelling up in my spirit. I didn't know what it was, but my eyes would begin to fill up and tears would run down my round cheeks. This emotion, this exuberance, this *Presence* would overpower me. It was like a celebration in my heart. It was a party! . . .

Most of the time, as soon as my feet hit the floor in the morning, I turn on praise music. I love gospel music; it gets me going! . . . There's something about listening to praise music that opens up the portals of heaven on earth and reassures me that I'm surrounded by God's loving presence.

THELMA WELLS
Boundless Love

Evening

· · · · · · · · ·

Why are you cast down, O my soul?
And why are you disquieted within me?
Hope in God;
For I shall yet praise Him,
The help of my countenance and my God.

PSALM 43:5

The LORD is my rock and my fortress and my deliverer;
My God, my strength, in whom I will trust;
My shield and the horn of my salvation, my stronghold.

PSALM 18:2

I will call upon the LORD, who is worthy to be praised;
So shall I be saved from my enemies.

2 SAMUEL 22:4

A Lesson from the Orchestra

An orchestra, to be worthy of its name, is like love. It demands *doing* as well as *feeling*.

And it *takes practice, practice,* PRACTICE. Its members may not feel like correcting the mistakes, but they do—until the problem is resolved. They may not feel that they can endure going over and over the areas in which they continue to make mistakes, but they do—until they can communicate, share, and encourage the other members in spite of the difficulties. Only then can they become a "whole." . . .

Each instrument occupies a special "chair." Each adds a unique movement. Yet each must retain its individual beauty. And oh, how fine-tuned each instrument must be! . . .

We form an orchestra, too. Each of us is an integral part of the whole with our families, coworkers, friends. . . . To create a symphony, we must keep our ears tuned to one another, our eyes focused on the Director.

JUNE MASTERS BACHER

The Quiet Heart

Evening

. . . .

Comfort each other and edify one another, just as you
also are doing. . . . Be at peace among yourselves.

1 THESSALONIANS 5:11, 13

"I will be a Father to you,
And you shall be My sons and daughters,
Says the LORD Almighty."

2 CORINTHIANS 6:18

As each one has received a gift, minister
it to one another, as good stewards
of the manifold grace of God.

1 PETER 4:10

Morning

. . . .

God's Unfailing Love

There are two kinds of love: human love and God's love. Human love can fall short; God's love never does. . . .

I experienced that love when I was imprisoned in a concentration camp during the Second World War. Each morning they held roll call. The supervisor used that time to demonstrate her cruelty. One morning I could hardly bear to see and hear what was happening in front of me. Then a lark started to sing in the air. All the prisoners looked up. I looked up too and listened to the bird, but I looked further and saw heaven. I thought of Psalm 103:11, "For as high as the heavens are above the earth, so great is his love for those who fear him" (NIV). I suddenly saw that the ocean of God's great love is greater than human cruelty. God sent the lark every day for three weeks to teach us to direct our eyes to Him.

CORRIE TEN BOOM

Messages of God's Abundance

I bow my knees to the Father of our Lord Jesus
Christ . . . that Christ may dwell in your hearts
through faith; that you, being rooted and grounded
in love, may be able to comprehend with all the saints
what is the width and length and depth and height—to
know the love of Christ which passes knowledge;
that you may be filled with all the fullness of God.

EPHESIANS 3:14, 17—19

As high as the heavens are above the earth,
so great is his love for those who fear him.

PSALM 103:11 NIV

Because Your lovingkindness is better than life,
My lips shall praise You.
Thus I will bless You while I live;
I will lift up my hands in Your name.

PSALM 63:3—4

Morning

. . . .

Running to Jesus

At Jesus' invitation, the children came running. The little girl with long black curls skipped into His arms while a shy three-year-old quietly peeked around His shoulder. The tough toddler with dirt on his shirt climbed up onto Jesus' knee and a bright young boy gently sat at His feet. Jesus opened His arms, received each one, and placed His hand of blessing upon them. . . .

When was the last time we responded to God's love unhindered by self-consciousness? At what age did we decide we were too old to seek His touch? Somewhere, somehow we began to believe that to ask is to need, to need is to be weak, to be weak is to be vulnerable, and to be vulnerable is to be hurt.

Children do not accept these flawed, self-protective assumptions. Without shame they make their need for affection known. "I want to be with you," they declare loudly without embarrassment or apology. "Hold me!" they request boldly with their arms confidently lifted in the air.

God longs for the same childlike affection from us.

ALICIA BRITT CHOLE

Sitting in God's Sunshine

Evening

"Let the little children come to Me, and do not forbid them; for of such is the kingdom of God. Assuredly, I say to you, whoever does not receive the kingdom of God as a little child will by no means enter it."

Luke 18:16–17

We love Him because He first loved us.

1 John 4:19

He is our God,
And we are the people of His pasture,
And the sheep of His hand.

Psalm 95:7

Morning

. . . .

Strengthening Your Marriage

God requires the husband to *love* his wife, but the wife is required to have *respect* for her husband. I assume no woman would marry a man she didn't love, but too often a wife loses respect for her husband after they've been married awhile. Loss of respect seems to precede loss of love and is more hurtful to a man than we realize. . . .

If this has already happened to you, and you know you've shown disrespect for your husband, confess it to God right now. Say, "Lord, I confess I do not esteem my husband the way Your Word says to. There is a wall in my heart that I know was erected as a protection against being hurt. But I am ready to let it come down so that my heart can heal." . . .

Praying like this will free you to see your man's potential for greatness as opposed to his flaws. It will enable you to say something positive that will encourage, build up, give life, and make the marriage better.

STORMIE OMARTIAN

The Power of a Praying Wife

Evening

• • • • • • • • •

Let each one of you in particular so love
his own wife as himself, and let the wife
see that she respects her husband.

Ephesians 5:33

[Let] older women . . . be reverent in behavior, not
slanderers, not given to much wine, teachers of
good things—that they admonish the young women
to love their husbands, to love their children.

Titus 2:3—4

An excellent wife is the crown of her husband.

Proverbs 12:4

Morning

. . . .

Love Is a Commitment

We all want to love and be loved in a way that feels good.

Greeting card companies make millions from our desire to somehow express a love that is different from all others, a love that is deeply committed. All of us probably have a drawer where there is a little stack of sentimental cards with words of undying love swirled across the front of each delicate offering. Yet whether they are cards that we have given and saved after the object of our love has read them, or cards that we have received, let's face it, that drawer full of cards is not what love is all about.

The major myth about love and a love relationship is that it always looks pretty and feels good. We want the objects of our love to be pretty, act pretty, and make us feel good. That is just the raw bottom line. Because of that myth, too often we are faced with the fact that real love has nothing to do with "prettiness" or "good feelings." Real love has to do with commitment and choices. It is the over-arching principle in a meaningful relationship.

JAN SILVIOUS

Moving Beyond the Myths

Evening

· · · · · · · · · ·

"Greater love has no one than this, than
to lay down one's life for his friends."

JOHN 15:13

"Whoever desires to become great among you
shall be your servant. And whoever of you desires
to be first shall be slave of all. For even the Son
of Man did not come to be served, but to serve,
and to give His life a ransom for many."

MARK 10:43—45

Whoever has this world's goods, and sees his brother
in need, and shuts up his heart from him, how does
the love of God abide in him? . . . Let us not love
in word or in tongue, but in deed and in truth.

1 JOHN 3:17—18

FEBRUARY 14

93

God's Cleansing Love

As I learned more about God with my head and experienced His love with my heart, I was absolutely overwhelmed. His love was so big that it crowded out my shame. For a lifetime, I'd tried to be "good enough." . . .

Now I knew I simply *couldn't* be good enough. What a relief to cheerfully admit my inadequacy! On my own, I could never be in a relationship with a perfect, holy God. But Jesus was good enough. Perfectly good. And because of His death on the cross, in my place, for my sins, God credited Christ's perfect righteousness to my account. My debt was paid in full. Cancelled. . . .

I didn't have to get rid of my shame by the power of positive thinking. . . . That weight was lifted from me, freeing me and leaving me lighter than air.

God's love for me was like a cleansing flood, washing away the sad little rags of shame. I was freed from the need to try to be "good enough" to earn anyone's favor. I knew I was loved with an everlasting love simply because of Jesus.

DENISE JACKSON

It's All About Him

We know how dearly God loves us, because he has
given us the Holy Spirit to fill our hearts with his
love. When we were utterly helpless, Christ came
at just the right time and died for us sinners. Now,
most people would not be willing to die for an
upright person, though someone might perhaps
be willing to die for a person who is especially
good. But God showed his great love for us by sending
Christ to die for us while we were still sinners.

ROMANS 5:5—8 NLT

"I have loved you with an everlasting love;
Therefore with lovingkindness I have drawn you."

JEREMIAH 31:3

Purge me with hyssop, and I shall be clean;
Wash me, and I shall be whiter than snow.

PSALM 51:7

Morning

. . . .

Remembering God's Faithfulness

To most of us who live in northern climates, spring seems to follow winter at a snail's pace. But eventually flowers peek through chilled soil and bird songs replace the scrape of snowplows. Bulky coats and boots hide in closets or attics, and screens replace storm windows and doors. . . .

Eventually, in the heat of August, winter may even seem like a long overdue friend. But come next January, when spring hides like buried treasure, remember . . . as sure as winter came, it will eventually leave. The same holds true for the winter of the soul. One day God will surprise you with the sight and song of spring.

In the darkest winter God can surprise you with spring.

JAN CARLBERG

The Hungry Heart

Therefore know that the LORD your God, He is
God, the faithful God who keeps covenant and
mercy for a thousand generations with those
who love Him and keep His commandments.

DEUTERONOMY 7:9

Mercy shall be built up forever;
Your faithfulness You shall establish in the very heavens.

PSALM 89:2

God is faithful, by whom you were called into the
fellowship of His Son, Jesus Christ our Lord.

1 CORINTHIANS 1:9

Jesus Loves Me!
Part 1

My Maker's words make me feel better about myself. Sure, I value the positive opinions my husband and my children have about my looks. But beneath all the layers, at the core of my being, the opinion that really matters is God's. The question is, will I choose to receive what God says about me? After all, it's not what *they* think of me that counts. It's *His* love and strength that perfect me. . . . When I set my mind on Him, He makes me "completely whole" (Isaiah 26:3 MSG).

And the truth is, often people will see the person I am *choosing* to reflect. So if I move through this life feeling unloved, fat, unhealthy, stupid, or whatever, that is how people are going to unconsciously see me. But when I truly choose to reflect the beautiful-and-beloved-princess attitude, people unconsciously see me that way. I have a lot to do with how others see me—and not just what I do to myself (good or bad) physically, but also mentally. Proverbs 23:7 reminds us that what we think, we become.

SANDI PATTY

Layers

Evening

· · · · · · · · · ·

For as he thinks in his heart, so is he.

PROVERBS 23:7

You will keep him in perfect peace,
Whose mind is stayed on You,
Because he trusts in You.

ISAIAH 26:3

Let love be without hypocrisy. Abhor what is evil.
Cling to what is good. Be kindly affectionate
to one another with brotherly love, in honor
giving preference to one another; not lagging in
diligence, fervent in spirit, serving the Lord.

ROMANS 12:9—11

Morning

. . . .

Jesus Loves Me!
Part 2

I've learned a lot of valuable lessons as I work through my layers. For one, I know without a doubt that God thinks I am wonderful. He thinks you are wonderful too. . . . "I praise you because I am fearfully and wonderfully made; your works are wonderful, I know that full well" (Psalm 139:14).

So when I look in the mirror with Sandi's eyes, I may see an overweight woman with a puffy face and droopy flesh. But when I look at my reflection with God's eyes, I recognize myself as one of His works and remember that all His works are wonderful. After all, a mirror is just a reflection; it isn't the real me. So what if I choose—ah, there's that word again—to be a reflection of His grace and His love, instead of—or in addition to—what I see in the mirror? That's where real beauty resides. Deep inside, I know that to be true. Now I want to *live* it as intensely as I *believe* it.

SANDI PATTY

Layers

Evening

· · · · · · · · ·

Do not let your adornment be merely outward—
arranging the hair, wearing gold, or
putting on fine apparel—rather let it
be the hidden person of the heart, with the
incorruptible beauty of a gentle and quiet spirit,
which is very precious in the sight of God.

1 PETER 3:3—4

Many, O LORD my God, are Your wonderful works
Which You have done;
And Your thoughts toward us
Cannot be recounted to You in order;
If I would declare and speak of them,
They are more than can be numbered.

PSALM 40:5

As in water face reflects face,
So a man's heart reveals the man.

PROVERBS 27:19

Morning

. . . .

God's Steadfast Love

In order to be a child of God, we have to change; that's what Jesus said. We have to admit we can't get there the way we are and be willing to humble ourselves and change. . . .

Remember that God's love for you is absolutely steadfast, and unlike humans, He does not give or take away His love based on your performance or your qualifications. It will not take God by surprise when you discover an area in your life that is less than what it should be. He knows it already, and even knowing all there is to know about you, His love and concern for you have not budged one inch.

MARY WHELCHEL
How to Thrive from 9 to 5

Evening

· · · · · · · · ·

If we say that we have no sin, we deceive ourselves,
and the truth is not in us. If we confess our sins,
[God] is faithful and just to forgive us our sins
and to cleanse us from all unrighteousness.

1 JOHN 1:8—9

Be doers of the word, and not hearers
only, deceiving yourselves.

JAMES 1:22

"I am the vine, you are the branches. He who
abides in Me, and I in him, bears much fruit;
for without Me you can do nothing."

JOHN 15:5

FEBRUARY 20

God Rejoices in You!

What brings God great joy and genuine pleasure? His people! He delights in those who have pledged their loyalty to Him and recognize His position as Almighty God, Author of history, Deliverer, Redeemer, and King. He delights in those people who acknowledge Jesus as their Savior and then choose to serve Him as their Lord. Further delight comes when His people obey Him and when they persevere in their faith during tough and challenging days.

Consider again the wonderful promises of Zephaniah 3:17. This Mighty [God] will save: He will bring peace, redemption, guidance, and hope to any and every situation you, His child, find yourself in. When you choose to walk in obedience to Him, He will rejoice over you with gladness and song. He will also come alongside to quiet you with His love when circumstances call for that.

The Lord your God is a God of joy. Know that He rejoices in you!

100 Favorite Bible Verses

Evening

The LORD your God in your midst,
The Mighty One, will save;
He will rejoice over you with gladness,
He will quiet you with His love,
He will rejoice over you with singing.

ZEPHANIAH 3:17

The LORD was my support.
He also brought me out into a broad place;
He delivered me because He delighted in me.

PSALM 18:18—19

Jesus [is] the author and finisher of our faith,
who for the joy that was set before Him endured
the cross, despising the shame, and has sat
down at the right hand of the throne of God.

HEBREWS 12:2

Morning

· · · · · · · ·

You Are Treasured!

Stepped into a Tiffany's jewelry store lately? Tiffany's is in the business of taking your breath away. Counter after counter lined with diamonds and jewels makes every girl gasp, not to mention drool. The way a twenty-karat diamond takes your breath away is the same way you take God's breath away every time He looks at you. The way your eyes twinkle at an unblemished, perfectly clear diamond is the way God' eyes twinkle when He sees you. Because of Jesus, the hard rock of sin that surrounded you was chiseled away, turning you into the most valuable of gems. No matter what mistakes you have made or how many people have told you that you don't amount to anything, know this: you are treasured by the Creator of the stars. He loves you!

So if you struggle with knowing you are valuable, march up to the Tiffany's window and say to yourself, "I'm more important to God than the finest of diamonds." And keep saying it until you believe it.

JENNA LUCADO BISHOP
Redefining Beautiful

Evening

· · · · · · · · ·

Now therefore, if you will indeed obey My voice and
keep My covenant, then you shall be a special treasure
to Me above all people; for all the earth is Mine.

EXODUS 19:5

"They shall be Mine," says the LORD of hosts,
"On the day that I make them My jewels.
And I will spare them
As a man spares his own son who serves him."

MALACHI 3:17

"For God so loved the world that He gave His
only begotten Son, that whoever believes in Him
should not perish but have everlasting life."

JOHN 3:16

Morning

· · · · · · · · ·

An Unglued Moment
Part 1

Oh, if only I were more in the habit of having a thankful heart full of praises instead of a grumbling heart consumed with circumstances. The hard thing is, I just don't feel very thankful in that moment when problems start bumping into my happy. I just don't feel like busting out in a praise song. I wish I did. But I don't.

In the midst of an unglued moment, how do I shift from *having an attitude to walking in gratitude*? I need a go-to script that will redirect my perspective to a better place. And I think I have just the thing. I say out loud to myself, "If this is the worst thing that happens to me today, it's still a pretty good day."

LYSA TERKEURST

Unglued

Evening

· · · · · · · ·

In everything give thanks; for this is the
will of God in Christ Jesus for you.

1 THESSALONIANS 5:18

Oh, give thanks to the Lord!
Call upon His name;
Make known His deeds among the peoples!
Sing to Him, sing psalms to Him;
Talk of all His wondrous works!

1 CHRONICLES 16:8—9

Oh, give thanks to the LORD, for He is good!
For His mercy endures forever.

1 CHRONICLES 16:34

An Unglued Moment
Part 2

My friend just hurt my feelings. If this is the worst thing that happens to me today, it's still a pretty good day. Praise You, God.

My husband is running late at work, and now I have to stay with the kids and miss the fun girls' night out I'd been planning to attend. If this is the worst thing that happens to me today, it's still a pretty good day. Praise You, God. . . .

I can't authentically praise God for anything that is wrong or evil, but I sure can shift my focus to all that is right and praise Him for that. . . . Oh, how powerful it is to shift from an attitude to gratitude and to praise our God in the midst of it all. When I do this, my circumstances may not instantly change, but the way I look at those circumstances certainly does. I stop being blind to all that's right and see so many more reasons to praise God. And when my heart is full of praise, my emotions aren't nearly as prone to coming unglued!

LYSA TERKEURST

Unglued

Evening

Sing praise to the Lord, you saints of His,
And give thanks at the remembrance of His holy name.
For His anger is but for a moment,
His favor is for life;
Weeping may endure for a night,
But joy comes in the morning.

PSALM 30:4—5

Praise the Lord!
Oh, give thanks to the Lord, for He is good!
For His mercy endures forever.
Who can utter the mighty acts of the Lord?
Who can declare all His praise?

PSALM 106:1—2

We, Your people and sheep of Your pasture,
Will give You thanks forever;
We will show forth Your praise to all generations.

PSALM 79:13

Morning

· · · · · · · · ·

Become a Hit

Most people suffer from chronic performance anxiety. Is that the case with you? Are you constantly wondering what kind of reviews you will receive from your family, your boss, or your coworkers? If so, here's a little stage wisdom to help you cope.

Kill the foot lights and turn up the house lights. When you do, you will see that there is only one VIP in the audience—God. Ultimately, His review is the only one that matters. Live your life in a manner that is pleasing to Him. Doing so will build your confidence because you will be establishing your life on something solid instead of on the shifting sands of people's opinions. So, chase away your anxiety and live your life for God. You're bound to be a hit with Him.

Living God's Way

Evening

• • • • • • • •

Be diligent to present yourself approved
to God, a worker who does not need to be
ashamed, rightly dividing the word of truth.

2 TIMOTHY 2:15

I am persuaded that neither death nor life, nor angels
nor principalities nor powers, nor things present
nor things to come, nor height nor depth, nor any
other created thing, shall be able to separate us from
the love of God which is in Christ Jesus our Lord.

ROMANS 8:38–39

"His lord said to him, 'Well done, good
and faithful servant.'"

MATTHEW 25:21

An Acquired Taste

Will I ever be content? . . . Yes. It's something I have to choose daily. I know there will be moments when I'll get a bee in my bonnet about replacing our countertops or I'll grumble because I have white appliances and not stainless steel. In those times, I have to stop focusing on everything I want and focus on what I have. I'm not saying that getting to a place of complete contentment is easy, but I know that I am much happier (and so is my family) when I'm not consumed with my wish list.

If you've struggled to find contentment as I have, you don't have to wallow in your past shortcomings. We've all had those moments when we're in a funk because we feel like we should have hardwood floors instead of the beige carpet the previous owners installed that is now spotted with stains. . . . But even on bad days with bad carpet, we can set our sights on the things that really matter—such as friendship, family, and faith—and live our lives with a spirit of contentment.

MARIAN PARSONS

Inspired You

Evening

. . . .

I have learned in whatever state I am, to be content.

PHILIPPIANS 4:11

Godliness with contentment is great gain. For
we brought nothing into this world, and it
is certain we can carry nothing out.

1 TIMOTHY 6:6—7

Let your conduct be without covetousness; be content
with such things as you have. For He Himself has
said, "I will never leave you nor forsake you."

HEBREWS 13:5

· · · · · · · · ·

Gaze at the Lord

The dog has tracked Alpo all over the kitchen floor. Your husband has called to say he'll be late. The saucepans are boiling over, and the burning casserole is staining your oven. Teenagers are wrestling in the bedroom above your kitchen. Little wonder you stand there with the dish towel in your hand, droop-shouldered and dumbfounded, not knowing what to do.

What we need here is more than a prayer mumbled in obligation. . . . We need a different focus. . . .

Consider Jesus. He had one heavy cross to bear, but He fixed His sight on the joy before Him. And we are to do the same.

So what about the burning casserole, the dirty kitchen floor, and the screaming kids upstairs? They haven't changed. But your focus has. Don't gaze at your problems while you only glance at the Lord. Get life in focus. Gaze at the Lord—behold Him—and your problems won't cause you to grow weary and lose heart.

JONI EARECKSON TADA

Seeking God

Evening

· · · · · · · · ·

Let us run with endurance the race that is set before
us, looking unto Jesus, the author and finisher
of our faith, who for the joy that was set before Him
endured the cross, despising the shame, and has
sat down at the right hand of the throne of God.

HEBREWS 12:1–2

One thing I have desired of the LORD,
That will I seek:
That I may dwell in the house of the LORD
All the days of my life,
To behold the beauty of the LORD.

PSALM 27:4

Who among all these does not know
That the hand of the LORD has done this,
In whose hand is the life of every living thing,
And the breath of all mankind?

JOB 12:9–10

Morning

. . . .

Stop Looking for the *Why*

Sometimes it's a job, an opportunity, or a dream—the thing we wanted so badly . . . and prayed for [that] goes up in smoke. Sometimes we get fired when we've been model employees. Sometimes a person we have loved and invested our time, energy, affection, and trust in walks away and leaves us in the dust with little to no explanation. . . .

Stop trying to solve the mystery. . . . Stop looking for the *why* and start looking for the *good* in good-bye—because it's there. . . . The exit of that person, thing, or dream was a boarding pass to somewhere new, somewhere better, somewhere you need to be that you weren't going to reach without losing some of the baggage. Realize that if a door closed, it's because what was behind it wasn't meant for you.

Every time you release your hold on what is old, you issue an invitation to God to fill up that space with something new. The place you were might've been great, but it can't hold a candle to where you can go.

MANDY HALE

The Single Woman

Evening

· · · · · · · · ·

"My thoughts are not your thoughts,
Nor are your ways My ways," says the LORD.
"For as the heavens are higher than the earth,
So are My ways higher than your ways,
And My thoughts than your thoughts."

ISAIAH 55:8—9

You number my wanderings;
Put my tears into Your bottle;
Are they not in Your book?
When I cry out to You,
Then my enemies will turn back;
This I know, because God is for me.

PSALM 56:8—9

In God I have put my trust;
I will not be afraid.
What can man do to me?

PSALM 56:11

Morning

. . . .

Like Cats or Dogs?

When I pat my dog, [Cobi] goes into a state of ecstasy. He closes his eyes and leans into me with his body. He revels in loving and being loved. . . .

In contrast, our cat, Pepper, just pretends to love me. She'll snake back and forth around my feet, rubbing against me . . . But as soon as I reach for her she's gone . . .

What if we greeted each other with the same enthusiasm and joy with which our pets greet us? (Sniffing excluded!) What if we were as quick to forgive and forget? What if we exhibited the joy for life that Cobi exhibits as he bounds up and down the stairs?

What if we were as loyal? What if we reveled in being loved the way they do? What if we loved enthusiastically? What if, no matter how severely we were wronged, we just kept coming back to love and be loved? What if?

KEN DAVIS

Lighten Up!

Owe no one anything except to love one another,
for he who loves another has fulfilled the law.

ROMANS 13:8

For I say, through the grace given to me, to everyone
who is among you, not to think of himself more
highly than he ought to think, but to think soberly,
as God has dealt to each one a measure of faith.

ROMANS 12:3

"Judge not, and you shall not be judged. Condemn
not, and you shall not be condemned. Forgive,
and you will be forgiven. Give, and it will be
given to you: good measure, pressed down,
shaken together, and running over will be put
into your bosom. For with the same measure
that you use, it will be measured back to you."

LUKE 6:37—38

March

My soul shall be joyful in the Lord;
It shall rejoice in His salvation.

PSALM 35:9

Our Unchanging, Unchangeable God

Think about this: if the character of God could change, it must necessarily change to become better (meaning He is not perfect now) or worse (meaning He is corruptible). If His character, His plans, intentions, and promises, aren't fully trustworthy and perfect now, why would we believe His Word or trust in His plan for salvation? No, God is unchangeable. He is perfect. We can trust that He won't take a different view of His saving grace tomorrow or change His promise that "all things work together for good to those who love God, to those who are called according to His purpose" (Romans 8:28).

The heavens change, though very slowly. Jesus saw a slightly different shape to the constellation of Orion the Hunter than the one Abraham saw or the one we see now. But God's plans and promises do not change. Let's rejoice today that God is unchangeable and worship Him for His unchanging nature the next time we look up and consider the heavens.

KEVIN HARTNETT

The Heavens

Evening

· · · · · · · · · ·

Jesus Christ is the same yesterday, today, and forever.

HEBREWS 13:8

Of old You laid the foundation of the earth,
And the heavens are the work of Your hands.
They will perish, but You will endure;
Yes, they will all grow old like a garment;
Like a cloak You will change them,
And they will be changed.
But You are the same,
And Your years will have no end.

PSALM 102:25—27

Finding Joy in Your Work

Work should always be associated with joy. . . .

The story is told of three women washing clothes. A passerby asked each what she was doing.

"Washing clothes" was the first answer.

"A bit of household drudgery" was the second.

"I'm mothering three young children who someday will fill important and useful spheres in life, and washday is a part of my grand task in caring for these souls who shall live forever" was the third.

Ordinary work, which is what most of us do most of the time, is ordained by God every bit as much as is the extraordinary. All work done for God is spiritual work and therefore not merely a duty but a holy privilege.

ELISABETH ELLIOT
The Shaping of a Christian Family

Evening

Whatever you do, do it heartily, as
to the Lord and not to men.

COLOSSIANS 3:23

I can do all things through Christ
who strengthens me.

PHILIPPIANS 4:13

In all labor there is profit.

PROVERBS 14:23

The LORD will give strength to His people;
The LORD will bless His people with peace.

PSALM 29:11

Adoption into God's Family

As Christians, we are adopted as God's children. To change metaphors, we are grafted into the Vine. This process begins when we enter into relationship with Christ; we immediately benefit from becoming part of His family.

In telling the parable of the vine and the branches, Jesus explained, "I am the vine; you are the branches. Whoever abides in me and I in him, he it is that bears much fruit, for apart from me you can do nothing" (John 15:5).

When we abide in Jesus, we start taking on characteristics of His life flowing through us—the inward evidence of His influence and the indwelling work of His Spirit. The "fruit" Jesus spoke of is the outward change that comes as a result of adoption into His family.

We who are followers of Christ receive many benefits when we choose to live aligned with Jesus' goodness and righteousness. Our Lord's desires become our desires; His plans for us become plans of our own. We are shaped—reshaped—by Him as we allow His influence into every area of our lives.

A Jane Austen Devotional

"Abide in Me, and I in you. As the branch cannot
bear fruit of itself, unless it abides in the vine,
neither can you, unless you abide in Me."

JOHN 15:4

Behold what manner of love the Father has bestowed
on us, that we should be called children of God!

1 JOHN 3:1

You received the Spirit of adoption by whom we
cry out, "Abba, Father." The Spirit Himself bears
witness with our spirit that we are children of God.

ROMANS 8:15—16

Deep Water, Fiery Trials, God's Faithfulness

All God's children go through deep waters and trials by fire. There's no if—only when. But with the *when* comes a *Who*. God never allows His children to swim alone. His buddy system is sink- and fireproof. More sure than the when is the Who. It is God who assures His children, *"I will be with you"*—when!

Can you see God in your trials by water or fire? God says to you, "I will be with you whenever, wherever, and forever."

JAN CARLBERG

The Hungry Heart

Evening

· · · · · · · · ·

"Lo, I am with you always, even to the end of the age."

MATTHEW 28:20

"When you pass through the waters,
I will be with you;
And through the rivers,
they shall not overflow you.
When you walk through the fire,
you shall not be burned,
Nor shall the flame scorch you."

ISAIAH 43:2

Though I walk through the valley of
the shadow of death,
I will fear no evil;
For You are with me;
Your rod and Your staff, they comfort me.

PSALM 23:4

MARCH 5

Yield Up the Pieces

How many times . . . has the Lord said, "Yield up the pieces, the scraps, the leftovers of your lives. All you've got is all I need to make a mountain from your molehill of faith"?

He said that through Elisha to a woman who came to the prophet in great distress. Her sons were about to be sold into slavery as a settlement for her late husband's debts (2 Kings 4:1–7).

The widow had one small container of oil—nothing else of value.

"Gather up all of your empty vessels—whatever old pots and pitchers you can find or borrow," the prophet commanded, "and begin to fill them with oil."

The widow did as she was bid, and she found to her amazement that there was enough oil to fill every vessel—enough to pay the debt and keep her family for life. . . .

God stands ready to transform all that we offer (when it is all that we have) into all that we need.

CLAIRE CLONINGER
When God Shines Through

Evening

· · · · · · · · ·

[Jesus] took the five loaves and the two fish, and
looking up to heaven, He blessed and broke and gave
the loaves to the disciples; and the disciples gave to
the multitudes. So they all ate and were filled, and
they took up twelve baskets full of the fragments
that remained. Now those who had eaten were about
five thousand men, besides women and children.

MATTHEW 14:19—21

You do not desire sacrifice, or else I would give it;
You do not delight in burnt offering.
The sacrifices of God are a broken spirit,
A broken and a contrite heart—
These, O God, You will not despise.

PSALM 51:16—17

As for God, His way is perfect;
The word of the LORD is proven;
He is a shield to all who trust in Him.

2 SAMUEL 22:31

133

Brokenness Has Its Blessings

Our lives aren't just random, unconnected collections of scenes without meaning. They have purpose, and as we become more and more tuned in to who God is, we can have peace in the plot's strange twists and turns. . . .

Many of us have chapters that we would prefer had never been written. . . . But the hard chapters show God's power in a way that the happy ones do not. Brokenness moves my story forward in a way that peaceful times do not. It's in the difficulties that I became desperate to really know God, to cry out to Him.

When everything is going well, we often can't hear God, because the music all around us is turned up too loud. But when the party stops—in those moments of crashing pain, sorry, and sudden silence—we begin to hear His voice. . . .

God is with you no matter what. He is stronger than the challenges in front of you. You can trust Him. Even though you can't see how your story will turn out, know that the end is in His hands.

DENISE JACKSON

The Road Home

Evening

. . . .

The righteous cry out, and the LORD hears,
And delivers them out of all their troubles.
The LORD is near to those who have a broken heart,
And saves such as have a contrite spirit.
Many are the afflictions of the righteous,
But the LORD delivers him out of them all.

PSALM 34;17—19

"I am the Alpha and the Omega, the Beginning
and the End," says the Lord, "who is and who
was and who is to come, the Almighty."

REVELATION 1:8

Your Maker is your husband,
The LORD of hosts is His name;
And your Redeemer is the Holy One of Israel;
He is called the God of the whole earth.

ISAIAH 54:5

Gnarled Beauty

While spending time painting in . . . Tuscany, I became accustomed to seeing grape vines growing on the hillsides. The older gnarled vines were beautiful to sketch because of their knotty twists and bends. Over the course of time, the winds, rains, and sun—the weathering effects of the seasons—had forced their shapes. The most luscious growth came from these rugged old vines . . . grapes so heavy and bountiful they seemed to invite people to pick them.

In another vineyard were young plants which had suffered no ill effects of nature at all. They offered no particular beauty or character and were hardly worthy of my pencil or paintbrush.

As it is in nature, so it is in God's kingdom. From the winds and rains of adversity comes abundant growth and a beautiful life worth painting.

Do not be afraid to suffer. . . . It is from being shaken apart and not being destroyed that one becomes strong and courageous.

LAURA LEWIS LANIER

All Things Bright and Beautiful

Now thanks be to God who always leads us in
triumph in Christ, and through us diffuses the
fragrance of His knowledge in every place.

2 CORINTHIANS 2:14

Though I walk in the midst of trouble,
You will revive me;
You will stretch out Your hand
Against the wrath of my enemies,
And Your right hand will save me.

PSALM 138:7

Beloved, do not think it strange concerning the
fiery trial which is to try you, as though some
strange thing happened to you; but rejoice to the
extent that you partake of Christ's sufferings.

1 PETER 4:12—13

The Work of God

Years ago, I read that the average woman today has the equivalent of *fifty* full-time servants, in the form of modern, timesaving devices and equipment. That figure may or may not be accurate, but we certainly have many conveniences available to us that were unknown to women of past generations. Imagine going back to the days when there were no dishwashers, microwaves, washing machines, dryers, or automobiles. . . .

So why are our lives more harried and hurried than ever? Why are we so stressed out? . . .

In Jesus' words, we find a clue—a powerful Truth that sets us free from the bondage of hurry and frustration about all we have to do. Notice what work Jesus completed in the thirty-three years He was here on the earth: "I have finished the work *which thou gavest me to do*" (John 17:4 KJV). That is the secret. Jesus didn't finish everything His disciples wanted Him to do. . . . He didn't finish everything the multitudes wanted Him to do. . . . But He did finish the work that *God* gave Him to do.

NANCY LEIGH DEMOSS

Lies Women Believe

Evening

· · · · · · · · ·

As for me and my house, we will serve the LORD.

JOSHUA 24:15

Six days you shall labor and do all your work, but
the seventh day is the Sabbath of the LORD your
God. In it you shall do no work. . . . For in six
days the LORD made the heavens and the earth,
the sea, and all that is in them, and rested
the seventh day. Therefore the LORD blessed
the Sabbath day and hallowed it.

EXODUS 20:9—11

A woman who fears the LORD, she shall be praised. . . .
And let her own works praise her in the gates.

PROVERBS 31:30—31

Finding Light for the Path

We are all travelers, whether we want to be or not. Life forces us to hit the road in search of doctors, banks, dry cleaners, groceries, and many other things. [My husband] Les and I divide our time between Texas and Michigan, which means for me, a non-mapper, that I seldom know where I am, much less where the bank is in relationship to our home. So sweet Les, in an attempt to simplify my perpetual lostness, chose the bank directly across the street from our subdivision. No missing piece there— out the driveway, into the bank. Now, if only life were that simple!

Thank heavens for Jesus, who offers to walk with us wherever we are. He promises to guide our steps and light our path. Jesus is there for us if, like Zacchaeus, we are out on a limb. He's there for us if, like Eve, we've taken the wrong path. He's there for us if we are wandering aimlessly or high-stepping with certainty.

PATSY CLAIRMONT

All Cracked Up

Evening

· · · · · · · · ·

I will instruct you and teach you in the way
you should go.

PSALM 32:8

"I am with you always, even to the end of the age."

MATTHEW 28:20

Though I walk through the valley of the shadow of death,
I will fear no evil;
For You are with me.

PSALM 23:4

Your word is a lamp to my feet
And a light to my path.

PSALM 119:105

Morning

. . . .

Choosing a Positive Attitude

Your attitude is your choice. It always is.

We live in an age that has developed the art of shifting blame to very high levels, and sometimes we get caught up in that same tendency. "Well, if you had my job you wouldn't be so positive." "If you had my kids, you wouldn't feel so good." "If only my boss were different, I could be a positive person." In other words, "My bad attitude is not my fault!"

The truth is, however, your attitude and mine are always our choice. No matter how bad things are, no one can force you to have a bad attitude if you don't want to, and no matter how good things are, no one can force you to have a good attitude if you don't want to. Now that should come as really good news because it says our attitudes don't have to be the victims of our circumstances or of other people. We choose our responses.

MARY WHELCHEL
How to Thrive from 9 to 5

Evening

· · · · · · · · ·

Now may the God of hope fill you with all joy
and peace in believing, that you may abound
in hope by the power of the Holy Spirit.

ROMANS 15:13

Be glad in the LORD and rejoice, you righteous;
And shout for joy, all you upright in heart!

PSALM 32:11

"As the Father loved Me, I also have loved you;
abide in My love. If you keep My commandments,
you will abide in My love, just as I have kept My
Father's commandments and abide in His love.
These things I have spoken to you, that My joy may
remain in you, and that your joy may be full."

JOHN 15:9—11

143

A Smiling Heart

A smile on your heart means a smile on your face. Some people wear their hearts on their sleeves. What goes on inside, shows up outside. Have you ever asked a junior-high daughter to help you with the housework? Her face tells the story. Her heart is definitely not in it!

When your heart has Jesus as its guest, it smiles. How can it do anything else? When your heart houses the one who is our joy, it cannot help grinning at grief, laughing at loads, and smiling at sorrows. Even when we are called to suffer, we cannot be sad or sour because we discover that we have been saved to sing. . . .

"But," you may object, "how can I even smile when I'm suffering, much less sing about it?" Look at Jesus! Can you look at Jesus and remain sober? When I'm in trouble, and I meet Him in the secret place and He smiles at me, that mends my heart so I can mend others. He sets my heart singing.

JILL BRISCOE
Quiet Times with God

Evening

· · · · · · · · ·

The LORD is my strength and my shield;
My heart trusted in Him, and I am helped;
Therefore my heart greatly rejoices,
And with my song I will praise Him.

PSALM 28:7

I will give thanks to You, O LORD . . .
And sing praises to Your name.

2 SAMUEL 22:50

The LORD is great and greatly to be praised;
He is also to be feared above all gods.

1 CHRONICLES 16:25

Sin—Forgiven and Forgotten

It's been said that there is only one thing God cannot do, and that is to remember your sin and mine that has been forgiven. When I come to Him humbly, through faith in Jesus, He erases my sin from His memory much more effectively than I erase things from my computer. Even Satan can't retrieve it from the inner workings of my spiritual hard drive!

Corrie ten Boom, author of *The Hiding Place* and survivor of the Nazi concentration camps during World War II, once remarked that God has cast our sins into the depths of the sea and posted a sign that says, "No Fishing Allowed."

ANNE GRAHAM LOTZ

I Saw the Lord

Evening

· · · · · · · · ·

For as the heavens are high above the earth,
So great is His mercy toward those who fear Him;
As far as the east is from the west,
So far has He removed our transgressions from us.
As a father pities his children,
So the LORD pities those who fear Him.

PSALM 103:11–13

In Him we have redemption through
His blood, the forgiveness of sins,
according to the riches of His grace.

EPHESIANS 1:7

If we walk in the light as He is in the light, we
have fellowship with one another, and the blood
of Jesus Christ His Son cleanses us from all sin.

1 JOHN 1:7

A Matter of Perspective

No one could convince you that black is white or up is down. But Paul does a good job of making a case that heavy is light.

A burden is heavy when its presence is pointless, when traveling with it is lonely, and when the journey is long. But life's afflictions are purposeful, not pointless. God uses our hardships to make us more like Jesus.

Furthermore we need not travel alone during this lifelong process of transformation. Fellow believers have their own afflictions, and we can be physical reminders that God is sovereign.

Finally, walking with fellow believers can help us keep focused on the unseen and eternal reward that God has for His people.

Trust in God's sovereign goodness, walk with His people, and remind yourself that the unseen and eternal are far more important than the seen and temporary. Life's afflictions will then be lighter.

100 Favorite Bible Verses

Evening

. . . .

Our light affliction, which is but for a moment, is
working for us a far more exceeding and eternal
weight of glory, while we do not look at the things
which are seen, but at the things which are not seen.

2 CORINTHIANS 4:17—18

Bear one another's burdens, and so fulfill the
law of Christ. For if anyone thinks himself to be
something, when he is nothing, he deceives himself.

GALATIANS 6:2—3

Two are better than one,
Because they have a good reward for their labor.
For if they fall, one will lift up his companion.
But woe to him who is alone when he falls,
For he has no one to help him up.

ECCLESIASTES 4:9—10

The Future Belongs to God

The thing I keep trying to remember about giving the future over to God is that . . . it belongs to Him anyway. Through blindness or selfishness, I can stumble around trying my best to ruin God's plan for my life, but as long as I am living in Him, the future takes care of itself, no matter what I do. If God is the Destination of our spiritual journey, then we are freed from the fear of making bad choices. The present moment is all that matters. The future snuggles right into the present and gives us peace.

LESLIE WILLIAMS

Night Wrestling

Evening

· · · · · · · · ·

Mark the blameless man, and observe the upright;
For the future of that man is peace.

PSALM 37:37

I know the thoughts that I think toward you,
says the LORD, thoughts of peace and not of
evil, to give you a future and a hope.

JEREMIAH 29:11

A thousand years in Your sight
Are like yesterday when it is past,
And like a watch in the night.

PSALM 90:4

Gardening Instructions for Life

Plant seeds of hope by expecting the best. Don't have ridiculous expectations, but do look for God's hand at work wherever you are . . . because it is.

Weed out regret. Once you make your decision to plow a certain field (new job, home, school, etc.), don't second-guess yourself. You will only stir up yellow jackets of insecurity. . . .

Water your mind and words generously with gratitude. Find as many things as you can each day to be thankful for . . . like the smell of fresh coffee, new leather, old lavender. . . .

Remember, rooting takes both time and tilling. One part, the tilling, is up to us; the other, time, we have to wait on. Like spring.

Yep, becoming a garden means you will crawl in the dirt, lie dormant through some seasons, be resurrected in the spring, and blossom till the freeze comes. The circle of life.

PATSY CLAIRMONT

Stained Glass Hearts

You visit the earth and water it,

You greatly enrich it;

The river of God is full of water;

You provide their grain,

For so You have prepared it.

You water its ridges abundantly,

You settle its furrows;

You make it soft with showers,

You bless its growth.

You crown the year with Your goodness.

PSALM 65:9—11

I planted, Apollos watered, but God gave the increase.
So then neither he who plants is anything, nor he who
waters, but God who gives the increase. Now he who
plants and he who waters are one, and each one will
receive his own reward according to his own labor.
For we are God's fellow workers; you are God's field.

1 CORINTHIANS 3:6—9

Countercultural Jesus

Women were the first to be present at Jesus' birth, the last present at Jesus' crucifixion, and the first to be given the incredible privilege of sharing the great and good news of the Resurrection. Throughout His life Jesus treated women with great respect and dignity. . . .

In a day and time when the Orthodox Jew would include in his morning prayers, "I thank Thee, God, I am not a slave, I am not a Gentile, I am not a woman," Jesus made firm friends and followers of slaves, Gentiles, and women! . . . Women from all levels of society were involved in Christ's life and ministry. They ranked among His closest earthly friends (Mary and Martha) and assisted and traveled with Him on His tours of ministry, helping to support Him out of their own means (Luke 8:1–3).

Women who were sinners found forgiveness, women who were sick found health, and women who were dead found life!

JILL BRISCOE

Heartstrings

Evening

· · · · · · · · ·

There is neither Jew nor Greek, there is neither
slave nor free, there is neither male nor
female; for you are all one in Christ Jesus.

GALATIANS 3:28

Then the rib which the LORD God had taken from man
He made into a woman,
And He brought her to the man. And Adam said:
"This is now bone of my bones
And flesh of my flesh;
She shall be called Woman,
Because she was taken out of Man."

GENESIS 2:22—23

There were also women looking on from afar,
among whom were Mary Magdalene, Mary the
mother of James the Less and of Joses, and
Salome, who also followed Him and ministered
to Him when He was in Galilee, and many other
women who came up with Him to Jerusalem.

MARK 15:40—41

Rest—and Appreciate Life!

Some of you will appreciate my newfound area of excellence: doing nothing and resting afterward. It flies in the face of the Puritan work ethic we've all been taught and feels more decadent than a five-pound box of Godiva chocolates all to yourself. I would love to start a new habit amongst us perpetually tired women: ritualized resting.

Doesn't it seem that Sunday afternoons were specially made for napping? . . . I've always felt cheated that we live in a country that doesn't embrace the afternoon siesta. . . .

I love that the Bible tells us God didn't create Sabbath for Himself but that it was a life principle we human beings were desperately in need of. It seems that one of the most difficult things to do is to truly cease from all of our efforts and then relax and enjoy our life apart from the work of it. . . . I challenge you to start taking a day once a week to truly rest and appreciate the life God has given you.

ANITA RENFROE
The Purse-Driven Life

Evening

. . . .

"Come to Me, all you who labor and are
heavy laden, and I will give you rest."
MATTHEW 11:28

Remember the Sabbath day, to keep it holy.
EXODUS 20:8

"In six days the LORD made the heavens and
the earth, the sea, and all that is in them, and
rested the seventh day. Therefore the LORD
blessed the Sabbath day and hallowed it."
EXODUS 20:11

Facebook vs. Face-to-Face

One of the ironies of modern life is that the more technically interconnected we get, the more isolated and disconnected we seem to be. . . . I won't dispute that there is great value to the social networks and cyberfriends we enjoy. . . .

But when God wanted to demonstrate His love for us, it required nothing less than flesh meeting flesh. . . . In order to communicate His love, He sent Jesus to meet people face-to-face. The tablets and burning bushes were replaced with dinners, embraces, personal touch, and holy blood spilled on barren ground.

I'm so glad God didn't text, e-mail, or tweet His message of love to us. Only the appearance of God in the flesh could consummate the relationship He desired with us. It was this act of love that gave us the ability to lighten up and live fully alive.

KEN DAVIS

Fully Alive

Evening

. . . .

"For God so loved the world that He gave His
only begotten Son, that whoever believes in Him
should not perish but have everlasting life."

JOHN 3:16

Christ Jesus, who, being in the form of God, did
not consider it robbery to be equal with God, but
made Himself of no reputation, taking the form
of a bondservant, and coming in the likeness of
men. And being found in appearance as a man,
He humbled Himself and became obedient to the
point of death, even the death of the cross.

PHILIPPIANS 2:5–8

There is a friend who sticks closer than a brother.

PROVERBS 18:24

Sinned Against

Forgiving means we stop pressing rewind and play. Forgiving means we refuse to let our minds house the moldy leftovers of other's sins against us.

Jesus makes it clear: rehash of the past is a spiritual poison that hinders us from receiving God's forgiveness. Can anything be worth that price? Why do we hold on to what Jesus has called us to release?

For many, refusing to forgive is a weapon, the only form of punishment we think the offender will ever receive. But in truth, the weapon of unforgiveness points a sword at our own soul. . . .

Jesus knows what it's like to be sinned against. He was slandered, betrayed, abused, mocked, misrepresented, beaten, and rejected. Yet He stayed on the cross and paid the price to offer forgiveness even to those who would never admit their guilt or whisper, "I'm sorry."

ALICIA BRITT CHOLE

Sitting in God's Sunshine

Evening

. . . .

"Judge not, and you shall not be judged.
Condemn not, and you shall not be condemned.
Forgive, and you will be forgiven."

LUKE 6:37

We know Him who said, "Vengeance is Mine,
I will repay," says the Lord. And again, "The
LORD will judge His people." It is a fearful thing
to fall into the hands of the living God.

HEBREWS 10:30—31

"Be angry, and do not sin": do not let the sun go
down on your wrath, nor give place to the devil.

EPHESIANS 4:26—27

MARCH 19

161

Like a Cool Shower

Forgiving well means moving through the hurt and the legitimate anger that tells us we've been hurt, to a choice to release the person who inflicted the injury. Notice that I didn't say excuse. There's no effort to gloss over something here. Forgiveness is about looking the pain straight in the eye and saying, "God is bigger than this."

I find, personally, that there is nothing quite so helpful as a blank legal pad and a couple of hours. It's so helpful that about twice a year I take out my yellow pad and start to write, even when I can't think of anyone to forgive! I ask God to show me if there is anything I am holding against anyone, and I let my pencil do the talking. . . . Then I tear up the paper into a dozen little yellow pieces and go about my day. It's like taking a cool shower after jogging on a hot day.

PAULA RINEHART

Strong Women, Soft Hearts

Evening

· · · · · · · · · ·

"If you forgive men their trespasses, your
heavenly Father will also forgive you. But if you
do not forgive men their trespasses, neither
will your Father forgive your trespasses."

MATTHEW 6:14–15

Be kind to one another, tenderhearted, forgiving
one another, even as God in Christ forgave you.

EPHESIANS 4:32

"Blessed are the merciful,
For they shall obtain mercy."

MATTHEW 5:7

Misery Is Optional

Pain is inevitable for all of us, but we have an option as to how we react to the pain. It is no fun to suffer; in fact, it can be awful. We are all going to have pain, but misery is optional. We can decide how we react to the pain that inevitably comes to us all.

Since learning that I have diabetes, I have read a dozen books and even watched some video tapes to learn all I could about how to cope with this chronic, debilitating disease. The most important thing I learned is that having a proper mental attitude works wonders. If you take care of yourself and do all the things that you must do to keep it in control so that it doesn't control you, you can live a happy, productive life.

BARBARA JOHNSON

Stick a Geranium in Your Hat and Be Happy

Evening

· · · · · · · · ·

MARCH 21

Though I walk in the midst of trouble,
You will revive me;
You will stretch out Your hand
Against the wrath of my enemies,
And Your right hand will save me.

PSALM 138:7

What then shall we say to these things? If God is for
us, who can be against us? He who did not spare His
own Son, but delivered Him up for us all, how shall
He not with Him also freely give us all things?

ROMANS 8:31 32

I will mention the lovingkindnesses of the LORD
And the praises of the LORD,
According to all that the LORD has bestowed on us.

ISAIAH 63:7

165

Refuse, Replace, Repeat

Patsy Clairmont had to make some tough choices to overcome a longtime struggle with agoraphobia. She used a three-word principle to help her choose, one decision at a time, the right path. Those three words were *refuse, replace, repeat*.

She refused the negative thought that tempted her to make the wrong choice. She replaced the negative pull with something God assured her was true. And then she repeated that practice every time she was confronted by that mental fork in the road. Thinking about Patsy's advice, I . . . would *refuse* that negative choice—*Oh, you are so ugly. Nobody could love you*—and choose instead to *replace* it with what God (and Don) have convinced me is true: *Don is crazy about me, and God loves me more than anything I could ever imagine*. Then I repeat that truth again and again. . . .

I need to always perceive that I'm one choice away from heading in the right direction—and snap myself into making the choice God would have me make even when it's the hard choice.

SANDI PATTY

Layers

I can do all things through Christ
who strengthens me.

PHILIPPIANS 4:13

Charm is deceitful and beauty is passing,
But a woman who fears the LORD, she shall be praised.

PROVERBS 31:30

Do not let your adornment be merely outward—
arranging the hair, wearing gold, or
putting on fine apparel—rather let it
be the hidden person of the heart, with the
incorruptible beauty of a gentle and quiet spirit,
which is very precious in the sight of God.

1 PETER 3:3—4

Happily Ever After

Happily ever after has a wonderful ring to it, and many people do their best to try to secure that happy ending. They have their rabbit's foot, their lucky hat, or their not-to-be-varied pregame routine. Some of us Christians don't worry about having a rabbit's foot, but we do grab onto Romans 8:28 as something of a good luck charm.

But is this verse truly a happily-ever-after promise? God works for the good of those who love Him (criterion #1) and whom He has called according to His purpose for them (criterion #2). Verse 29 explains that purpose: God wants His people to become more like Jesus.

Jesus is sinless, holy, and pure. Jesus is patient and kind; He is not envious, boastful, rude, self-centered, irritable, or evil thinking.

God uses every event, relationship, challenge, and hurt that we experience to make us more like Jesus. No one can improve on that happily ever after.

100 Favorite Bible Verses

All things work together for good to those who
love God, to those who are the called according
to His purpose. For whom He foreknew, He also
predestined to be conformed to the image of His Son,
that He might be the firstborn among many brethren.

ROMANS 8:28—29

You are a chosen generation, a royal priesthood, a
holy nation, His own special people, that you may
proclaim the praises of Him who called you out of
darkness into His marvelous light; who once were not
a people but are now the people of God, who had not
obtained mercy but now have obtained mercy.

1 PETER 2:9—10

"You are the light of the world. . . . Let your light
so shine before men, that they may see your good
works and glorify your Father in heaven."

MATTHEW 5:14, 16

MARCH 24

Pouring God's Grace on Others

We human beings have an overwhelming tendency to jump to conclusions, to expect the worst in order to avoid disappointment, and to turn our backs on people who hurt us. Yet the Bible says, "Love never gives up, never loses faith, is always hopeful, and endures through every circumstance" (1 Corinthians 13:7 NLT).

The extent to which we are able to demonstrate this kind of love requires God's operative grace in our lives. We can love with this kind of love when we remember that life is *not about us*; it's about dying to self and surrendering our sinful tendencies to Christ. When we do, we are freed up to love one another as we want to be loved ourselves, and we get a taste of how we are loved by Christ.

Think about whom you struggle most to love. Pray about that relationship, surrender it to Christ, and begin letting His love flow through you to other imperfect humans.

A Jane Austen Devotional

"A new commandment I give to you, that
you love one another; as I have loved you,
that you also love one another."

JOHN 13:34

Let nothing be done through selfish ambition
or conceit, but in lowliness of mind let each
esteem others better than himself. Let each
of you look out not only for his own interests,
but also for the interests of others.

PHILIPPIANS 2:3—4

"Whoever desires to become great among you
shall be your servant. And whoever of you
desires to be first shall be slave of all."

MARK 10:43—44

Fight for Love

Throughout history, there have been heroes and warriors of every nation and creed, but no one fought harder for love—and won—than Jesus Christ.

Even when it became deadly for Him to love rebellious, self-centered, and hateful people, Jesus never quit. He fought, died, and rose again—because of love. But it wasn't just any love. It was a higher love—an absurd, illogical, crazy love not common to this world.

It's that kind of love we're going for. Bring that love to mind when you are tempted to give up on a difficult person, relationship, job, church, or calling.

Pursue love. Make love a habit. Fight to see it rise again.

More Than a Bucket List

Evening

· · · · · · · · ·

God demonstrates His own love toward us, in that
while we were still sinners, Christ died for us.

ROMANS 5:8

By this we know love, because He
laid down His life for us.

1 JOHN 3:16

In this is love, not that we loved God, but
that He loved us and sent His Son to be the
propitiation for our sins. Beloved, if God so
loved us, we also ought to love one another.

1 JOHN 4:10—11

The Fragrant Knowledge of God

I love crisp, cold days when you can smell the smoke of a cherry-wood fire from a neighbor's chimney. . . . I love the smell of fresh, damp laundry that you hang outside on the line. . . .

In 2 Corinthians 2:14 Paul wrote, "But thanks be to God, who always leads us in triumphal procession in Christ and through us spreads everywhere the fragrance of the knowledge of him."

That idea was borrowed from the ancient Roman parades of triumph. The apostle Paul compared himself, first, to one of the prisoners led in long chains behind the conqueror's chariot: then, to a servant bearing incense; and lastly, to the incense itself that rose all along the procession of triumph.

Paul knew the power behind a sweet fragrance. It is as though he were saying, . . . "I want my words and deeds to bring to the mind of God those wonderful, similar memories of the earthly life of Jesus."

JONI EARECKSON TADA

Seeking God

Let your heart therefore be loyal to the LORD
our God, to walk in His statutes and keep
His commandments, as at this day.

1 KINGS 8:61

Let us not grow weary while doing good, for in
due season we shall reap if we do not lose heart.

GALATIANS 6:9

Be doers of the word, and not hearers
only, deceiving yourselves.

JAMES 1:22

Real Strength

We have all known women who were strong, but not very honorable. Our television screens [and movies] are filled with them. And there are women who are honorable, but frankly, not very strong. The first setback or the first perceived threat, and they fold up like a card table.

The kind of women most of us long to be are both strong and honorable, clothed with the kind of power that comes from on high, certain of our value in God's eyes, definite in our calling, and moving forward with complete assurance. Francis De Sales said, "Nothing is so strong as gentleness, nothing so gentle as real strength."

LIZ CURTIS HIGGS
Only Angels Can Wing It

Let your gentleness be known to all men.

PHILIPPIANS 4:5

"Be strong and of good courage; do
not be afraid, nor be dismayed, for the LORD your
God is with you wherever you go."

JOSHUA 1:9

In you, O LORD, I put my trust;

Let me never be put to shame.

Deliver me in Your righteousness,

and cause me to escape;

Incline Your ear to me, and save me. . . .

For You are my hope, O Lord GOD,

You are my trust from my youth.

PSALM 71:1–2, 5

Accomplishing Goals

Ah, the joy of accomplishment! Aim for a goal and stick to it. And when you reach that goal, the natural result is to celebrate. We like to finish things, don't we? And to absolutely know we've finished, there's nothing like beating the drums, popping the corks, throwing the confetti, and commemorating the victory. If we realize a celebration is down the road . . . the tests along the way are easier to bear. Personally, I find I am more willing to defer rewards when I anticipate a big event at the end of the journey. That event serves as an incentive toward which I aim. It is part of the spoils of victory.

I love that thought. Many a time it has kept me going when all other inducements were dropping by the wayside. People were no longer cheering me on. My initial enthusiasm was waning. I was tired or discouraged. . . .

Rewards are the touchstones in our lives physically, materially, academically, financially, and even spiritually. They affirm our growth and the alchemy of our hearts.

LUCI SWINDOLL

You Bring the Confetti

Evening

· · · · · · · · ·

Do you not know that those who run in a race
all run, but one receives the prize? Run in such
a way that you may obtain it. And everyone
who competes for the prize is temperate in all
things. Now they do it to obtain a perishable
crown, but we for an imperishable crown.

1 CORINTHIANS 9:24 25

I do not count myself to have apprehended; but
one thing I do, forgetting those things which are
behind and reaching forward to those things
which are ahead, I press toward the goal for the
prize of the upward call of God in Christ Jesus.

PHILIPPIANS 3:13—14

Now may the God of peace Himself sanctify
you completely; and may your whole spirit,
soul, and body be preserved blameless at
the coming of our Lord Jesus Christ. He who
calls you is faithful, who also will do it.

1 THESSALONIANS 5:23—24

MARCH 28

179

Morning

· · · · · · · · ·

Words That Refresh

Job's friends pelted him with unrelenting words. Like torrential rains on parched soil, their words gouged deep gullies. Job attempted to escape like a tired swimmer, only to be crushed with a fresh wave of words. His comforters rapped him with anger, guilt, idle chatter, ignorance, and faulty conclusions. And he remained crushed instead of wrapped in comfort.

Do your words rain down comfort? Love chooses to cover instead of condemn. Job's choice confronts us daily. Some people provoke us to exchange blow for blow, gossip for gossip, curse for curse, rebuke for rebuke. To speak as Job's comforters spoke requires no wisdom or strength from God. That kind of speech comes naturally. But if we choose to use our words to encourage and comfort, we will need supernatural strength.

God is ready when you are.

JAN CARLBERG

The Hungry Heart

The heart of the wise teaches his mouth,
And adds learning to his lips.
Pleasant words are like a honeycomb,
Sweetness to the soul and health to the bones.

PROVERBS 16:23—24

A soft answer turns away wrath,
But a harsh word stirs up anger.
The tongue of the wise uses knowledge rightly,
But the mouth of fools pours forth foolishness.

PROVERBS 15:1—2

For we all stumble in many things. If anyone
does not stumble in word, he is a perfect
man, able also to bridle the whole body.

JAMES 3:2

MARCH 30

Trouble Trusting?

Think about all the different people to whom we entrust our lives. We trust pharmacists to give us the right pills from a prescription we can't read. We trust pilots we don't know to take us to the right destination. . . . As we soar down the interstate, we trust other drivers to stay alert and follow the road. We trust our lives to engineers and road construction crews, believing the bridges will hold. We make countless decisions to trust people we don't even know every single day.

Yet people have trouble trusting God. They often say, "I can't see Him." Do we see the engineers who designed the bridge? Do we know the pilots? Not usually. Yet God, our Creator, who loves us more than anyone, who even sacrificed His Son for us to have forgiveness of sin and eternal life, is difficult to trust. It's amazing. It just doesn't make sense to trust imperfect men and women and not to trust a perfect God. From the love He shows us through His Son, it just makes sense to trust Him.

BRYANT WRIGHT

Right from the Heart

Evening

· · · · · · · ·

I will say of the LORD, "He is my refuge and my fortress;
My God, in Him I will trust."

PSALM 91:2

Oh, taste and see that the LORD is good;
Blessed is the man who trusts in Him!
Oh, fear the LORD, you His saints!
There is no want to those who fear Him.

PSALM 34:8—9

The LORD is good,
A stronghold in the day of trouble;
And He knows those who trust in Him.

NAHUM 1:7

God Is Close

The answer to our deepest desires is not the seemingly perfect life . . . not the most romantic husband . . . not the smartest and most well-behaved kids . . . not the bigger house . . not the better job . . . not the awards and recognition of people . . . not in trying to feel our way to God.

It's making the choice to recognize God is close. Whether we're at a big concert, on a playground in the middle of a sorry kickball game, running the streets of our neighborhood, or sitting in a chair in our den—God is there. Loving. Assuring. Teaching. Calling. Choosing to spend time with us.

Becoming more than a good Bible study girl means never settling for needing to feel our way to God or to limit our experience of Him to those few minutes we call our quiet time. It's being able to sit in the noise of the arena of life with every worldly distraction imaginable bombarding you and suddenly thinking of Him—talking with Him, smiling with Him . . . The One who chooses you.

LYSA TERKEURST

Becoming More Than a Good Bible Study Girl

You are a chosen generation, a royal priesthood, a holy nation, His own special people, that you may proclaim the praises of Him who called you out of darkness into His marvelous light.

1 PETER 2:9

"Are not two sparrows sold for a copper coin? And not one of them falls to the ground apart from your Father's will. But the very hairs of your head are all numbered. Do not fear therefore; you are of more value than many sparrows."

MATTHEW 10:29–31

We love [God] because He first loved us.

1 JOHN 4:19

April

I will greatly rejoice in the Lord,
My soul shall be joyful in my God.

ISAIAH 61:10

. . . .

"Let Us Rejoice!"

Psalm 118 is part of the traditional Jewish Passover celebration Jesus celebrated the night He was arrested. One
can only imagine what was racing through His mind as
He read "the stone that the builders rejected has become
the cornerstone" (v. 22 ESV), "the LORD is on my side; I
will not fear. What can man do to me?" (v. 6 ESV), "This
is the gate of the LORD; the righteous shall enter through
it" (v. 20 ESV).

But buried in the psalm, and meant to give Him courage in that fateful hour, is this profession of astounding
faith: "This is the day that the LORD has made; let us
rejoice and be glad in it" (v. 24 ESV). Because Jesus knew
that God the Father loved and was for Him, He was able
to trust His Father and humbly obey His will—even unto
death. God created that awesome, astronomical day just
as He created today. If the Lord has made it and given it to
us with the promise of His inseparable love, let us rejoice
and be glad in it.

KEVIN HARTNETT

The Heavens

Evening

· · · · · · · · ·

For thus says the LORD,
Who created the heavens,
Who is God,
Who formed the earth and made it,
Who has established it,
Who did not create it in vain,
Who formed it to be inhabited:
"I am the LORD, and there is no other."

ISAIAH 45:18

"Where were you when I laid the foundations of the earth?
Tell Me, if you have understanding.
Who determined its measurements?
Surely you know!
Or who stretched the line upon it?
To what were its foundations fastened? . . .
Or who shut in the sea with doors,
When it burst forth and issued from the womb; . . .
Have you commanded the morning since your days began,
And caused the dawn to know its place . . .
Can you bind the cluster of the Pleiades,
Or loose the belt of Orion?"

JOB 38:4—6, 8, 12, 31

APRIL 2

Ransomed by Jesus

Can you think of someone in your life who has joy? I met someone recently whose body radiated joy. If someone had not told me, I never would have known she had three terminal diseases. Her life wasn't pain-free, but she had complete joy. Our first conversation explained why. She was in love with Jesus.

My friend had been ransomed! She realized exactly what Jesus had done for her and knew there would come a time when sorrow and sighing would flee away. In Luke 2:10, the angel says, "I bring you good tidings of great joy." What was this joy? It was Jesus! You, too, have been ransomed by Jesus—the only One who could possibly save you.

DENISE JONES

Women of Faith Devotional Bible

Evening

· · · · · · · · ·

"Fear not, for I have redeemed you;
I have called you by your name;
You are Mine.
When you pass through the waters, I will be with you;
And through the rivers, they shall not overflow you.
When you walk through the fire, you shall not be burned,
Nor shall the flame scorch you.
For I am the LORD your God,
The Holy One of Israel, your Savior."

ISAIAH 43:1–3

You were not redeemed with corruptible
things, like silver or gold, from your aimless
conduct received by tradition from your
fathers, but with the precious blood of Christ, as
of a lamb without blemish and without spot.

1 PETER 1:18–19

The ransomed of the LORD shall return,
And come to Zion with singing,
With everlasting joy on their heads.
They shall obtain joy and gladness;
Sorrow and sighing shall flee away.

ISAIAH 51:11

APRIL 3

An Anchor
Through Change

Spinning! Spiraling! Up! Down! Round and round! Nothing seems to stay the same. As soon as you're comfortable, things change. If it feels like things are moving too fast for you these days, you may have to work at slowing the pace. Being intentional about finding a few quiet moments to let the world simply go by is a good thing. The One who made order out of chaos is still in control.

Change often makes fear into an ally. Fear likes to remind you that you're out of your comfort zone. It heckles you about why things can't stay the same. The other voice of change is opportunity. It gives you a chance to stop and look at where you've been and where you want to go. Go to God! He's the same yesterday, today, and forever!

Memorize one of these scriptures. Write it on a note card, and repeat it several times a day until it really moves from your head to your heart. Let it echo in your mind every time you become anxious about life. Give yourself a moment to breathe in the small, still voice of God.

Your Promises from God Today

Evening

. . . .

Of old You laid the foundation of the earth,
And the heavens are the work of Your hands.
They will perish, but You will endure;
Yes, they will all grow old like a garment;
Like a cloak You will change them,
And they will be changed.
But You are the same,
And Your years will have no end.

PSALM 102:25–27

Be still, and know that I am God;
I will be exalted among the nations,
I will be exalted in the earth!
The LORD of hosts is with us;
The God of Jacob is our refuge.

PSALM 46:10–11

And the LORD, He is the One who goes before
you. He will be with you, He will not leave you
nor forsake you; do not fear nor be dismayed.

DEUTERONOMY 31:8

"Follow Me"

What I like about Jesus is that He didn't try to recruit people or use spin. Neither He nor His disciples ever said they were going on a mission trip, because they weren't. He just invited everyone and said they could follow Him. He didn't use big words or Christian code to cue people that He was in the club or that He wanted to protect His reputation. Or talk about all of the things He was going to do or the number of people He was going to have "pray the prayer" to accept Him. He didn't present God's plan like a prospectus promising a return on investment. He just asked people to join the adventure. It's almost like Jesus came to say, among other things, that a relationship with Him isn't supposed to make complete sense or provide security. Faith isn't an equation or a formula or a business deal that gets you what you want. In short, there's nothing on the other side of the equals sign, just Jesus.

BOB GOFF

Love Does

Evening

Jesus, walking by the Sea of Galilee, saw two
brothers, Simon called Peter, and Andrew his
brother, casting a net into the sea; for they
were fishermen. Then He said to them, "Follow
Me, and I will make you fishers of men." They
immediately left their nets and followed Him.

MATTHEW 4:18–20

"My sheep hear My voice, and I know them,
and they follow Me. And I give them eternal
life, and they shall never perish."

JOHN 10:27–28

Jesus said to His disciples, "If anyone desires
to come after Me, let him deny himself,
and take up his cross, and follow Me."

MATTHEW 16:24

Growing Spiritually

True knowledge of Christ comes only as we are willing to give up our dreams of glory, praying to be identified with Him on the cross. . . . Are we really willing to let God take us through times of defeat and despair, when we experience communion with Him in His crucifixion?

The wonder of God's goodness is that He can use these "crosses" for our sanctification, just as He used the death of Jesus to advance His redemptive plan. "You meant evil against me, but God meant it for good," Joseph told his brothers (Genesis 50:20). Christians sometimes think it a matter of piety to deny the evil done to them—to cover it up, say it wasn't so bad, wear a smile in public.

Yet Joseph did not shrink from calling his brothers' actions evil, and neither should we. In this world, we too will be rejected by people with sinful motives, and for the sake of truth we should call it what it is. But we can also turn it to good by realizing that suffering gives us a chance to enter spiritually upon the journey that Jesus mapped out for us: rejected, slain (spiritually), and, finally, raised.

NANCY PEARCEY

Total Truth

Evening

· · · · · · · · ·

We also glory in tribulations, knowing that
tribulation produces perseverance; and
perseverance, character; and character, hope.
Now hope does not disappoint, because the
love of God has been poured out in our hearts
by the Holy Spirit who was given to us.

ROMANS 5:3—5

"If anyone desires to come after Me, let him deny
himself, and take up his cross daily, and follow Me."

LUKE 9:23

We do not lose heart. Though outwardly we are
wasting away, yet inwardly we are being renewed day
by day. For our light and momentary troubles
are achieving for us an eternal glory that far
outweighs them all. So we fix our eyes not on what
is seen, but on what is unseen, since what is seen
is temporary, but what is unseen is eternal.

2 CORINTHIANS 4:16—18 NIV

The Letter A

[In Nathaniel Hawthorne's classic novel *The Scarlet Letter*,] Hester Prynne, a "fallen woman" during Colonial times, is forced by her Puritan community to wear the red letter A on the bodice of her dress as punishment for the sin of bearing a child out of wedlock.

My friend imagined that big scarlet letter A being worn by all the women today "who feel unworthy to hold their heads up as God's daughters." Now, thinking about that image, let me ask you: Are you one of us? If you are what does that A stand for? Abuse? Adultery? Abortion? Appetite? Anger? Abandonment? Avoidance? Adoption? Alcohol?

Maybe it did originally. . . . I hope you see instead that as Christians that A stands for something altogether different: *atonement*. . . .

All those mistakes we made, all those sins we committed are forgiven and forgotten, paid for in full by Jesus' death on the cross. And because of another wonderful A-word—*arisen!*—we have the promise of a gloriously wonderful life in heaven with God—*always*.

SANDI PATTY

Layers

Evening

. . . .

"I will establish My covenant with you. Then you shall know that I am the LORD . . . when I provide you an atonement for all you have done," says the Lord GOD.

EZEKIEL 16:62—63

In mercy and truth
Atonement is provided for iniquity;
And by the fear of the LORD one departs from evil.

PROVERBS 16:6

We have been sanctified through the offering of the body of Jesus Christ once for all. . . . Every priest stands ministering daily and offering repeatedly the same sacrifices, which can never take away sins. But this Man, after He had offered one sacrifice for sins forever, sat down at the right hand of God. . . . For by one offering He has perfected forever those who are being sanctified.

HEBREWS 10:10—12, 14

From Abandoned to Embraced

We will never know what it meant for Christ to have His own Father throw Him into that cauldron of deepest evil . . . [and turn] away from His Son. As Jesus bore the sin of the world, He endured an indescribable abandonment. The innocent shed His blood for the guilty.

There simply was no other way.

Millennia before, when Adam and Eve disobeyed God . . . their sin ripped a chasm between a holy God and a broken people. They felt it in the garden: abandoned, alone, ashamed. Since then, each one of us has felt it, and so we have cried out, "Why?" . . .

On the cross, Jesus uttered the question that so many of us have asked of God in our own darkest nights, "Why have You forsaken me?" The question hung in the air, held there by pure, raw, uncomprehending agony. . . . "It is finished!" He cried (John 19:30) a little later. And then, finally, "Father, into your hands I commit my spirit" (Luke 23:46).

From abandoned to embraced. And so shall it be for us.

SHEILA WALSH

God Loves Broken People

Evening

· · · · · · · · ·

[God] made Him who knew no sin to be sin for us, that
we might become the righteousness of God in Him.

2 CORINTHIANS 5:21

Now from the sixth hour until the ninth hour there
was darkness over all the land. And about the ninth
hour Jesus cried out with a loud voice, saying, "Eli,
Eli, lama sabachthani?" that is, "My God, My God,
why have You forsaken Me?" . . . Then, behold,
the veil of the temple was torn in two from top to
bottom; and the earth quaked, and the rocks were
split. . . . When the centurion and those with him,
who were guarding Jesus, saw the earthquake
and the things that had happened, they feared
greatly, saying, "Truly this was the Son of God!"

MATTHEW 27:45—46, 51, 54

We love Him because He first loved us.

1 JOHN 4:19

APRIL 7

201

God Shows Us What Is Good

God's most powerful illustration of what is good is His own Son. Jesus overturned the tables of the money changers who had made His Father's house a den of thieves. He paid taxes—with money He got from a fish's mouth. And He spoke out openly against the hypocrisy of Jewish church leaders who used their power for their own good. Jesus did justly.

Jesus healed the sick, made the blind see, and enabled the lame to walk. He freed people from demons and illness. He reached out to Samaritans, prostitutes, and tax collectors, to sinners like you and me. Jesus loved mercy.

Jesus submitted to God's will to the point of dying on a cross. After His agonized prayers in Gethsemane, Jesus ultimately agreed to do the Father's will, not His own. Jesus walked humbly with His God. May we walk in our Savior's footprints.

100 Favorite Bible Verses

He has shown you, O man, what is good;
And what does the LORD require of you
But to do justly,
To love mercy,
And to walk humbly with your God?

MICAH 6:8

[Jesus] said, "Abba, Father, all things are possible
for You. Take this cup away from Me; nevertheless,
not what I will, but what You will."

MARK 14:36

Humble yourselves in the sight of the
Lord, and He will lift you up.

JAMES 4:10

"Whoever desires to become great among you,
let him be your servant. And whoever desires to
be first among you, let him be your slave—just as
the Son of Man did not come to be served, but to
serve, and to give His life a ransom for many."

MATTHEW 20:26—28

APRIL 9

Abiding in Christ

It's not your circumstances that shape you. They are outside you and beyond you; they can't really touch you. It's
how you react to your circumstances that shapes you.
That's between your ears, and that affects the "real you."

And what controls your reactions? Abiding in Christ
(John 15:4–10 KJV). Staying there.

Then what if you find, for instance, a lump in your
breast? Of course you'll make a doctor's appointment
immediately—but that's external. What happens within?

*Lord, nothing important has changed. You love me. Your
eternal, perfect plans for me are continuing on schedule. I will
praise You; I will worship You. I will rest in all You're continuing
to do in my life.*

ANNE ORTLUND

Disciplines of the Heart

Evening

"Abide in Me, and I in you. As the branch cannot
bear fruit of itself, unless it abides in the vine,
neither can you, unless you abide in Me. I am the
vine, you are the branches. He who abides in Me, and
I in him, bears much fruit; for without Me you can
do nothing. . . . By this My Father is glorified, that
you bear much fruit; so you will be My disciples."

JOHN 15:4–5, 8

Now may our Lord Jesus Christ Himself, and our God
and Father, who has loved us and given us everlasting
consolation and good hope by grace, comfort your
hearts and establish you in every good word and work.

2 THESSALONIANS 2:16–17

God will wipe away every tear from their eyes;
there shall be no more death, nor sorrow,
nor crying. There shall be no more pain, for
the former things have passed away.

REVELATION 21:4

Worshiping God

Praise and worship of God are always acts of will. Sometimes our problems or the burdens we carry choke out our good intentions, so we have to make the effort to establish praise as a way of life. And it becomes a way of life when we make it our first reaction to what we face and not a last resort. That's when we find true freedom in the Lord. . . .

In the Old Testament, the people who carried the Ark of the Covenant stopped every six steps to worship. We, too, need to remind ourselves not to go very far without stopping to worship. For spiritual well-being, we have to be six-step persons and continually invite the presence of the Lord to rule in our situations. We have to be free to praise Him no matter what our circumstances.

STORMIE OMARTIAN
Praying God's Will for Your Life

Evening

· · · · · · · ·

Give unto the LORD, O you mighty ones,
Give unto the LORD glory and strength.
Give unto the LORD the glory due to His name;
Worship the LORD in the beauty of holiness.

PSALM 29:1–2

Oh come, let us worship and bow down;
Let us kneel before the LORD our Maker.
For He is our God,
And we are the people of His pasture,
And the sheep of His hand.

PSALM 95:6–7

"The hour is coming, and now is, when the true
worshipers will worship the Father in spirit and
truth; for the Father is seeking such to worship
Him. God is Spirit, and those who worship
Him must worship in spirit and truth."

JOHN 4:23–24

APRIL 10

APRIL 11

Made to Need Him

Would you send your only son to die for someone you just like a little? No! For goodness' sake, you'd only send him to die for those you can't bear to live for eternity without. The ones you are wildly in love with. For your beloved. For your baby girl. That's who God sent His only Son for.

God has known from the very beginning that you and I would need a Savior. He is well acquainted with our humanity. And He's *not mad about it*. We are the created, and He is the Creator. You need a Savior. I need a Savior. And I still need a Savior this very day to forgive me of my sins, to give guidance to my next decisions, to parent these children well, and to work by the power of the Holy Spirit to change me from the woman I have been into a woman who looks more like Him. . . .

You need a Savior, and He has never been mad that you were made to need Him.

ANGELA THOMAS
My Single Mom Life

"The Son of Man has come to save that which was lost."

MATTHEW 18:11

[Jesus said to His disciples,] "Children, how
hard it is for those who trust in riches to enter
the kingdom of God! It is easier for a camel
to go through the eye of a needle than for a
rich man to enter the kingdom of God."
And they were greatly astonished, saying among
themselves, "Who then can be saved?"
But Jesus looked at them and said, "With
men it is impossible, but not with God;
for with God all things are possible."

MARK 10:24—27

Christ died for the ungodly. For scarcely for a
righteous man will one die; yet perhaps for a good
man someone would even dare to die. But God
demonstrates His own love toward us, in that
while we were still sinners, Christ died for us.

ROMANS 5:6—8

APRIL 12

Jesus Is Enough

Jesus didn't live an easy life or die an easy death. The glory of Easter was preceded by the sorrow of absolute rejection. Our Redeemer knows what it feels like to be stripped of all comfort and ease. He experienced the betrayal of best friends. He sobbed alone, without a single person offering support. Yet, instead of trying to drown His sorrows with a margarita or spilling His guts to a sympathetic stranger on a plane, He endured. He shouldered the greatest possible anguish, being completely abandoned by everyone, including God, so we would never have to carry that burden ourselves.

I didn't used to believe Jesus was enough for me. . . . It wasn't until I hit the bottom that I found the love of Christ really is enough to sustain me, no matter what. Buckling under the weight of my own life is what helped me fall into the arms of God. I didn't just stumble into His grace; I collapsed there in a messy heap! And you know what? It's by far the best thing that's ever happened to me.

LISA HARPER

Stumbling into Grace

He is despised and rejected by men,
A Man of sorrows and acquainted with grief.
And we hid, as it were, our faces from Him;
He was despised, and we did not esteem Him.

ISAIAH 53:3

[Jesus] sat down with the twelve. Now as they were
eating, He said, "Assuredly, I say to you, one of you
will betray Me." . . . Jesus said to [Peter], "Assuredly,
I say to you that this night, before the rooster
crows, you will deny Me three times." . . .
[Jesus] began to be sorrowful and deeply distressed.
Then He said to [His disciples], "My soul is
exceedingly sorrowful, even to death. Stay here
and watch with Me." . . . He came to the disciples
and found them sleeping, and said to Peter, "What!
Could you not watch with Me one hour?"

MATTHEW 26:20—21, 34, 37—38, 40

Against You, You only, have I sinned, . . .
Purge me with hyssop, and I shall be clean;
Wash me, and I shall be whiter than snow.

PSALM 51:4, 7

211

APRIL 13

God's Glory in Our Lives

I have two containers for flowers. One is an old clay pot; the other is a beautiful cut-glass vase. Occasionally, I receive a lovely bouquet of roses. If I put them in the vase, the glory is shared. If I put them in the pot, attention is drawn to the blossoms. "What beautiful flowers!" exclaim my visitors, ignoring the container.

God chooses such earthen vessels that His glory may be better displayed. In fact, He has told us that He will not share His glory with another. He insists on receiving the honor due His name.

Sometimes I want to be the cut-glass vase and draw attention to myself. I have to be reminded that my sense of importance lies in the miracle of God's choosing me. He placed His roses in my vase. In this lies my value. What use is a vase without flowers?

JILL BRISCOE

Quiet Times with God

Evening

We have this treasure [of the knowledge of Jesus
Christ] in earthen vessels, that the excellence
of the power may be of God and not of us.

2 CORINTHIANS 4:7

Not unto us, O LORD, not unto us,
But to Your name give glory,
Because of Your mercy,
Because of Your truth.

PSALM 115:1

In God is my salvation and my glory;
The rock of my strength,
And my refuge, is in God.

PSALM 62:7

213

Morning

. . . .

Honesty, Transparency, and Grace

Perhaps God's most beautiful gift to the believer is His provision for forgiveness and reconciliation. It cost Him everything—the life and death of His Son. It costs us so little by comparison—only that we be willing to confess each wrong thought or deed or attitude and turn back to Him. Yet so often we let sins fester unconfessed beneath the surface of our lives.

One vital ingredient in our relationship with Jesus is our willingness to be honest with Him. He found it easy to be friends with harlots and tax collectors because they were honest with Him about their sinfulness. And He asks the same honesty of us. . . .

Christians whose lives are transparent before the Father see themselves as sinners. They understand grace and praise God for it. Because they know their forgiveness was not bought cheaply, they take it very seriously.

CLAIRE CLONINGER

When God Shines Through

Evening

. . . .

"Her sins, which are many, are forgiven,
for she loved much. But to whom little
is forgiven, the same loves little."

LUKE 7:47

Now all things are of God, who has reconciled us
to Himself through Jesus Christ, and has given us
the ministry of reconciliation, that is, that God
was in Christ reconciling the world to Himself.

2 CORINTHIANS 5:18–19

For it pleased the Father that in Him all the
fullness should dwell, and by Him to reconcile
all things to Himself, by Him, whether things
on earth or things in heaven, having made
peace through the blood of His cross.

COLOSSIANS 1:19—20

"Grace Be with You"

[The apostle] Paul normally closed his letters by saying, "Grace be with you." Now, it's interesting that Paul used that particular phrase because he had been a most unlikely candidate for receiving the grace of God. Paul spent his first career terrorizing first-century Christians. He literally persecuted the church and oversaw the killing of Christians. . . .

Then Christ appeared to him, forgave him and saved him. And Paul . . . focused on the grace of Christ because he knew he didn't deserve to be forgiven. . . . None of us does either. Not one of us deserves to have the God of the universe go to a cross and pay that awful penalty for us so that we might be forgiven and have eternal life. . . .

A Christ-centered church will focus on the grace of God that's found in what Jesus did for us on the cross. It will emphasize the grace of God, remembering the price Jesus paid in giving us something none of us deserves—forgiveness, salvation, and eternal life.

BRYANT WRIGHT

Right from the Heart

Evening

· · · · · · · · ·

And the Word became flesh and dwelt among us, and
we beheld His glory, the glory as of the only begotten
of the Father, full of grace and truth. . . .
For the law was given through Moses, but grace
and truth came through Jesus Christ.

JOHN 1:14, 17

By grace you have been saved through faith,
and that not of yourselves; it is the gift of God,
not of works, lest anyone should boast.

EPHESIANS 2:8–9

Let us therefore come boldly to the throne
of grace, that we may obtain mercy and
find grace to help in time of need.

HEBREWS 4:16

Morning

. . . .

Forgiven . . . and Forgiving

Forgiveness was the key to real freedom in my life. It unlocked all kinds of new blessings. . . .

I prayed, pouring out my concerns to God. . . . I asked Him to do things in my heart that I just could not do on my own. I asked Him to free me from rage. And I prayed that He would help me to be the loving, forgiving [person] that I wanted to be.

I knew I could not be that person through my own good intentions or willpower. I wasn't strong enough. But God was strong enough to do miracles in me. . . .

My ability to forgive . . . had a lot to do with realizing that I, too, was in need of forgiveness. . . . If I could begin to see how big and revolting my sins really were in God's eyes, and yet how He had wiped out every single one of them, then I'd have a big love for Him. . . . Out of the overflowing gratitude of realizing that *I'd* been totally forgiven, I could follow Jesus' lead and forgive the debts of others who owed me.

DENISE JACKSON

It's All About Him

Evening

· · · · · · · · ·

"Forgive, and you will be forgiven."

LUKE 6:37

"Forgive us our debts,
As we forgive our debtors."

MATTHEW 6:12

"Whenever you stand praying, if you have anything
against anyone, forgive him, that your Father in
heaven may also forgive you your trespasses."

MARK 11:25

Releasing Our Brokenness

We live in a world gone wrong, one that was created perfect but now suffers the ravages of sin: death, violated relationships, children born with disabilities and deformities, disease, man's inhumanity to man, moral failures, tragedies of major proportions, chaos. It is, indeed, a broken world. But it is one thing to shake our heads at the mess the world is in; it is quite another to confront the reality of it in our own lives. . . .

When we stand in the middle of a life storm, it seems as if the storm has become our way of life. We cannot see a way out. We are unable to chart a course back to smoother waters. We feel defeated—and broken. Will that brokenness produce a cynicism that will keep us forever in the mire of "if only" thinking? Or will we yield up that brokenness to the resources of One who calms the winds and the waves, heals the brokenhearted, and forgives the most grievous of sins? The choice is ours.

VERDELL DAVIS

Riches Stored in Secret Places

APRIL 17

The creation was subjected to futility, not
willingly . . . the creation itself also will be
delivered from the bondage of corruption into
the glorious liberty of the children of God. For
we know that the whole creation groans and
labors with birth pangs together until now.

ROMANS 8:20—22

The LORD is near to those who have a broken heart,
And saves such as have a contrite spirit.
Many are the afflictions of the righteous,
But the LORD delivers him out of them all.

PSALM 34:18—19

The ransomed of the LORD shall return,
And come to Zion with singing,
With everlasting joy on their heads.
They shall obtain joy and gladness,
And sorrow and sighing shall flee away.

ISAIAH 35:10

Morning

. . . .

Only One Yardstick

There's only one yardstick by which to measure our worth. You and I were made in the image of God. . . . Your combination of giftedness is absolutely unique. Mine is exceptionally weird. There's none other like either of us in the universe.

Here's a list of personal reminders I use:

- I will never play football and live to tell about it.
- I will never change the world with my deep philosophical contributions. . . .
- I will never beat my mother in a game of cards. . . .

Here is the most important fact concerning the above: IT DOESN'T MATTER. Here is all that matters:

- God made me in His image.
- God made me unique.
- God loves me.

We are significant because our Creator is significant.

KEN DAVIS

Lighten Up!

Evening

· · · · · · · · ·

APRIL 18

"I have called you by your name;
You are Mine."

ISAIAH 43:1

You formed my inward parts;
You covered me in my mother's womb.
I will praise You, for I am fearfully and wonderfully made.

PSALM 139:13—14

Present your bodies a living sacrifice, holy,
acceptable to God, which is your reasonable
service. And do not be conformed to this world,
but be transformed by the renewing of your
mind, that you may prove what is that good
and acceptable and perfect will of God.

ROMANS 12:1—2

223

Morning

. . . .

The Happiest Ending Possible

Since God loves us too much to see us die as a result of our sin, He had His Son take our place as a perfect sacrifice, so that all of our sins could be forgiven. . . .

Just when the demons of hell thought they were victorious because the Son of God was dead . . . the earth began to shake. . . . The stone that blocked the entrance to the tomb slowly began to roll away.

Jesus had risen from the dead! Jesus conquered death and conquered sin for us. . . . God has given us the gift of joining His family and living with Him forever.

I love a happy ending. . . . In this story, you and I receive the best ending ever: we are adopted daughters of God! . . . You and I are daughters of the same God who created the stars . . . who invented the concept of breathing . . . who formed the fish in the sea and the birds in the air! That's our Dad!

JENNA LUCADO BISHOP

Redefining Beautiful

Evening

· · · · · · · · · ·

Now after the Sabbath, as the first day of the
week began to dawn, Mary Magdalene and the
other Mary came to see the tomb. And behold,
there was a great earthquake; for an angel of
the Lord descended from heaven, and came and
rolled back the stone from the door, and sat on
it. His countenance was like lightning, and his
clothing as white as snow. And the guards shook
for fear of him, and became like dead men.
But the angel answered and said to the women, "Do
not be afraid, for I know that you seek Jesus who was
crucified. He is not here; for He is risen, as He said."

MATTHEW 28:1–6

When the fullness of the time had come, God sent
forth His Son, born of a woman, born under the
law, to redeem those who were under the law, that
we might receive the adoption as sons. And because
you are sons, God has sent forth the Spirit of His
Son into your hearts, crying out, "Abba, Father!"

GALATIANS 4:4–6

"O Death, where is your sting?
O Hades, where is your victory?"

1 CORINTHIANS 15:55

APRIL 19

225

Scandalous Grace

May I just say something and get it out into the open? We're all dysfunctional.

There isn't one of us who hasn't "functioned abnormally" at some point in time. There isn't one of us who has skated through life without an impairment of some sort tagging behind her. . . .

Listen: I struggle. I dream. I aspire to be more like Jesus.

And on other days? Well, I think I'm as much like Him as I care to be.

Ah, such is the marvelous journey of life.

I am convinced that most women could stand a heaping dose of scandalous grace that enables them to cut themselves—as well as one another—some serious slack. . . . It is this grace . . . that truly becomes the icing on the cake of life—freeing us as women and provoking us to live outwardly with mercy and forgiveness toward one another and ourselves.

JULIE ANN BARNHILL

Scandalous Grace

Have mercy upon me, O God,
According to Your lovingkindness;
According to the multitude of Your tender mercies,
Blot out my transgressions.
Wash me thoroughly from my iniquity,
And cleanse me from my sin.

PSALM 51:1—2

Since we are receiving a kingdom which cannot be
shaken, let us have grace, by which we may serve
God acceptably with reverence and godly fear.

HEBREWS 12:28

[The Lord] said to me [Paul], "My grace is
sufficient for you, for My strength is made
perfect in weakness." Therefore most gladly
I will rather boast in my infirmities, that the
power of Christ may rest upon me. Therefore I
take pleasure in infirmities, in reproaches, in
needs, in persecutions, in distresses, for Christ's
sake. For when I am weak, then I am strong.

2 CORINTHIANS 12:9—10

Morning

. . . .

New Beginnings

Many situations in life—graduation, starting a new job, moving out on your own—are brand-new beginnings, a fresh start, a chance to try again or to try something completely new.

These aren't the only fresh starts you'll experience in life, however. God offers you a "beginning-again" ceremony every time you need a second chance. Whenever you blow it, make a poor choice, or even all-out rebel, God says, "Let's begin again." You don't have to go to a job interview or sign a new lease. All God asks is that you come to Him in honest repentance and ask His forgiveness. From that moment, the past truly is history. All is forgiven, and your fresh start is ready to commence.

Living God's Way

Evening

. . . .

"I, even I, am He who blots out your
transgressions for My own sake;
And I will not remember your sins."

ISAIAH 43:25

If we confess our sins, He is faithful and
just to forgive us our sins and to cleanse
us from all unrighteousness.

1 JOHN 1:9

For as the heavens are high above the earth,
So great is His mercy toward those who fear Him;
As far as the east is from the west,
So far has He removed our transgressions from us.

PSALM 103:11—12

Taking a Break from Heartache

I have yet to meet a humorist, a comedian, or a clown who didn't have some deep hurt at the heart of his or her humor. When we laugh at something, we are in essence saying, "I identify with that!" If someone stood up and described all their blessings, we would be disgusted. When they stand up and share all their faults and foibles, we laugh and love them for it. Rosita Perez kindly encouraged me in a letter with these words: "Whoever says laughter isn't healing just hasn't hurt enough."

Laughter does not mean you are ignoring pain, living in denial, or just not aware of the troubles around you. . . . For me, laughter is how we take a much-needed break from the heartache, such that when we turn to face it again, it has by some miracle grown smaller in size and intensity, if not disappeared altogether.

LIZ CURTIS HIGGS
Only Angels Can Wing It

APRIL 22

The LORD also will be a refuge for the oppressed,
A refuge in times of trouble.
And those who know Your name will put their trust in You;
For You, LORD, have not forsaken those who seek You.

PSALM 9:9—10

Weeping may endure for a night,
But joy comes in the morning.

PSALM 30:5

The fruit of the Spirit is love, joy, peace,
longsuffering, kindness, goodness,
faithfulness, gentleness, self-control.

GALATIANS 5:22—23

"I Will Never Be Shaken"

The Bible doesn't whitewash human nature or paint a picture of a pain-free world. Life is difficult, and the Bible doesn't suggest otherwise.

David was facing difficult times when he penned Psalm 62—"Truly he is my rock and my salvation; he is my fortress, I will never be shaken" (v. 2 NIV). Whatever the circumstances, David chose to focus on God. He reminded himself that God was his rock, a secure foundation for life.

Now consider the last part of this verse. Sounding entirely confident in his God, David proclaimed, "I will never be shaken." Nothing would rattle his faith! But the English Standard Version offers a glimpse of David's humanness: "I shall not be greatly shaken." This translation may be more real-life. Acknowledging at least implicitly the reality that events can shake—at least a little bit—the faith of even the most devoted follower, the psalmist vowed to "not be *greatly* shaken." The shaking doesn't last long. After all, the psalmist knows to turn to his Lord, who is his rock, his salvation, his fortress.

Evening

· · · · · · · · ·

"In the world you will have tribulation; but be
of good cheer, I have overcome the world."

JOHN 16:33

"I am with you always, even to the end of the age."

MATTHEW 28:20

The LORD is my rock and my fortress and my deliverer;
My God, my strength, in whom I will trust;
My shield and the horn of my salvation, my stronghold.

PSALM 18:2

No Better News!

The night my husband and I told my parents that we were expecting our first child, we had tickets for all of us to see *Oklahoma*. Before we left, I made an insert to go into the playbill about a show coming in March called *A Baby Story*. The flyer listed that I'd be playing the part of "Mom," my husband, "Dad," and my parents, the "doting grandparents." We got there early to stuff our announcement into playbills for my parents. I'll never forget their joy when they saw the spring lineup! . . .

But honestly, that's exactly how we should feel every day as we carry in our hearts the joy of the gospel. The word *gospel* literally means "good news." And what better news could there be than that through Christ, our sins can be forgiven, our lives made new, and our access to God opened wide. Does your heart burst to share Christ? If not, ask God to renew the joy of your salvation and your eagerness to share His gospel.

CATHERINE CLAIRE LARSON
Waiting in Wonder

Evening

Restore to me the joy of Your salvation,
And uphold me by Your generous Spirit.
Then I will teach transgressors Your ways,
And sinners shall be converted to You.

PSALM 51:12—13

"God so loved the world that He gave His only
begotten Son, that whoever believes in Him
should not perish but have everlasting life."

JOHN 3:16

[Jesus] answered [the Pharisees] and said to them, "I
tell you that if these [people lining the road] should
keep silent, the stones would immediately cry out."

LUKE 19:40

APRIL 24

235

APRIL 25

Gardening Joy

The garden looks as rumpled as clothes left in the dryer too long. It looks at you with the same accusing eyes. Enough beans remain for tonight's vegetable dish, but in this unpredicted heat wave isn't it easier to take something from the freezer? . . . Why bother? . . . Working in the garden offers an intimate contact with God through the earth and its power for growing things. . . .

If [you have] never known the thrill of growing things, try it! You have no need for a course in botany, biology, or chemistry. Just read the seed catalogues, the directions on the seed packets, start digging, raking, smoothing, and praying. There! Do you feel the surge of life beneath your hands? You are helping this earth (that God Himself planted in the beginning) to perpetuate life. Something happens between you and God that's very special and very intimate. Then, with the harvest, there comes a certain knowing that you have been in direct touch with the Creator. What joy!

JUNE MASTERS BACHER

Quiet Moments for Women

God blessed them, and God said to them. . . . "See,
I have given you every herb that yields seed which
is on the face of all the earth, and every tree whose
fruit yields seed; to you it shall be for food."

GENESIS 1:28–29

The heavens declare the glory of God;
And the firmament shows His handiwork.

PSALM 19:1

Since the creation of the world [God's]
invisible attributes are clearly seen, being
understood by the things that are made, even His
eternal power and Godhead, so that [the unrighteous]
are without excuse [for not believing].

ROMANS 1:20

Morning

· · · · · · · ·

The Beauty
of God

I remember standing in St. Isaac's Cathedral in St. Petersburg once and feeling awash with the majesty of God. Beautiful paintings depicting classic Bible stories filled the walls—a visual feast to the illiterate eyes of Russian peasants from another century. Incense and music enveloped me. I have never been more tangibly aware of the splendor of a high and holy God. Worship is really the only rational response we can have to beauty of this magnitude. . . .

But there is another aspect of that beauty that awes. That this high and holy God, who owes us nothing, would come in search of us—now that is worth stopping in your tracks to absorb.

PAULA RINEHART

Strong Women, Soft Hearts

Evening

. . . .

"You shall be holy, for I the LORD your God am holy."

LEVITICUS 19:2

One thing I have desired of the LORD,
That will I seek:
That I may dwell in the house of the LORD
All the days of my life,
To behold the beauty of the LORD.

PSALM 27:4

Let the beauty of the LORD our God be upon us,
And establish the work of our hands for us;
Yes, establish the work of our hands.

PSALM 90:17

Morning

Our Empathetic Hero

Mouthy, well-intentioned Peter, who'd vowed to stick to Jesus like Velcro, fell asleep while the Messiah mourned under those gnarled trees in the Garden of Gethsemane. Our Savior was bereft of companionship. No one dropped by with a pint of chicken soup. No one wrote Him a note expressing his or her condolences. Every single person abandoned Him during His time of deepest need. And that's why the author of Hebrews was able to preach, "God is the One who made all things, and all things are for his glory. He wanted to have many children share his glory, so he made the One who leads people to salvation perfect through suffering. . . . And now he can help those who are tempted, because he himself suffered and was tempted" (Hebrews 2:10, 18 NCV). Jesus didn't supernaturally skip to the front of the pain line. He chose instead to be an empathetic hero, sharing perfectly in the frailty and loneliness of our humanity.

LISA HARPER

Stumbling into Grace

Evening

. . . .

Christ Jesus, who, being in the form of God, did
not consider it robbery to be equal with God, but
made Himself of no reputation, taking the form
of a bondservant, and coming in the likeness of
men. And being found in appearance as a man,
He humbled Himself and became obedient to the
point of death, even the death of the cross.

PHILIPPIANS 2:5—8

Christ also suffered once for sins, the just for the
unjust, that He might bring us to God, being put
to death in the flesh but made alive by the Spirit.

1 PETER 3:18

Surely He has borne our griefs
And carried our sorrows;
Yet we esteemed Him stricken,
Smitten by God, and afflicted.
But He was wounded for our transgressions,
He was bruised for our iniquities;
The chastisement for our peace was upon Him,
And by His stripes we are healed.

ISAIAH 53:4—5

APRIL 27

Morning

. . . .

Recapturing Joy

Is celebrating really that important anyway?

Yes, it is!

Life today is difficult. Problems challenge us, and we worry about our children's futures.

It's easy to fall into the trap of taking ourselves too seriously, of worrying about success, jobs, acceptance, parenting, illnesses, and so on. It's easy to lose our ability to laugh. It's easy to forget the simple ways of purely enjoying one another. Celebration keeps us balanced in a difficult world, renews our perspective, and enables us to recapture joy. It provides us with an easy means of building friendships within the family. A real benefit of celebration is that it can be very simple and yet the dividends are so great.

SUSAN ALEXANDER YATES

A House Full of Friends

Evening

. . . .

Make a joyful shout to the LORD, all you lands!
Serve the LORD with gladness;
Come before His presence with singing.
Know that the LORD, He is God;
It is He who has made us, and not we ourselves;
We are His people and the sheep of His pasture.
Enter into His gates with thanksgiving,
And into His courts with praise.
Be thankful to Him, and bless His name.
For the LORD is good;
His mercy is everlasting,
And His truth endures to all generations.

PSALM 100:1—5

Rejoice always, pray without ceasing, in
everything give thanks; for this is the
will of God in Christ Jesus for you.

1 THESSALONIANS 5:16—18

A merry heart does good, like medicine.

PROVERBS 17:22

Morning

· · · · · · · · ·

Living Steadfastly for Christ

A friend of mine recently climbed to the top of Mount Rainier for the first time. He said that the important thing in such a long climb was for the team to keep moving up, slowly but surely. . . .

My friend told me after his return from Mount Rainier of the exhilaration of reaching the top, even in a blizzard, and of being hardly able to realize that he had actually made it. It was very disappointing, then, that because of the storm, his team had to come back down immediately. The hope of our walk as Christians is that we are also moving toward the top. We are on our way to meeting [God] there, face to face. But when we arrive, we won't ever have to come back down. Now it is our purpose to keep on walking and not to faint.

MARVA DAWN

To Walk and Not Faint

Evening

. . . .

Blessed is the man
Who walks not in the counsel of the ungodly,
Nor stands in the path of sinners,
Nor sits in the seat of the scornful;
But his delight is in the law of the LORD,
And in His law he meditates day and night.
He shall be like a tree
Planted by the rivers of water,
That brings forth its fruit in its season,
Whose leaf also shall not wither;
And whatever he does shall prosper.

PSALM 1:1—3

And let us not grow weary while doing good, for in
due season we shall reap if we do not lose heart.

GALATIANS 6:9

I press toward the goal for the prize of the
upward call of God in Christ Jesus.

PHILIPPIANS 3:14

. . . .

APRIL 30

God's Never-Ending Love

Have you heard the story of the old woman whose life had been a constant struggle against poverty, and who had never seen the ocean? On being taken to the seaside for the first time, she exclaimed, "Thank God there's something there's enough of!"

Scripture is one long, beautiful story of God's patient, perfect, lavish love for humankind. . . . Sometimes His love doesn't look the way we want it to at the moment . . . but His grace is ever-present and His love is never-ending.

It's been said that the Christian life is like the dial of a clock. The hands are God's hands, passing over and over again, the short hand of discipline and the long hand of mercy. . . . And the hands are fastened to one secure pivot: the great, unchanging heart of our God of love.

Now that's something there's always more than enough of!

BARBARA JOHNSON

Boundless Love

Evening

· · · · · · · · ·

Know that the LORD your God, He is God, the
faithful God who keeps covenant and mercy
for a thousand generations with those who
love Him and keep His commandments.

DEUTERONOMY 7:9

The LORD is good;
his steadfast love endures forever,
and his faithfulness to all generations.

PSALM 100:5 ESV

You, O Lord, are a God full of compassion, and gracious,
Longsuffering and abundant in mercy and truth.
Oh, turn to me, and have mercy on me!
Give Your strength to Your servant.

PSALM 86:15–16

247

May

Make a joyful shout to God, all the earth!
Sing out the honor of His name;
Make His praise glorious.

PSALM 66:1-2

MAY 1

With All Your Strength

The first *commandment* came after the first *commitment*. In the beginning God loved us first. When we understand His love for us, we don't have to be commanded to love Him; we simply respond to what He has already given. Second, we give away what we have been given. Everything flows from God's loving the world first. We love Him in return and love others with the overflow of His love. Without God loving us first, there would be nothing to respond to, and there would be no overflow. He started it flowing down; we stand under the waterfall to receive and then share.

NICOLE JOHNSON

Women of Faith Devotional Bible

"'You shall love the LORD your God with all your
heart, with all your soul, with all your mind,
and with all your strength.' This is the first
commandment. And the second, like it, is this:
'You shall love your neighbor as yourself.'"

MARK 12:30—31

We love Him because He first loved us.

1 JOHN 4:19

Faith by itself, if it does not have works, is dead.

JAMES 2:17

Feeding Your Soul

Think about that feeling of satisfaction you get when you've eaten a good meal of your favorite foods and you wisely choose to stop eating before you go from full to stuffed.

That's how God wants you to feel about life. A job well done, a dream fulfilled, a relationship healed, a confidence in knowing how much God loves you—there are numerous things God can bring your way that satisfy your heart.

God knows every one of your deepest desires. Trying to fill these desires on your own can lead to frustration—or even lead you away from God. But letting God fill your desires in His way and in His time leads to satisfaction that lasts.

Living God's Way

Evening

· · · · · · · · ·

Delight yourself also in the LORD,
And He shall give you the desires of your heart.

PSALM 37:4

I will bless You while I live;
I will lift up my hands in Your name.
My soul shall be satisfied as with marrow and fatness,
And my mouth shall praise You with joyful lips.

PSALM 63:4—5

Now to Him who is able to do exceedingly abundantly
above all that we ask or think, according to the
power that works in us, to Him be glory.

EPHESIANS 3:20—21

MAY 3

Useless or Useful?

A woman makes an enormous leap forward in her spiritual development when she determines that being useful is more important than being noticed. I am appalled at how often our culture urges us to place priority attention on our physical appearance. We thus become mindful of the things that are evaluated in terms of size and shape. And listening to this "cultural mandate," we can be tempted to try to become very beautiful—and useless. . . .

If there is a beginning point in spiritual development, it is the choice one makes to become useful to God and, therefore, to others. I have a right to make this choice because I begin with the assumption that having been made by God, I am alive for a purpose.

GAIL MACDONALD
High Call, High Privilege

Evening

· · · · · · · · ·

"You shall worship the LORD your God,
and Him only you shall serve."

MATTHEW 4:10

"Do not lay up for yourselves treasures on earth,
where moth and rust destroy and where thieves break
in and steal; but lay up for yourselves treasures in
heaven, where neither moth nor rust destroys and
where thieves do not break in and steal. For where
your treasure is, there your heart will be also."

MATTHEW 6:19—21

"Well done, good and faithful servant;
you were faithful over a few things. . . .
Enter into the joy of your lord."

MATTHEW 25:21

MAY 3

255

MAY 4

Seeing God in Nature

Creation is a vivid expression of God's glory, power, and beauty. Those who recognize and appreciate the natural world as God's masterpiece are often quick to exclaim their admiration of it. How can we be silent in the presence of such magnificent beauty as a breathtaking sunset, a soaring mountain, or a raging river?

Indeed, natural beauty is one of the most unmistakable ways God reveals His character to us. Isn't the fact that He wants us to know Him enough to make you rejoice? The psalmist was rejoicing when he wrote the words, "I lift up my eyes to the hills. From where does my help come? My help comes from the LORD, who made heaven and earth" (Psalm 121:1–2).

When you look at creation, recognize God's greatness. The same God who created spectacular vistas and towering precipices is the God who comforts you in moments of weakness . . . who knew you before you were born . . . who offered His Son's life in exchange for yours. Consider His splendor, celebrate His glory, and rejoice!

A Jane Austen Devotional

For since the creation of the world His
invisible attributes are clearly seen, being understood
by the things that are made, even His eternal power
and Godhead, so that they are without excuse.

ROMANS 1:20

"Where were you when I laid the foundations of the earth?
Tell Me, if you have understanding.
Who determined its measurements?
Surely you know!
Or who stretched the line upon it?
To what were its foundations fastened?
Or who laid its cornerstone,
When the morning stars sang together,
And all the sons of God shouted for joy?"

JOB 38:4—7

The heavens declare the glory of God;
And the firmament shows His handiwork.

PSALM 19:1

A Matter of the Heart

C. S. Lewis once said, "No clever arrangement of bad eggs ever made a good omelet." What we truly are will dictate our choices, no matter how we try to camouflage or hide it, and no amount of moral effort will make us choose rightly if our hearts aren't right. . . .

Morality would be a cumbersome burden if each decision of our lives had to be carefully checked against some itemized, written code. We would be in constant turmoil worrying about whether some code was overlooked or misinterpreted. The joy of right living would be strangled in legalism. But it is exactly this sort of system that was in effect before Jesus brought the renovation of the human heart and motives through His death and resurrection and then provided us with the live-in support of the Holy Spirit. . . .

Good choices come most freely from the purist possible motives; these come from a heart repossessed by the transforming power of love. Love does what law could never do.

GLORIA GAITHER
Decisions

Evening

· · · · · · · · · · ·

Owe no one anything except to love one another,
for he who loves another has fulfilled the law.
For the commandments, "You shall not commit
adultery," "You shall not murder," "You shall
not steal," "You shall not bear false witness,"
"You shall not covet," and if there is any other
commandment, are all summed up in this saying,
namely, "You shall love your neighbor as yourself."

ROMANS 13:8—9

Sin shall not have dominion over you, for
you are not under law but under grace. What
then? Shall we sin because we are not under
law but under grace? Certainly not!

ROMANS 6:14—15

MAY 5

259

MAY 6

Courage for "Such a Time as This"

In the Old Testament we can read the story of Esther. Her history had been one of sorrow and loss. Caught up in the captivity, she found herself chosen to compete in a beauty queen contest. She had no choice at all in the matter. After all, she was a foreign slave—and she was a woman! Suddenly, her entire future was determined, and her own dreams of marriage and family were undoubtedly dashed. What thoughts went through her mind when she was chosen to be queen of Persia? Even as royalty, Esther would be forced to play out a role she'd had no role in creating.

Esther—whose name means "star"—could have hung up her joy early on when she was orphaned and taken prisoner, but she didn't. She sang a song of purity, piety, and poise that made her captors gasp. It was her sweet song of Zion spirituality. Although her masters understood it only dimly, her song won her the queen's crown. . . . Esther persevered. She refused to be or do anything less than her best for the God she served.

JILL BRISCOE

Heartstrings

The king loved Esther more than all the other women,
and she obtained grace and favor in his sight more
than all the virgins; so he set the royal crown upon
her head and made her queen. . . . Letters were sent
by couriers into all the king's provinces, to destroy,
to kill, and to annihilate all the Jews, both young
and old, little children and women, in one day . . .
Mordecai told . . . Esther . . . "If you remain completely
silent at this time, relief and deliverance will arise
for the Jews from another place, but you and your
father's house will perish. Yet who knows whether you
have come to the kingdom for such a time as this?"

ESTHER 2:17; 3:13; 4:13—14

Gird up the loins of your mind, be sober, and
rest your hope fully upon the grace that is to be
brought to you at the revelation of Jesus Christ; as
obedient children, not conforming yourselves to
the former lusts, as in your ignorance; but as He who
called you is holy, you also be holy in all your conduct,
because it is written, "Be holy, for I am holy."

1 PETER 1:13—16

MAY 7

The Weed of Unforgiveness

I learned to forgive in a garden. As a child, I had an argument with my younger cousin. She told me if I didn't apologize, I couldn't come to her fifth birthday party that day. I was too proud, even at age six, to say "I'm sorry." I decided instead to miss my cousin's party.

Later that afternoon, as I sat sullenly on the sofa, hearing the birthday festivities next door, my grandmother designed a teachable moment to talk with me about forgiveness. She took me to her gardens. We often talked and prayed as we walked hand-in-hand through her fragrant blooms on long summer afternoons. . . .

"Unforgiveness is like a weed in my garden," she told me as she knelt down to pull up a handful of wild plants. "Watch for them, 'Nisey. Pull 'em up as soon as they start to seed. Don't let them grow for one minute in your garden. Or they'll ruin your flower beds."

DENISE GEORGE

Cultivating a Forgiving Heart

Evening

· · · · · · · · · ·

"Forgive us our debts,
As we forgive our debtors."

MATTHEW 6:12

"Love one another; as I have loved you, that you also
love one another. By this all will know that you are
My disciples, if you have love for one another."

JOHN 13:34—35

"Be angry, and do not sin": do not let the sun go
down on your wrath, nor give place to the devil.

EPHESIANS 4:26—27

MAY 7

263

. . . .

Which Way Was I Going?

When you were a kid, you may have dreamed about what you'd be when you grew up. At five, you pictured yourself as a superhero or a cowgirl. When you were fifteen, you might have imagined being a cheerleader or a drum major leading the band. Ultimately, you began a vocation after high school or college and thought you might have that job as a career for the rest of your life.

The problem is the rest of your life may change quickly. Devastating things happen in life and leave you feeling hopeless! You're suddenly set adrift, with nowhere to go and nowhere you want to go. You imagine the system has failed you or that God has left you.

Whatever the circumstances that bring a loss of your life direction, there is still reason to maintain a sense of hope. This kind of hope is built on trust in your Creator. He holds you up and has a plan for your life. He has your present and your future in His hands. Take comfort in that knowledge. He will plant new seeds of hope in your heart. Trust Him!

Little Seeds of Hope

Evening

· · · · · · · · · ·

Peace I leave with you, My peace I give to you; not
as the world gives do I give to you. Let not your
heart be troubled, neither let it be afraid.

JOHN 14:27

Are not two sparrows sold for a copper coin?
And not one of them falls to the ground apart
from your Father's will. But the very hairs of your
head are all numbered. Do not fear therefore;
you are of more value than many sparrows.

MATTHEW 10:29—31

We also glory in tribulations, knowing that
tribulation produces perseverance; and
perseverance, character; and character, hope.

ROMANS 5:3—4

MAY 9

Planting Hope

Five years ago I planted over three hundred bulbs around a brick pathway and in varying places in our yard. I told my husband that I'd be able to manage the winter somehow if I could look forward to a spring and summertime filled with the vibrant colors of crocuses, daffodils, tulips, snowdrops, and lilies.

In a sense, I planted hope. The hope of new life. The products of sun and warmth.

When I feel my spirits drooping, I . . . envision all the lovely red, white, purple, pink, orange, and blue flowers that will explode in a wild proliferation of joy all over my yard, come spring.

When I can't find hope, hope has an exquisite way of finding me . . . through the promises of what will be.

JULIE ANN BARNHILL
Exquisite Hope

I will hope continually,
And will praise You yet more and more.
PSALM 71:14

Let love be without hypocrisy. . . . Be kindly
affectionate to one another with brotherly
love, in honor giving preference to one
another; . . . rejoicing in hope, patient in
tribulation, continuing steadfastly in prayer.
ROMANS 12:9–10, 12

Hope in the LORD;
For with the LORD there is mercy,
And with Him is abundant redemption.
PSALM 130:7

Rain Clouds and Blue Skies

While flying to a conference recently, I was leafing through the airline's magazine, which has items you can purchase through a catalog. I spied a darling ad showing a black umbrella. The description said, "Gray skies are gonna clear up!" The umbrella opened to reveal a blue sky with white fluffy clouds floating by. It was like moving out from under dismal rain clouds to a clear bright day at the touch of a button.

I had to order that umbrella, of course, because it was such an encouragement to me! When it arrived in the mail, it was even better than depicted in the advertisement. . . .

None of us can avoid the gray skies and dreariness in life. At times we get absolutely drenched with troubles. But you know what? They're gonna clear up! Nothing lasts forever. The stuff we go through is only temporary. There will be lots of clearings along the way. And one day we will enjoy blue skies forever.

BARBARA JOHNSON

Extravagant Grace

Evening

· · · · · · · · ·

Through the LORD's mercies we are not consumed,
Because His compassions fail not.
They are new every morning;
Great is Your faithfulness.

LAMENTATIONS 3:22—23

God said: "This is the sign of the covenant which I
make between Me and you, and every living creature
that is with you, for perpetual generations: I set
My rainbow in the cloud, and it shall be for the
sign of the covenant between Me and the earth."

GENESIS 9:12—13

The wolf also shall dwell with the lamb,
The leopard shall lie down with the young goat,
The calf and the young lion and the fatling together;
And a little child shall lead them. . . .
The earth shall be full of the knowledge of the LORD
As the waters cover the sea.

ISAIAH 11:6, 9

Single and Content

Friends offer all sorts of advice to single women: don't be too aggressive or too backward, too friendly or too hard-to-get, too intellectual or too dumb, too earthly or too heavenly. "Hang around till the bitter end of the singles' barbecue—he might want to take you home." Or "Don't go to the singles' barbecue at all. Just stay home where you read your Bible and pray." It's terribly confusing.

"Is my Father God in charge here, or am I supposed to take over?" He is in charge if you want Him to be. He will not invade your freedom to choose to take over. But if you want His way—nothing more, nothing less, and nothing else—you've got to leave it to Him. It's easy to be deceived here telling ourselves we really want His will, but meaning "I want [God's will] so long as it includes marriage!"

God gives the very best to those who leave the choice with Him.

ELISABETH ELLIOT

Keep a Quiet Heart

Evening

· · · · · · · · ·

I know the plans I have for you, declares
the LORD, plans for welfare and not for
evil, to give you a future and a hope.

JEREMIAH 29:11 ESV

"Your kingdom come.
Your will be done
On earth as it is in heaven."

MATTHEW 6:10–22

Again, a second time, [Jesus] went away and prayed,
saying, "O My Father, if this cup cannot pass away
from Me unless I drink it, Your will be done."

MATTHEW 26:42

Trust in the LORD with all your heart,
And lean not on your own understanding;
In all your ways acknowledge Him,
And He shall direct your paths.

PROVERBS 3:5–6

271

MAY 12

Loved by God

One of my favorite television commercials has no words. A young woman walks into a shop and admires a bathing suit on a mannequin. With a look of self-satisfaction, she picks up a suit like it, disappears into a dressing room, throws her own clothes over the door, then, after a couple seconds, lets out a blood-curdling scream. It's a powerhouse endorsement of the diet the commercial recommends. I laugh every time I see it as I munch away on my Snickers. . . .

The next time you stand in front of a mirror and want to scream, try to remember that God made that face. That smile. Those big eyes . . . and chubby cheeks. You are His creation, called to reflect Him. Spiritual transformation doesn't come from a diet program, a bottle, a makeover, or mask. It comes from an intimate relationship with the Savior. He . . . appreciates us for who we really are. So we can too.

LUCI SWINDOLL
Extravagant Grace

He chose us in Him before the foundation of the
world, that we should be holy and without blame
before Him in love, having predestined us to
adoption as sons by Jesus Christ to Himself,
according to the good pleasure of His will, to
the praise of the glory of His grace, by which
He made us accepted in the Beloved.

EPHESIANS 1:1–6

I am fearfully and wonderfully made.

PSALM 139:14

Teach me Your way, O LORD;
I will walk in Your truth;
Unite my heart to fear Your name.
I will praise You, O Lord my God, with all my heart,
And I will glorify Your name forevermore.
For great is Your mercy toward me,
And You have delivered my soul from the depths of Sheol.

PSALM 86:11–13

Our Thorns, God's Grace

No one knows what the thorn in Paul's flesh was (2 Corinthians 12:7). Whatever that affliction actually was does not matter. The truth God had taught Paul—and that Paul then taught us—matters greatly.

And what was that truth? That Jesus' grace was all he needed, whatever life's demands. Christ's power clearly rested on Paul in his weakness and enabled him to do what he wouldn't have been able to do on his own.

Paul had experienced God faithfully giving him strength when he was weak, insulted, persecuted, and struggling.

When we are aware of our weaknesses, of our need for Jesus, we yield ourselves more fully to God. We give Him room to move in and room to work. And He works not only in circumstances but also in our hearts. May we then, as Paul himself did, find delight in those weaknesses that help us know more fully God's great strength at work in us and through us.

100 Favorite Bible Verses

I can do all things through
Christ who strengthens me.

The LORD repay your work, and a full reward
be given you by the LORD God of Israel, under
whose wings you have come for refuge.

RUTH 2:12

To keep me grounded and stop me from becoming
too high and mighty due to the extraordinary
character of these revelations, I was given a thorn in
the flesh—a nagging nuisance of Satan, a messenger
to plague me! I begged the Lord three times to
liberate me from its anguish; and finally He said
to me, "My grace is enough to cover and sustain
you. My power is made perfect in weakness." . . . I
am at peace and even take pleasure in any
weaknesses, insults, hardships, persecutions, and
afflictions for the sake of the Anointed because
when I am at my weakest, He makes me strong.

2 CORINTHIANS 12:7–10 THE VOICE

Authentic Love

A Zogby/Forbes ASAP poll asked respondents, *What would you like most to be known for? Being intelligent? Good looking? Having a great sense of humor?* A full half of respondents checked off an unexpected answer: They said they would like a reputation for "being authentic." In a world of spin and hype, the postmodern generation is searching desperately for something real and authentic. They will not take Christians seriously unless [we] demonstrate an authentic way of life. . . .

In the days of the early church, the thing that most impressed their neighbors in the Roman Empire was the community of love they witnessed among believers. "Behold how they love one another," it was said. In every age, the most persuasive evidence for the gospel is not words or arguments but a living demonstration of God's character through Christians' love for one another, expressed in both their words and their actions.

NANCY PEARCEY

Total Truth

Evening

· · · · · · · · ·

Fulfill my joy by being like-minded, having the
same love, being of one accord, of one mind.

PHILIPPIANS 2:2

Love suffers long and is kind; love does not envy;
love does not parade itself, is not puffed up; does
not behave rudely, does not seek its own, is not
provoked, thinks no evil; does not rejoice in iniquity,
but rejoices in the truth; bears all things, believes
all things, hopes all things, endures all things.

1 CORINTHIANS 13:4–7

All who believed were together, and had all things
in common, and sold their possessions and goods,
and divided them among all, as anyone had need.
So continuing daily with one accord in the
temple, and breaking bread from house to
house, they ate their food with gladness and
simplicity of heart, praising God and having
favor with all the people. And the Lord added to
the church daily those who were being saved.

ACTS 2:44–47

MAY 14

277

Be a Kid Again

When Jesus said, "Let the little children come to me," He was talking to adults as well as kids. He was telling us to mimic the kids, to fling our hearts open wide and obliterate the boxes we've put God in. To embrace faith with wild abandon, be teachable, and trust God as a child would trust a parent. Sounds easy enough, right?

What can we learn from kids? To express our ideas boldly, to dream ginormous dreams, to live fully in the moment, to taste crazy foods, to take risks, to be wildly creative and contagiously optimistic, and to trust God wholeheartedly.

More Than a Bucket List

Evening

· · · · · · · · ·

But Jesus said, "Let the little children come to
Me, and do not forbid them; for of
such is the kingdom of heaven."

MATTHEW 19:14

"Whoever comes to Me, and hears My sayings and
does them, I will show you whom he is like: He is like
a man building a house, who dug deep and laid the
foundation on the rock. And when the flood arose,
the stream beat vehemently against that house, and
could not shake it, for it was founded on the rock."

LUKE 6:47—48

[Cast] all your care upon Him, for He cares for you.

1 PETER 5:7

279

Just Like Jesus

Everyone who has ever walked on this earth has been criticized—even the only perfect Person who ever lived. Jesus came to Earth to walk among us, to show us what the Father was like, and also to let us know He understood what it was like to live as we do, rubbing shoulders with difficult people.

No matter what Jesus did, He couldn't please the religious leaders of the day. If He healed, it was on the wrong day. If He ate dinner, it was with the wrong people. If He told the truth about Himself, He was called a liar. . . . He knows what it feels like to take it on the chin, day after day. . . .

Criticism is part of life. But just because "they said," it doesn't make it so. Remember that. And the next time "they say," take the mercy and accept the help that Jesus offers—and then keep on going. It's part of the journey.

JAN SILVIOUS

Look at It This Way

Evening

"In quietness and confidence
shall be your strength."

ISAIAH 30:15

"If you were of the world, the world would love
its own. Yet because you are not of the world, but
I chose you out of the world, therefore the world
hates you. Remember the word that I said to you,
'A servant is not greater than his master.' If they
persecuted Me, they will also persecute you."

JOHN 15:19—20

If you are reproached for the name of Christ, blessed
are you, for the Spirit of glory and of God rests upon
you. . . . If anyone suffers as a Christian, let him not
be ashamed, but let him glorify God in this matter.

1 PETER 4:14, 16

MAY 16

281

"Pray Without Ceasing"

Prayer is sort of like an unlocked door. . . . Inside is the storehouse of all that God is. He invites us to share it all. He doesn't intend for us to stay on the outside and struggle all alone with the perplexities of life, and He not only invites us to come in but to stay in, in order that His "grace and peace be yours in fullest measure, through the knowledge of God and Jesus our Lord" (2 Peter 1:2 NEB). . . .

It is an ongoing process, not just an occasional religious-sounding speech we make to a nebulous divinity "out there somewhere." Prayer is meant to be a part of our lives, like breathing and thinking and talking.

GLORIA GAITHER

Decisions

Evening

. . . .

"I say to you, ask, and it will be given to you; seek, and you will find; knock, and it will be opened to you. For everyone who asks receives, and he who seeks finds, and to him who knocks it will be opened. If a son asks for bread from any father among you, will he give him a stone? Or if he asks for a fish, will he give him a serpent instead of a fish?"

LUKE 11:9–11

Evening and morning and at noon
I will pray, and cry aloud,
And He shall hear my voice.

PSALM 55:17

Rejoice always, pray without ceasing, in everything give thanks; for this is the will of God in Christ Jesus for you.

1 THESSALONIANS 5:16–18

Going Home

Let's be honest. Old age entails suffering. I'm acutely aware of this now as I watch my mother, once so alive and alert and quick, now so quiet and confused and slow. She suffers. We who love her suffer. We see the "preview of coming attractions," ourselves in her shoes, and ponder what this interval means in terms of the glory of God in an old woman. . . .

We look at what's happening—limitations of hearing, seeing, moving, digesting, remembering; distortions of countenance, figure, and perspective. If that's all we could see, we'd certainly want a face-lift or something.

But we're on a pilgrim road. It's rough and steep, and it winds uphill to the very end. We can lift up our eyes and see the unseen: a Celestial City, a light, a welcome, an ineffable Face. We shall behold Him. We shall be like Him. And that makes a difference in how we go about aging.

ELISABETH ELLIOT

On Asking God Why

Evening

· · · · · · · · · ·

God will wipe away every tear from their eyes;
there shall be no more death, nor sorrow, nor
crying. There shall be no more pain, for the former
things have passed away. Then He who sat on the
throne said, "Behold, I make all things new."

REVELATION 21:4—5

Behold what manner of love the Father has
bestowed on us, that we should be called children of
God! Therefore the world does not know us, because
it did not know Him. Beloved, now we are children
of God; and it has not yet been revealed what we
shall be, but we know that when He is revealed, we
shall be like Him, for we shall see Him as He is.

1 JOHN 3:1—2

Morning

. . . .

Sojourners on Earth

As believers, we understand the heart of the psalmist's declaration, "I am a sojourner on the earth" (Psalm 119:19 ESV); we simply aren't home yet. We are travelers, doing battle every day with failing bodies, corrupt political systems, poverty, squalor, chaos—all the deficiencies of living in a fallen world.

Do you ever feel an unexplainable homesickness? God designed us not to feel at peace in this world, but to always harbor homesickness. Our final resting place, heaven, will be the full manifestation of perfection. We will finally enjoy all that is missing here.

Though it's easy to get comfortable when our lives are going well, we should invite that longing. It is the living hope that something better awaits us. Remember, we're foreigners here. An existence not marred by imperfection or inadequacy is coming. A place that will know no more tears, no more sorrow. An eternity of communing freely with the God of the universe.

A Jane Austen Devotional

Now I saw a new heaven and a new earth, for the first
heaven and the first earth had passed away. Also there
was no more sea. Then I, John, saw the holy city, New
Jerusalem, coming down out of heaven from God,
prepared as a bride adorned for her husband. And
I heard a loud voice from heaven saying, "Behold,
the tabernacle of God is with men, and He will
dwell with them, and they shall be His people. God
Himself will be with them and be their God.
REVELATION 21:1—3

Our citizenship is in heaven, from which we also
eagerly wait for the Savior, the Lord Jesus Christ.
PHILIPPIANS 3:20

"I, Jesus, have sent My angel to testify to you these
things in the churches. I am the Root and the
Offspring of David, the Bright and Morning Star."
And the Spirit and the bride say, "Come!" And let him
who hears say, "Come!" And let him who thirsts come.
Whoever desires, let him take the water of life freely.
REVELATION 22:16—17

The Big Picture

The great evangelist Leonard Ravenhill was the last person on the planet you'd ever accuse of mincing words. "Five minutes after you die, you'll know how you should have lived."

You've got 1,440 minutes today; 43,200 this month; and 525,600 this year to determine your priorities and how you should be living. Even those minutes aren't guaranteed. So how will you live?

As distracted as we sometimes get, we can't afford to lose sight of the bigger picture—that heaven, our true home, awaits. Today carries real pain, struggle, and obligations, but never cast aside your "light and momentary troubles" for the eternal glory that outweighs them all (2 Corinthians 4:17)! Your citizenship in heaven begins on earth. Live a life that has heaven's flavor all over it.

More Than a Bucket List

Our citizenship is in heaven.

PHILIPPIANS 3:20

"Let not your heart be troubled; you believe in God,
believe also in Me. In My Father's house are many
mansions; if it were not so, I would have told you. I
go to prepare a place for you. And if I go and prepare
a place for you, I will come again and receive you to
Myself; that where I am, there you may be also."

JOHN 14:1–3

Then He who sat on the throne said,
"Behold, I make all things new."

REVELATION 21:5

MAY 21

What If?

As an act of grace toward yourself, on this day imagine yourself to be the person you aspire to be. Spend the whole day walking in the blessing and persona of that person. What would you talk about? Where would you go? What kind of attitude would you have? How would you respond to the people around you? In what ways would your life look different?

What if you . . .

Dropped the spirit of criticism? Stopped blaming others? Were less defensive? Held your tongue this time? Jumped to a grace-filled conclusion instead? Had the courage to speak up for the underdog? Were brave enough to have that heart-stopping conversation?

Allow this one day to launch a lifetime of living as the person you aspire to be.

More Than a Bucket List

Evening

· · · · · · · · · · ·

Be filled with the Spirit, speaking to one another
in psalms and hymns and spiritual songs,
singing and making melody in your heart to the
Lord, giving thanks always for all things to God
the Father in the name of our Lord Jesus Christ.

EPHESIANS 5:18—20

"The righteous will answer Him, saying, 'Lord, when
did we see You hungry and feed You, or thirsty and
give You drink? When did we see You a stranger and
take You in, or naked and clothe You? Or when did
we see You sick, or in prison, and come to You?' And
the King will answer and say to them, 'Assuredly,
I say to you, inasmuch as you did it to one of the
least of these My brethren, you did it to Me.'"

MATTHEW 25:37—40

"You shall love your neighbor as yourself."

MATTHEW 19:19

MAY 22

Jesus' Prayer for You

[In the Upper Room] Jesus knew what was coming for Him, and He stopped to pray for His disciples, for you, and for me. What a powerful example. His very actions show us that we can face suffering best by not giving in to it or pulling into ourselves, but by reaching out and looking up and holding on to this promise. Trouble is knit into the very fabric of this life, but Christ has overcome. The call to take heart implies action, a consciousness. . . . Remember that Christ prepared us for the fact that trouble will come, so [we are to] gather up everything we are feeling and tuck ourselves into His shelter, the Cleft of the Rock, for He has overcome. . . .

No matter how alone we may feel at moments, because of what Jesus has done for us, we are never alone. Even in the eye of the storm, we call our heart to remember that no matter how hard life gets, we win.

SHEILA WALSH

The Shelter of God's Promises

Evening

. . . .

"My prayer is not that you take them out of the world
but that you protect them from the evil one."

JOHN 17:15 NIV

Thomas answered and said to Him,
"My Lord and my God!"
Jesus said to him, "Thomas, because you have
seen Me, you have believed. Blessed are those
who have not seen and yet have believed."

JOHN 20:28—29

"The Helper, the Holy Spirit, whom the Father will
send in My name, He will teach you all things, and
bring to your remembrance all things that I said
to you. Peace I leave with you, My peace I give to
you; not as the world gives do I give to you. Let not
your heart be troubled, neither let it be afraid."

JOHN 14:26—27

293

MAY 23

Known, Broken, Forgiven

Secrets lurk inside most of us like buried treasure, even though their value is dubious. Some people assume their secrets are safe, since they remain convinced that God does not exist. Others are too busy covering their sins to consider the consequences. However we handle our secrets, two truths remain: nothing hides from God, and no one escapes the woe of secret sins. Trust God with your confessions and repentance. The God who sees and knows your secret sins also sees and knows your broken heart. And He forgives.

JAN CARLBERG

The Hungry Heart

Search me, O God, and know my heart;
Try me, and know my anxieties;
And see if there is any wicked way in me,
And lead me in the way everlasting.

PSALM 139:23—24

There is therefore now no condemnation to
those who are in Christ Jesus, who do not walk
according to the flesh, but according to the Spirit.
For the law of the Spirit of life in Christ Jesus has
made me free from the law of sin and death.

ROMANS 8:1—2

If we confess our sins, He is faithful and
just to forgive us our sins and to cleanse
us from all unrighteousness.

1 JOHN 1:9

MAY 24

He Carries Me

I admit that some days the weight of [my physical] blindness falls heavy upon me. Sometimes even a simple thing like wearing matching socks can seem like a monumental challenge. . . . When those times come, blindness becomes an uninvited guest that stifles my dreams by turning ordinary routines into such extraordinary tasks that they leave me worn out and discouraged. On those mornings, when the list of questions is longer than the list of answers, my fatigue seems more powerful than my faith, and not even sheer grit seems enough to propel me out of bed to face the day.

So guess what I do?

Before I get up, I fall down. . . .

The *ultimate* fall is the one that happens in my heart when, with complete abandon, I yield my entire self and fall before my heavenly Father. He finds me there in my weakness and lovingly lifts me. . . . On days when I can't rise, He *carries* me.

JENNIFER ROTHSCHILD

Lessons I Learned in the Dark

Evening

· · · · · · · · ·

We do not have a High Priest who cannot sympathize
with our weaknesses, but was in all points tempted
as we are, yet without sin. Let us therefore come
boldly to the throne of grace, that we may obtain
mercy and find grace to help in time of need.

HEBREWS 4:15–16

"Listen to Me, O house of Jacob,
And all the remnant of the house of Israel,
Who have been upheld by Me from birth,
Who have been carried from the womb:
Even to your old age, I am He,
And even to gray hairs I will carry you!
I have made, and I will bear;
Even I will carry, and will deliver you. . . .
For I am God, and there is no other;
I am God, and there is none like Me."

ISAIAH 46:3–4, 9

"Put On the New Man"

Caterpillars. These little butterflies-in-the-making are really vulnerable when they're fat little worms. They can't flutter out of the way of someone's foot or scurry away from a bird's hungry beak. But God didn't intend for them to be so vulnerable forever. So He taught them to build a cocoon of layers around themselves. Those layers are made of silk, which can be something good. Every woman I know loves the luxurious texture of silk against her skin.

But as the caterpillar layers itself with all this good silk, it creates something that eventually becomes distasteful. As far as I know, there aren't any creatures that like to eat cocoons. Some of them are hard and brittle; others have scratchy outside coverings that also make them unappealing.

If the caterpillar remained inside those protective layers of good stuff, it would die. There comes a point when it has to peel back those layers and climb out of the cocoon. And when it does . . . It becomes a butterfly.

SANDI PATTY

Layers

Evening

. . . .

Be renewed in the spirit of your mind, and that you
put on the new man which was created according
to God, in true righteousness and holiness.

EPHESIANS 4:23—24

If anyone is in Christ, he is a new creation; old things
have passed away; behold, all things have become new.

2 CORINTHIANS 5:17

"Are not two sparrows sold for a copper coin?
And not one of them falls to the ground apart
from your Father's will. But the very hairs of your
head are all numbered. Do not fear therefore;
you are of more value than many sparrows."

MATTHEW 10:29—31

God's Standards

In God's kingdom, comparisons are not allowed. Women make a terrible mistake comparing. God does not have a standard by which He measures us against each other. We do that. His standard is far higher. Holy God measures each of us against His Son, Jesus. That should change your focus. God will not ask us if we wear specific clothing labels. He will want to know if we are clothed in Christ Jesus.

The biblical truth is that each woman of God is uniquely created and gifted for the purpose of bringing glory to God. This sets us apart from the world. We don't take our standard from the world's fashion designers. We take our standard from the Master Designer!

ESTHER BURROUGHS

Splash the Living Water

Evening

· · · · · · · · ·

If God is for us, who can be against us? He
who did not spare His own Son, but delivered
Him up for us all, how shall He not with
Him also freely give us all things?

ROMANS 8:31—32

God created man in His own image; in the image of
God He created him; male and female He created
them. Then God blessed them. . . . God saw everything
that He had made, and indeed it was very good. So
the evening and the morning were the sixth day.

GENESIS 1:27—28, 31

So get yourselves ready, prepare your minds
to act, control yourselves, and look forward in
hope as you focus on the grace that comes when
Jesus the Anointed returns and is completely
revealed to you. Be like obedient children as you
put aside the desires you used to pursue when you
didn't know better. Since the One who called you
is holy, be holy in all you do. For the Scripture
says, "You are to be holy, for I am holy."

1 PETER 1.13—16 THE VOICE

Morning

. . . .

A Gracious Heart

No sooner had I turned forty, than I started receiving [e-mails] promoting products guaranteed to combat the effects of aging—they promise me younger, clearer skin; fewer wrinkles; no more dark shadows; more energy; prettier nails and hair; and improved eyesight and hearing. The implication is that, as I get older, what matters most is looking and feeling younger.

However, the fact is, I am getting older, and in this fallen world, that means my body is slowly deteriorating. I look in the mirror and see lines that weren't there ten years ago; I am definitely gray-headed. . . .

But I refuse to buy into the lie that those things are ultimate tragedies or that my biological clock can somehow be reversed. I am not trying to hasten my physical decline, but neither am I going to get consumed with fighting off the inevitable. As I get older, I want to focus on those things that God says matter most—things like letting His Spirit cultivate in me a gracious, wise, kind, loving heart.

NANCY LEIGH DEMOSS

Lies Women Believe

Evening

. . . .

Our citizenship is in heaven, from which we
also eagerly wait for the Savior, the Lord Jesus
Christ, who will transform our lowly body that
it may be conformed to His glorious body.

PHILIPPIANS 3:20–21

A gracious woman retains honor.

PROVERBS 11:16

As the elect of God, holy and beloved, put
on tender mercies, kindness, humility,
meekness, longsuffering.

COLOSSIANS 3:12

Morning

. . . .

Undeserved!
Part 1

While many of us know Paul's explanation of salvation by heart—"For it is by grace you have been saved, through faith—and this is not from yourselves, it is the gift of God" (Ephesians 2:8 NIV)—most of us still water the plant of self-righteousness on the windowsill of our hearts. We may be thinking to ourselves that we're spiritually cleaner than the chick who smells like cigarette smoke in our Beth Moore Bible study. We may be assuming that our regular church attendance is adding up like divine frequent-flyer miles. Or we may secretly believe that we somehow *deserve* God's acceptance and approval more than the stinkers we rub shoulders with on a regular basis. . . .

I tend to see myself as more "forgiveness worthy" than people like my stepdad. I've made a habit of stroking and feeding an inner pet idol of *deservedness*. Sometimes I even buy little sweaters for it.

LISA HARPER

Stumbling into Grace

All have sinned and fall short of the glory of God.

ROMANS 3:23

Remember, O LORD, Your tender mercies
and Your lovingkindnesses,
For they are from of old.
Do not remember the sins of my youth, nor my transgressions;
According to Your mercy remember me,
For Your goodness' sake, O LORD.

PSALM 25:6—7

"The Pharisee stood and prayed thus with himself,
'God, I thank You that I am not like other men—
extortioners, unjust, adulterers, or even as this
tax collector.' . . . The tax collector, standing afar
off, would not so much as raise his eyes to heaven,
but beat his breast, saying, 'God, be merciful
to me a sinner!' I tell you, this man went down
to his house justified rather than the other; for
everyone who exalts himself will be humbled,
and he who humbles himself will be exalted."

LUKE 18:11, 13—14

Morning

. . . .

Undeserved!
Part 2

One of my dear friends had a daddy who was so mean she actually prayed for God to go ahead and take him out, if He wasn't planning on saving him. Of course, she was wholly undone when her father walked an aisle and gave his crooked heart to Jesus at the age of eighty-four! People. Messy people. Mistake-prone people. Even mean, old daddies. God loves them all. It is His will that none of us should perish. And He goes to extravagant lengths to accomplish His will.

May I [offer] a suggestion from one stinker to another? Make a short list of the people in your life story who appear to be the least deserving of God's forgiveness. Pray for them by name—that they will stumble into the redemptive grace of Jesus Christ—at least once a week. And for goodness' sake, instead of praying for God to take them out if He's not going to save them, ask Him to kill the idol of deservedness in your own heart!

LISA HARPER

Stumbling into Grace

The Lord is not slack concerning His promise
[to return], as some count slackness, but is
longsuffering toward us, not willing that any should
perish but that all should come to repentance.

2 PETER 3:9

If you confess with your mouth the Lord Jesus
and believe in your heart that God has raised
Him from the dead, you will be saved.

ROMANS 10:9

"Look to Me, and be saved,
All you ends of the earth!
For I am God, and there is no other."

ISAIAH 45:22

Morning

. . . .

Don't Miss the View

"Let's pause a minute and enjoy the view," the guide said as the hikers stopped for breath on a nature walk at the Grand Canyon.

Everyone gasped in awe at the splendor spread below. The *huff-puff* of the steep mountain trail robbed the procession of a chance to see the cathedral-like monuments . . . time had carved along the way.

"Were those formations there when we passed?" one of the tourists teased.

The guide nodded seriously. "They were. But in our struggle to reach the top, we missed the view."

Guilty as charged. . . . Are we in such a rush to climb the ladder of success that we never look over our shoulders? So we reach the top . . . so we bump our heads on the very ceiling of achievement? How sad to realize one day that the rush to a destination robbed us of the joy of traveling.

JUNE MASTERS BACHER

The Quiet Heart

[Jesus] said to [the apostles], "Come aside by yourselves to a deserted place and rest a while." For there were many coming and going, and they did not even have time to eat. So they departed to a deserted place in the boat by themselves.

MARK 6:31–32

Be still, and know that I am God.

PSALM 46:10

The LORD is my shepherd;
I shall not want.
He makes me to lie down in green pastures;
He leads me beside the still waters.
He restores my soul.

PSALM 23:1–3

God Will Not Let Us Go

Do you sometimes have a hard time finishing a project you start? Fortunately, our heavenly Father is not like that at all.

When God enables us to recognize our sin and our need for forgiveness, He won't stop until He finishes. And He won't consider Himself finished until the final product meets His high standards of purity, holiness, and—in eternity—Christlikeness. Furthermore, God is not surprised by the challenges that come with our lack of cooperation or the roadblocks we erect with our sinful ways and selfish desires. He expects hardened hearts and too-busy schedules. He knows we'll make wrong choices and have wrong priorities. Yet God will not let us go.

The Master Artist's signature reads *Yahweh*, and it's written on your heart, just as your name is written on the palms of His Son's hands. And the Artist who began that good work in you will indeed see it through to completion.

100 Favorite Bible Verses

Evening

· · · · · · · · ·

I am persuaded that neither death nor life, nor angels
nor principalities nor powers, nor things present
nor things to come, nor height nor depth, nor any
other created thing, shall be able to separate us from
the love of God which is in Christ Jesus our Lord.

ROMANS 8:38–39

Have you not known?
Have you not heard?
The everlasting God, the LORD,
The Creator of the ends of the earth,
Neither faints nor is weary.
His understanding is unsearchable.
He gives power to the weak,
And to those who have no might He increases strength.

ISAIAH 40:28–29

Being confident of this very thing, that
He who has begun a good work in you will
complete it until the day of Jesus Christ.

PHILIPPIANS 1:6

June

Be glad in the Lord and
rejoice, you righteous;
And shout for joy,
all you upright in heart!

PSALM 32:11

Morning

. . . .

Making a Difference

You are a walking, talking message of hope. Whether you realize it or not, your character, words, and actions are all preaching a sermon to those you meet along the road of life. The closer you follow God, the more visible He'll be to others through you.

You may never know how wide your influence really goes. An act of kindness, a word of encouragement, or a job well done could be what moves a close friend, or even a stranger, one step closer to knowing God.

Take a moment to thank God for the people who've had a positive influence on your life. Then ask God to help you become someone else's reason for thanks.

Living God's Way

Do all things without complaining and
disputing, that you may become blameless and
harmless, children of God without fault in the
midst of a crooked and perverse generation,
among whom you shine as lights in the world.

PHILIPPIANS 2:14–15

Let nothing be done through selfish ambition
or conceit, but in lowliness of mind let each
esteem others better than himself. Let each
of you look out not only for his own interests,
but also for the interests of others.

PHILIPPIANS 2:3–4

"Let your light so shine before men, that they may see
your good works and glorify your Father in heaven."

MATTHEW 5:16

JUNE 2

Rejoice—and Keep on Rejoicing

Paul is not being redundant when he says, "Rejoice, and again I say rejoice" (Philippians 4:4). He effectively creates a picture for us. Imagine the sight of a little lamb coming out of the barn and jumping up once, then jumping up again. He leaps across the fields and hills, jumping as if for the sheer fun of it. So we are to rejoice and keep on rejoicing, not because things are wonderful, but because of the joy that comes from knowing the Lord is in the middle of things that are going on. . . .

No matter how much you might want to be like Scarlett O'Hara and deal with life's realities tomorrow, that is no way to live. No matter your circumstances, rejoice and rejoice again, because God is the author and finisher of life. He is in the middle of everything you face, no matter what.

JAN SILVIOUS

Big Girls Don't Whine

Evening

· · · · · · · · · ·

I will rejoice in the LORD,
I will joy in the God of my salvation.

HABAKKUK 3:18

My soul magnifies the Lord,
And my spirit has rejoiced in God my Savior.

LUKE 1:46–47

The LORD has done great things for us,
And we are glad.

PSALM 126:3

Love and Mercy— and Joy

God is always the Initiator of love and mercy—of the kind of strength that fills in our weaknesses, the kind of perfection that covers our flaws, and the kind of shelter that says, "I'm going to keep you and love you through all your failings." God is the One who pursues us, who woos us to this place of grace, the shelter of His promises. . . .

Where we mess up, He mends it. Where we are weak, He is strong. Where we struggle with imperfections, He rushes in to touch us and lovingly shows us the way He sees us and calls us to be. He patiently listens to our doubts and fears and proclaims, *With all My heart, I'm telling you that you are loved just the same on the days when you feel you've done a good job as on the days when you know that you have blown it. You are loved and always will be loved, and I am going to love you and forgive you to the very end.*

SHEILA WALSH

The Shelter of God's Promises

Evening

· · · · · · · · ·

"What man of you, having a hundred sheep, if he loses one of them, does not leave the ninety-nine in the wilderness, and go after the one which is lost until he finds it? And when he has found it, he lays it on his shoulders, rejoicing. And when he comes home, he calls together his friends and neighbors, saying to them, 'Rejoice with me, for I have found my sheep which was lost!' I say to you that likewise there will be more joy in heaven over one sinner who repents than over ninety-nine just persons who need no repentance."

LUKE 15:4–7

"I am the good shepherd. The good shepherd gives His life for the sheep."

JOHN 10:11

Grace, mercy, and peace will be with you from God the Father and from the Lord Jesus Christ, the Son of the Father, in truth and love.

2 JOHN 1:3

319

Morning

. . . .

God Is at Work

I spent most of my life trying unsuccessfully to live up to unrealistic expectations—and pretending I'd already achieved them. The whole thing left me wading in guilt and totally confused. Was I the only one struggling with the process of becoming everything God created me to be? . . .

Every once in a while, someone would come clean. And their moments of honesty were never discouraging. . . . They were a refreshing affirmation of some important truths. I was *not* an aberration of nature. Life was actually a process for other human beings as well as for me.

It was also wonderful to realize that God is at work in the lives of imperfect people. Hope is the end result of seeing people be honest about their lives. If God cares about imperfect people, then He cares about me. What an encouragement to discover He has the power and He'll help me change—one step at a time. . . .

There is hope for change. . . . Lighten up and live!

KEN DAVIS

Lighten Up!

Evening

· · · · · · · · ·

What I am doing, I do not understand. For what I will
to do, that I do not practice; but what I hate, that I do.

ROMANS 7:15

"The things which are impossible with
men are possible with God."

LUKE 18:27

We all, with unveiled face, beholding as in
a mirror the glory of the Lord, are being
transformed into the same image from glory
to glory, just as by the Spirit of the Lord.

2 CORINTHIANS 3:18

JUNE 4

321

JUNE 5

Satisfied in Christ

There's nothing quite like the satisfaction of a glass of cold spring water on a hot afternoon. A cold shower after mowing the lawn. A dive into a stream after a long, tiring hike. Sometimes a glass of lemonade fresh out of the refrigerator. Being satisfied means you've been filled, you want nothing more, and that the thirsty longing has been quenched.

That's exactly how Jesus satisfies. To have Him means that you have it all. To trust Him means that your needs are met. To know Him is to realize that He is your dearest, most faithful companion. . . .

The next time you pour a cold drink on a hot afternoon, pause and praise the Lord for the way He quenches your thirst. He, the Wellspring of Water, overcomes, subdues, fulfills, and satisfies like nothing else, like no one else.

JONI EARECKSON TADA

Diamonds in the Dust

Evening

"Whoever drinks of this water will thirst
again, but whoever drinks of the water that I shall
give him will never thirst. But the water that I
shall give him will become in him a fountain
of water springing up into everlasting life."

JOHN 4:13—14

God is our refuge and strength,
A very present help in trouble.

PSALM 46:1

He gives power to the weak,
And to those who have no might
He increases strength.

ISAIAH 40:29

Diversity Yet Unity

I see the color of God's creation not only in the visual beauty of the world around me. I am also learning to see it in the incredibly diverse beauty of His children as well. Each of us has been made so uniquely, designed so specifically, that there is not one other person on earth exactly like us. We truly are what my friend Mickey Smith calls "human snowflakes." Every finger on every hand on every person in every land who has ever lived contains a unique fingerprint!

What a colorful creation this is! Think of it. God has delighted to give each one of us a special identity, and yet many of us spend our lives trying to conform to some self-imposed "norm." We deny our own individuality and that of others. We insist on playing out God's drama in black and white, ignoring the many colorful brushstrokes of His hand.

If there is any place on earth where creativity and individuality should flourish, it should be in the church of Jesus Christ.

CLAIRE CLONINGER
When God Shines Through

Evening

· · · · · · · · ·

For as we have many members in one body, but
all the members do not have the same function,
so we, being many, are one body in Christ,
and individually members of one another.
Having then gifts differing according to the
grace that is given to us, let us use them.

ROMANS 12:4–6

There are diversities of gifts, but the same Spirit.
There are differences of ministries, but the same
Lord. And there are diversities of activities,
but it is the same God who works all in all.

1 CORINTHIANS 12:4–6

Repay no one evil for evil. . . . If it is possible,
as much as depends on you, live
peaceably with all men.

ROMANS 12:17–18

Weeping and Laughter

In Chaim Potok's novel *My Name Is Asher Lev*, a famous painter defines whether or not one is an artist by "whether or not there is a scream in him wanting to get out in a special way." His friend then immediately adds, "Or a laugh." Pondering that bit of dialogue I realize with repentance and with rapture that Christians have both. God's people know the scream, for it is painful to acknowledge that all flesh is grass and to live in its withered failures. We weep with the world's sorrows of brokenness and faded dreams.

But Christians also can't help but laugh. We laugh with victory over despair. We laugh eternally. We bubble with delight because we are God's children. We giggle in the freedom of divine approval. The promise stands forever that grace is the foundation of the world and undergirds our lives. God's eternal Word assures us of eternal life with Him—already begun.

MARVA DAWN
To Walk and Not Faint

Evening

· · · · · · · · ·

Oh come, let us sing to the LORD!
Let us shout joyfully to the Rock of our salvation.

PSALM 95:1

The humble also shall
increase their joy in the LORD.

ISAIAH 29:19

The ransomed of the LORD shall return,
And come to Zion with singing,
With everlasting joy on their heads.
They shall obtain joy and gladness,
And sorrow and sighing shall flee away.

ISAIAH 35:10

Talk to Jesus

We have every reason to be insecure, except that Jesus gave His life for us emotional ragamuffins. He came to give us a new self-concept based on His acceptance, which is vast. Christ sees us, knows us, and—get this—loves us.

So I invite Christ into my sitting room near the fireplace. The smell of lilacs wafts in from the terrace, and I see the last sparks playing in the fire that took the chill off the morning air. I tell Jesus of my failure, but He already knows. Before I can finish asking Him to forgive me, I can tell He already has. I feel the dark smudges on my heart disappear.

Find your summer place. Talk to Jesus. He is the only invincible One who can rescue us from ourselves and heal us of our insecurities.

PATSY CLAIRMONT

I Second That Emotion

Evening

. . . .

If we confess our sins, [God] is faithful
and just to forgive us our sins and to
cleanse us from all unrighteousness.

1 JOHN 1:9

Trust in Him at all times, you people;
Pour out your heart before Him;
God is a refuge for us.

PSALM 62:8

You understand my thought afar off.
You comprehend my path and my lying down,
And are acquainted with all my ways.
For there is not a word on my tongue,
But behold, O LORD, You know it altogether.

PSALM 139:2—4

329

Accepting What God Gives

For my birthday one year, my mother sent me a package.
. . . When I opened it, there was a gaudy, multicolored
Mexican straw basket inside, stuffed with tissue paper. . . .
I tossed out the tissue paper, wondered what in the world
I was going to do with the basket, then called to thank her
for her "gift." Mother laughed when I thanked her for the
basket [and] then asked what I thought about what was
inside it. I told her that nothing was inside except tissue
paper, and I had thrown that out. . . .

"Oh no, Anne! Inside that tissue paper is your real
birthday gift!"

I ran outside . . . and went through the garbage piece by
piece until I came up with the wad of tissue paper. Inside
was a small gold ring with a lapis lazuli stone. . . .

Sometimes God wraps His glory in hard circumstances or ugly obstacles or painful difficulties, and it just
never occurs to us that within those life-shaking events is
a fresh revelation of Him.

ANNE GRAHAM LOTZ

I Saw the Lord

Evening

· · · · · · · · · ·

"When you pass through the waters, I will be with you;
And through the rivers, they shall not overflow you.
When you walk through the fire, you shall not be burned,
Nor shall the flame scorch you.
For I am the LORD your God."

ISAIAH 43:2

Every good gift and every perfect gift is from above,
and comes down from the Father of lights, with
whom there is no variation or shadow of turning.

JAMES 1:17

"Do not judge according to appearance."

JOHN 7:24

Healing Your Heart

Whatever you put your heart into usually gives you hope and joy. Your heart glows with love and gives you a reason to wake up each morning. You know there's a risk, but you take it because when it works well, it's the best gift ever. How can God understand this? He understands because He took the greatest risk of all. He loved us first before we ever loved Him. He set the wheels of love in motion.

When your heart is broken, certainly you know that God grieves with you. He recognizes the hope and the love you put into your relationship and that you need His comfort. Rest! Give Him a chance to draw near to you and give you His peace in your current situation. He is the One who can mend broken hearts and bring you new joy.

Your Promises from God Today

Evening

· · · · · · · · ·

For God so loved the world that He gave His only
begotten Son, that whoever believes in Him
should not perish but have everlasting life.

JOHN 3:16

Draw near to God and He will draw near to
you. Cleanse your hands, you sinners; and
purify your hearts, you double-minded.

JAMES 4:8

Therefore know that the LORD your God, He is
God, the faithful God who keeps covenant and
mercy for a thousand generations with those
who love Him and keep His commandments.

DEUTERONOMY 7:9

Seeing Potential

Secondhand shopping hones your ability to see something that others may not—potential. The ability to see something not for what it is but instead for what it can be is a great gift. If I . . . bought the five-piece furniture set with matching lamps for each room in my house, it wouldn't really be worth mentioning. . . . If I piece together hand-me-downs and create a beautiful space, well, that's something special. I want to challenge you to start looking at things—and people and situations—for what they can be, not what they are. I think you'll find treasures in all aspects of your life, treasures that have been hiding right under your nose. . . .

I've always loved the fact that God sees potential in each of us, no matter how big we've messed up or how broken we are. Isn't it awesome that we can take that example and do the same thing—not only in castoff furniture, but in others and even in ourselves? I'm incredibly thankful for potential. It means that in the right hands, the ordinary can become extraordinary.

MARIAN PARSONS

Inspired You

334

The LORD said to Samuel, "Do not look at his appearance or at his physical stature, because I have refused him. For the LORD does not see as man sees; for man looks at the outward appearance, but the LORD looks at the heart."

1 SAMUEL 16:7

Blessed is the Lord God of Israel,
For He has visited and redeemed His people.

LUKE 1:68

I know that my Redeemer lives,
And He shall stand at last on the earth;
And after my skin is destroyed, this I know,
That in my flesh I shall see God.

JOB 19:25—26

God's Tapestry

God has been making arrangements for your part in His plan long before you were born. He is never unprepared.

- Your past does not surprise Him.
- Your present does not worry Him.
- Your future is not a mystery to Him.

No one is a second-class laborer in His harvest. You are precious to Him. He is the Almighty, you are His beloved child, and we are all part of the wonderful tapestry of His eternal purposes.

ALICIA BRITT CHOLE

Pure Joy

I know the thoughts that I think toward you,
says the LORD, thoughts of peace and not of
evil, to give you a future and a hope.

JEREMIAH 29:11

Who is God, except the LORD?
And who is a rock, except our God?
God is my strength and power,
And He makes my way perfect.
He makes my feet like the feet of deer,
And sets me on my high places.

2 SAMUEL 22:32—34

"A woman, when she is in labor, has sorrow because
her hour has come; but as soon as she has given
birth to the child, she no longer remembers the
anguish, for joy that a human being has been
born into the world. Therefore you now have
sorrow; but I will see you again and your heart will
rejoice, and your joy no one will take from you."

JOHN 16:21—22

JUNE 13

Love One Another

A Belgian poet once said that if the world is spherical, it is made that way so love and friendship and peace can go around it. I like that thought. And I've traveled enough to know there's truth to it. When we give love, it comes back to us; when we're friendly, others are friendly too; and when peace abounds, it reproduces itself. . . .

It's not just that Belgian poet who encourages us to share friendship, love, and peace, but we have been summoned by the Savior Himself to do it. We are commanded to introduce people to Him, train them in the way they should live under His love and protection, instruct them in His teachings. And when we do this, He has promised us His constant presence. What could be more loving and fulfilling than such a powerful assignment and such a personal promise?

LUCI SWINDOLL

Boundless Love

JUNE 13

Let us pursue the things which make for peace
and the things by which one may edify another.
ROMANS 14:19

He Himself is our peace, who has made both one,
and has broken down the middle wall of separation.
EPHESIANS 2:14

Walk worthy of the calling with which you were
called, with all lowliness and gentleness.
EPHESIANS 4:1–2

JUNE 14

Enjoying Friendship

When the chips are down, there's nothing like a good girlfriend. A friend is someone who accepts you—warts, wrinkles, weight, and all—unconditionally. She will listen to you cry or complain and do her best to look out for your best interests. . . . She supports you through thick and thin, but because there is mutual respect, she will not allow you to wallow in self-pity or manipulate her. She will encourage you to be your best self and allow you the freedom to make your own choices.

All women are born with the need to communicate at a deeper level with their mothers, grandmothers, sisters, daughters, aunts, cousins, and other significant females in their lives. Wholesome friendships among women promote sound mental and emotional health. Friends remind us we are part of something greater than ourselves, a larger world, and the right friends keep us on track.

BARBARA JENKINS

Wit and Wisdom for Women

Evening

A friend loves at all times.

PROVERBS 17:17

Faithful are the wounds of a friend.

PROVERBS 27:6

"This is My commandment, that you love one another
as I have loved you. Greater love has no one than
this, than to lay down one's life for his friends."

JOHN 15:12—13

Ointment and perfume delight the heart,
And the sweetness of a man's friend gives
delight by hearty counsel.

PROVERBS 27:9

JUNE 15

Becoming Strong in the Broken Places

To become strong in the broken places in our lives demands that we do two things, seeming opposites: hang in there, and let go. To somehow dig up the courage to keep going is the very courage that allows us to scoop up the broken pieces of our lives and lay them all at the feet of One who would do more in us than just get us through the storm. As James Means said, "He would take the fire that blackens our horizons and warm our souls with it. He would sharpen our vision in the darkness that oppresses us. He would use the despair of standing at a grave to deepen our trust. This we cannot do for ourselves."

Perhaps because our brokenness brings us to the end of ourselves, it is here, in these jars of clay that we offer up to His very special grace, that God's all-surpassing power is made known and He, indeed, makes us strong in our broken places.

VERDELL DAVIS

Riches Stored in Secret Places

I would have lost heart, unless I had believed
That I would see the goodness of the LORD
In the land of the living.
Wait on the LORD;
Be of good courage,
And He shall strengthen your heart;
Wait, I say, on the LORD!

PSALM 27:13—14

It is the God who commanded light to shine
out of darkness, who has shone in our hearts
to give the light of the knowledge of the glory of
God in the face of Jesus Christ. But we have this
treasure in earthen vessels, that the excellence
of the power may be of God and not of us.

2 CORINTHIANS 4:6—7

The LORD will perfect that which concerns me;
Your mercy, O LORD, endures forever;
Do not forsake the works of Your hands.

PSALM 138:8

JUNE 16

A Father's Job

It's not lost on me that of all of the names God could have asked us to call Him, we most often refer to Him as "Father." I think that's because He has the same kind of relationship in mind for us that I had in mind for my kids. I think a father's job, when it's done best, is to get down on both knees, lean over his children's lives, and whisper, "Where do you want to go?"

Every day God invites us on the same kind of adventure. It's not a trip where He sends a rigid itinerary, He simply invites us. God asks what it is He's made us to love, what it is that captures our attention, what feeds that deep indescribable need of our souls to experience the richness of the world He made. And then, leaning over us, He whispers, "Let's go do *that* together."

BOB GOFF

Love Does

Behold what manner of love the Father has bestowed
on us, that we should be called children of God!

1 JOHN 3:1

As many as are led by the Spirit of God, these are
sons of God. For you did not receive the spirit
of bondage again to fear, but you received the
Spirit of adoption by whom we cry out, "Abba,
Father." The Spirit Himself bears witness with
our spirit that we are children of God.

ROMANS 8:14—16

Because you are sons, God has sent forth the Spirit of
His Son into your hearts, crying out, "Abba, Father!"

GALATIANS 4:6

JUNE 17

Silver Lining

No doubt Noah felt the grace (unmerited favor) of God when he was delivered from the total destruction that wiped out sinful humankind. For Noah, God brought forth treasure in the darkness when the flood ended. Noah again heard the voice of God and beheld the bow in the clouds. Here was the assurance of God's presence and comfort, along with His faithfulness and ongoing promise.

Those same treasures are there for each of us as we come through crisis or struggle, for as we look for the silver lining in each cloud, we discover the treasure He has hidden there. All is not lost, and He is forever with us to comfort and encourage us no matter what happens on this earth. If we find our feet stuck in the cloud of passing crisis, perhaps it's God's way of asking us to go back and check for the silver lining!

LANA BATEMAN
Women of Faith Devotional Bible

Evening

. . . .

It shall be, when I bring a cloud over the earth, that
the rainbow shall be seen in the cloud; and I will
remember My covenant which is between Me and
you and every living creature of all flesh; the waters
shall never again become a flood to destroy all flesh.

GENESIS 9:14–15

Be strong and of good courage, do not fear
nor be afraid of them; for the LORD your
God, He is the One who goes with you. He
will not leave you nor forsake you.

DEUTERONOMY 31:6

David said to his son Solomon, "Be strong and of good
courage, and do it; do not fear nor be dismayed, for
the LORD God—my God—will be with you. He will not
leave you nor forsake you, until you have finished all
the work for the service of the house of the LORD."

1 CHRONICLES 28:20

Making God Supreme

When we begin to talk to people who say, "I live by the Ten Commandments, but I can do it without God," we are talking with people who are breaking the first and greatest commandment of all. The first commandment is all about God being supreme. God says it's a big sin to ignore Him and think you are big enough and clever enough and good enough to live life well enough to please God and get to heaven on your own merits. That is saying to God that you are good enough without God. Independence is the essence of sin! The first commandment is "You shall have no other gods before Me" (Exodus 20:3). Trying to live life without reference to God is making yourself God.

JILL BRISCOE

Here Am I, Lord

The LORD is the true God;
He is the living God and the everlasting King.
At His wrath the earth will tremble,
And the nations will not be able to endure His indignation.

JEREMIAH 10:10

The LORD had made a covenant and charged them,
saying: "You shall not fear other gods, nor bow
down to them nor serve them nor sacrifice to them;
but the LORD, who brought you up from the land
of Egypt with great power and an outstretched
arm, Him you shall fear, Him you shall worship,
and to Him you shall offer sacrifice."

2 KINGS 17:35—36

Whoever shall keep the whole law, and yet
stumble in one point, he is guilty of all.

JAMES 2:10

The Riches of God's Grace

When my friend Karen returned from England she told me about visiting the Tower of London and beholding the stunning crown jewels of Great Britain.

"I asked an attentive and well-accented Beefeater about the value of the crown jewels," she told me, "and instead of an answer, I received an education."

The guard explained . . . that the jewels lend their splendor to coronations and jubilees as symbols of royalty, authority, justice, and spirituality. They remain a tangible link, he said, between modern-day England and the kings and queens of long ago. . . . As to stated value, the storied jewels have none. That's hard to believe until you ask, How could you put a price on such magnificence? . . . They are irreplaceable and without comparison; no price tag could do them justice.

So it is with grace. . . . Grace has no equal and its value goes far beyond imagery, history, and tradition.

JENNIFER ROTHSCHILD

Lessons I Learned in the Dark

Evening

· · · · · · · · ·

In Him we have redemption through
His blood, the forgiveness of sins,
according to the riches of His grace.

EPHESIANS 1:7

You were not redeemed with corruptible
things, like silver or gold, from your aimless
conduct received by tradition from your fathers,
but with the precious blood of Christ, as of a
lamb without blemish and without spot.

1 PETER 1:18—19

He has not dealt with us according to our sins,
Nor punished us according to our iniquities.
For as the heavens are high above the earth,
So great is His mercy toward those who fear Him;
As far as the east is from the west,
So far has He removed our transgressions from us.

PSALM 103:10—12

A Picture of Faith

Look out several feet past the shore and you may see a group of people, even children, standing in what appears to be just a few feet of water. How is that possible, when you see others closer in, swimming in water that's over their heads?

Sandbars are formed at the break point of waves, and not all of them are visible. It's great fun to discover one beneath the ocean's surface. . . .

Our faith can be a lot like finding that "hidden" sandbar: we are willing to take that deep step, because we're certain it's out there—somewhere.

Understandably, sandbars are also navigational nightmares to boats and can cause considerable damage. . . .

From a faith perspective, it's an interesting visual. On one side of the sandbar, some are eager to swim toward it, unconcerned about the depth of the waters surrounding it. On the other side, others want nothing to do with it, and they change course at any hint of its presence. . . .

On which side of the sandbar does your faith reside?

MIRIAM DRENNAN
Devotions for the Beach

Evening

· · · · · · · · ·

Now faith is the substance of things hoped
for, the evidence of things not seen.

HEBREWS 11:1

In You, O LORD, I put my trust;
Let me never be ashamed;
Deliver me in Your righteousness.
Bow down Your ear to me,
Deliver me speedily;
Be my rock of refuge,
A fortress of defense to save me.
For You are my rock and my fortress;
Therefore, for Your name's sake,
Lead me and guide me.

PSALM 31:1–3

Moses called Joshua and said to him in the sight
of all Israel, "Be strong and of good courage. . . .
And the LORD, He is the One who goes before you.
He will be with you, He will not leave you nor
forsake you; do not fear nor be dismayed."

DEUTERONOMY 31:7–8

Letting Go of Shame

Maybe if I had been thinner, smarter, younger, more beautiful, more confident, more fit, funnier, more adventurous, more whatever . . . Many of us feel shame because of a lifelong feeling that we just don't measure up. . . .

As I learned more about [God] . . . and experienced His love . . . I was absolutely overwhelmed. His love was so big that it crowded out my shame. . . .

Now I knew that I simply couldn't be good enough. . . . But Jesus was good enough. Perfectly good. And because of His death on the cross, in my place, for my sins, God credited Christ's perfect righteousness to my account. . . . and I knew I was loved with an everlasting love simply because of Jesus.

The gospel tells us the truth that we are special and significant simply because we are children of God, not because of how we look or how many good things we've done. So take comfort in His perfect love no matter what storms you're facing.

DENISE JACKSON

The Road Home

Evening

· · · · · · · · ·

Blessed is he whose transgression is forgiven,
Whose sin is covered.
Blessed is the man to whom the LORD does not impute iniquity,
And in whose spirit there is no deceit.

PSALM 32:1—2

"Whoever hears these sayings of Mine, and does
them, I will liken him to a wise man who built his
house on the rock: and the rain descended, the floods
came, and the winds blew and beat on that house;
and it did not fall, for it was founded on the rock."

MATTHEW 7:24—25

I also count all things loss for the excellence of the
knowledge of Christ Jesus my Lord, for whom I have
suffered the loss of all things, and count them as
rubbish, that I may gain Christ and be found in Him,
not having my own righteousness, which is from
the law, but that which is through faith in Christ,
the righteousness which is from God by faith.

PHILIPPIANS 3:8—9

355

Present Sufferings, Future Glory

The apostle Paul dearly loved the elders of the Ephesian church, and when he visited them on his way to Jerusalem, he wasn't sure if he would ever see them again this side of heaven. Paul acknowledged the risks inherent in his trip: "chains and tribulations await me" (Acts 20:23).

Then came Paul's bold proclamation in verse 24: those dangers and risks were not going to keep him from going to Jerusalem. What mattered most to Paul was not how long his life lasted, but that—however many days God gave him—he would "finish [his] race with joy."

Paul was confident that the Lord had called him "to testify to the gospel of the grace of God," and he had faithfully fulfilled that calling, often at great cost to his physical health and safety. And he was willing to suffer some more.

What an example for us! May we, like Paul, finish our earthly race with joy!

100 Favorite Bible Verses

I consider that the sufferings of this present
time are not worthy to be compared with the
glory which shall be revealed in us. For the
earnest expectation of the creation eagerly
waits for the revealing of the sons of God.

ROMANS 8:18—19

We do not lose heart. Even though our
outward man is perishing, yet the inward
man is being renewed day by day. For our light
affliction, which is but for a moment, is working
for us a far more exceeding and eternal weight
of glory, while we do not look at the things which
are seen, but at the things which are not seen.
For the things which are seen are temporary,
but the things which are not seen are eternal.

2 CORINTHIANS 4:16—18

We also glory in tribulations, knowing that
tribulation produces perseverance; and
perseverance, character; and character, hope.

ROMANS 5:3—4

JUNE 23

Declaring Righteousness

Have you ever known any smorgasbord Christians? Along their journey they say, "I'll take a little of that and a small helping of this. I'd like a big portion of this, but you can keep that."

When it comes to walking with God, there are no options. You give Him your all, or you give Him nothing at all. You either embrace the truth, or you live a lie. The truth does not conform to situational ethics or political correctness. We conform to truth. The Lord delights in those who love truth, speak truth, and live truth.

BABBIE MASON

Women of Faith Devotional Bible

He who speaks truth declares righteousness, but
a false witness, deceit. . . . The tongue of the wise
promotes health. The truthful lip shall be established
forever, but a lying tongue is but for a moment.

PROVERBS 12:17—19

Be diligent to present yourself approved
to God, a worker who does not need to be
ashamed, rightly dividing the word of truth.

2 TIMOTHY 2:15

Teach me Your way, O LORD;
I will walk in Your truth;
Unite my heart to fear Your name.
I will praise You, O Lord my God, with all my heart,
And I will glorify Your name forevermore.

PSALM 86:11—12

Across the Miles

Events like graduation day, a big move, or a new job can bring excitement, change, expectation—and good-byes. A lot of the people you've grown close to over the past several years may not be headed the same direction that God is leading you. But that doesn't mean your friendships can't continue to grow.

Keeping in touch across the miles takes effort. However, an email, a crazy card, or a heartfelt phone call is all a friendship needs to spark many happy reunions. The friends God brings into your life are worth holding onto and praying for. That includes the ones you haven't met yet.

Along with those good-byes, you're also going to be saying a lot of glad-to-meet-yous. So open your heart. Some of your very best friends are waiting to meet you.

Living God's Way

Evening

· · · · · · · · · ·

"Greater love has no one than this, than
to lay down one's life for his friends."

JOHN 15:13

A friend loves at all times.

PROVERBS 17:17

Iron sharpens iron,
and one man sharpens another.

PROVERBS 27:17 ESV

The righteous should choose his friends carefully.

PROVERBS 12:26

• • • • • • • •

Living in Christ

Let every part of your life—your person, your style, your direction, your flavor—be in Him. When you're in Him, then you're based on truth. You'll be honest and genuine through and through; you'll be coordinated, all of a piece; you'll be in harmony with yourself. And then you can grow within yourself to unlimited dimensions—and all because you're in God.

Faddish lives age quickly. They're not based on God, who is greater than all culture and all generations, so twenty years from now they'll seem faded and "out of it." Anchor yourself to the great "I AM," and you will develop more and more into a woman who is ageless, whole, true, and at rest.

ANNE ORTLUND
Disciplines of the Heart

Evening

· · · · · · · · · ·

God said to Moses, "I AM WHO I AM."

EXODUS 3:14

[The Lord] is not far from each one of us; for in
Him we live and move and have our being.

ACTS 17:27—28

This is the victory that has overcome the world—
our faith. Who is he who overcomes the world, but
he who believes that Jesus is the Son of God?

1 JOHN 5:4—5

Morning

. . . .

Wise Choices

I am Eve, mother of every human being. If I close my eyes I can still remember the sweetness of walking with God in the cool of the day. That was before my heart flirted with temptation; before I made a fatal error.

Adam and I knew the serpent was crafty. But I underestimated the seductive power of his voice. I thought I could handle a conversation with him. How wrong I was. Conversations require cooperation. To cooperate you must grant authority to influence.

The serpent's influence was deadly. The more I spoke with him, the more reasonable his words became. . . .

The serpent was deceptive, but I held the power of choice. I chose to converse with him. I chose to make his words an option. I chose to elevate my desires above God's will. And my choice altered human history.

All choices do.

ALICIA BRITT CHOLE

Pure Joy

Evening

· · · · · · · · ·

Now the serpent was more crafty than any other
beast of the field that the LORD God had made.
He said to the woman, "Did God actually say,
'You shall not eat of any tree in the garden'? . . .
You will not surely die. For God knows that when
you eat of it your eyes will be opened, and you
will be like God, knowing good and evil."

GENESIS 3:1, 4—5 ESV

Choose for yourselves this day whom
you will serve. . . . But as for me and my
house, we will serve the LORD.

JOSHUA 24:15

Trust in the LORD with all your heart,
And lean not on your own understanding;
In all your ways acknowledge Him,
And He shall direct your paths.

PROVERBS 3:5—6

JUNE 27

Looking for Laughter and Joy

We can learn to look for laughter and joy in the many ordinary places where we go. When I go to our La Habra post office in the morning, the cement on the sidewalk outside is just plain blah gray. But if I go in the afternoon, when the sun hits it, the cement sparkles with a million transient diamonds! So, I usually go in the afternoon, looking for the joy that can bounce off that cement right into my life, to remind me of the sparkles all around us, if we are willing to look for them.

But I repeat, you have to LOOK for the joy. Look for the light of God that is hitting your life, and you will find sparkles you didn't know were there.

BARBARA JOHNSON

Stick a Geranium in Your Hat and Be Happy

Evening

· · · · · · · · · ·

Happy are the people whose God is the LORD!

PSALM 144:15

So they sang praises with gladness, and
they bowed their heads and worshiped.

2 CHRONICLES 29:30

Again there shall be heard in this place . . .
the voice of joy and the voice of gladness . . .
the voice of those who will say:
"Praise the LORD of hosts,
For the LORD is good,
For His mercy endures forever."

JEREMIAH 33:10—11

A merry heart makes a cheerful countenance.

PROVERBS 15:13

Dreams

The Bible tells the story of a dreamer named Joseph. He was a teenager, the youngest of twelve brothers, when he had a dream. Joseph told his brothers, "We were binding sheaves of grain out in the field when suddenly my sheaf rose and stood upright, while your sheaves gathered around mine and bowed down to it" (Genesis 37:6–7 NIV). Joseph's brothers did not like the idea of bowing to their younger brother. They hated Joseph for his dream, and they sold him into slavery. Still, Joseph believed that God had something great in store for him. After many trials, many years, and much patience, Joseph's dream came true: he became the chief minister (governor) of Egypt (Genesis 41:41–46), and his brothers did bow down to him when they visited Egypt desperate for food during a famine in Israel.

God has a plan for each of us. Often He instills dreams—ambitions—in our hearts and encourages us to reach for them. Whatever dream God puts on your heart, you can trust Him to lead you to it.

A Charles Dickens Devotional

Evening

· · · · · · · · ·

O LORD, I know the way of man is not in himself;
It is not in man who walks to direct his own steps.

JEREMIAH 10:23

Take great joy in the Eternal!
His gifts are coming, and they are all your heart desires!
Commit your path to the Eternal; let Him direct you.
Put your confidence in Him,
and He will follow through with you.

PSALM 37:4–5 THE VOICE

Your word is a lamp to my feet
And a light to my path.

PSALM 119:105

369

JUNE 29

Reflecting God

It's not just fingerprints that make us each so thoroughly unique. For His own glory God gives us different personalities, different gifts, and different callings. His absolute creativity and His vastness are reflected in the uniqueness of His creations. As we fully allow our personalities and gifts to be redeemed, developed, and used, we bring God glory in the greatest of ways. That's because in doing so we reflect another aspect of His complexity, diversity, and creativity as no other person has or ever will—because there's only one you. And when our gifts are being used, we are complementing one another not just for the purpose of doing good works, but also for the purpose of illuminating the bigger picture the world sees of who God is—a magnificent and vast Creator.

CATHERINE CLAIRE LARSON

Waiting in Wonder

You formed my inward parts;
You covered me in my mother's womb.
I will praise You, for I am fearfully and wonderfully made.

PSALM 139:13—14

For as the body is one and has many members,
but all the members of that one body, being
many, are one body, so also is Christ. . . . God
has set the members, each one of them, in the
body just as He pleased. And if they were all
one member, where would the body be? . . .
Indeed there are many members, yet one body.

1 CORINTHIANS 12:12, 18—20

God thunders marvelously with His voice;
He does great things which we cannot comprehend.
For He says to the snow, "Fall on the earth";
Likewise to the gentle rain and the heavy rain of His strength.
He seals the hand of every man,
That all men may know His work. . . .
He comes from the north as golden splendor;
With God is awesome majesty.

JOB 37:5—7, 22

Morning

· · · · · · · · ·

What Love Looks Like

Want to know what love looks like? Look at God. Consider His sacrifice, His patience, His comfort, His faithfulness, His generosity. God's creativity in expressing love is so great that it's almost incomprehensible.

Consider how your love stands up next to His. Don't get discouraged. You're not God. At times, your love still falters and fails—but God's love is always at work in your life. He's helping you love others in the same wonderful way He so deeply loves you.

Let God's creative compassion inspire you to love others well. Ask for His help in knowing the best way to express your love so that it meets needs, builds relationships, and warms hearts. Then take a moment to sit back and enjoy His love for you.

Living God's Way

Above all things have fervent love for one another,
for "love will cover a multitude of sins."

1 PETER 4:8

"God so loved the world that He gave His only
begotten Son, that whoever believes in Him
should not perish but have everlasting life."

JOHN 3:16

Love suffers long and is kind; love does not
envy; love does not parade itself, is not puffed
up; does not behave rudely, does not seek its own,
is not provoked, thinks no evil; does not rejoice
in iniquity, but rejoices in the truth; bears all
things, believes all things, hopes all things,
endures all things. Love never fails.

1 CORINTHIANS 13:4—8

July

Though now you do not see
Him, yet believing, you rejoice with
joy inexpressible and full of glory.

1 PETER 1:8

Anchored in the Gospel

We're deeply relational beings. Godless judgments about life made in reaction to people who have hurt us can predispose us toward fear, pride, or shame. Unthinkingly, we can be drawn into the sinful cycle of our own weaknesses—acting in self-pity, withdrawing from others, or perhaps even getting angry and attacking—as we reflexively crave the emotional satisfaction that only God can give us. . . .

When we choose to anchor ourselves in the gospel, we gain the deep satisfaction that we are "accepted in the Beloved" (Ephesians 1:6). We remember that God is our loving Father and we've been adopted into His family. We know that it is no longer us that lives but Christ that lives within us (Galatians 2:20). And daily we can learn to react as He would—forgiving the wrongs done to us by others, identifying and rejecting lies about God and others that lodge in our souls, filling our minds with the truth of God's Word, and glorifying God as our true source of joy.

KEVIN HARTNETT

The Heavens

"Sanctify [My disciples] by Your
truth. Your word is truth."

JOHN 17:17

I have been crucified with Christ; it is no longer I
who live, but Christ lives in me; and the life which
I now live in the flesh I live by faith in the Son of
God, who loved me and gave Himself for me.

GALATIANS 2:20

[God] chose us in Him before the foundation of
the world, that we should be holy and without
blame before Him in love, having predestined
us to adoption as sons by Jesus Christ to
Himself, according to the good pleasure of His
will, to the praise of the glory of His grace, by
which He made us accepted in the Beloved.

EPHESIANS 1:4—6

The Unique Bonds of Friendship

A poet once described friends as "the sunshine of life." I myself have found that the day is certainly much brighter when I'm sharing it with my friends. Enjoying fellowship is one of life's sweetest blessings and joys. What would we do without people and the many shadings of companionship and camaraderie? We need friends in our lives, friends with whom we not only discuss "deep" issues and confide our secrets, fears, or sorrows, but with whom we can laugh, play, and even cry. The best times in life are made a thousand times better when shared with a dear friend.

Camaraderie is definitely a part of friendship, and camaraderie itself can often produce friendships, too. When we reach out to others, they reach out to us. It's a two-way street, a street practically lined with balloons and streamers in celebration of the unique bonds of friendship.

LUCI SWINDOLL
You Bring the Confetti

Evening

. . . .

Two are better than one,
Because they have a good reward for their labor.
For if they fall, one will lift up his companion.
But woe to him who is alone when he falls,
For he has no one to help him up.

ECCLESIASTES 4:9—10

Let us consider one another in order to stir up love
and good works, not forsaking the assembling
of ourselves together, as is the manner of
some, but exhorting one another, and so much
the more as you see the Day approaching.

HEBREWS 10:24—25

If we walk in the light as He is in the light, we
have fellowship with one another, and the blood
of Jesus Christ His Son cleanses us from all sin.

1 JOHN 1:7

. . . .

JULY 3

The Gift of Hospitality

Some people have the gift of hospitality. This well-to-do woman from Shunem was one of them. She used her means to bless and refresh others. She had discerned that Elisha was God's prophet, but she also knew that he was hungry and tired. She and her husband anticipated his needs for rest, reflection, and reading. They gave the best they had, and God rewarded them by giving this childless couple a son. God rewarded her hospitality to His prophet with the desire of her heart.

When was the last time you were refreshed by the hospitality of one of God's thoughtful children? Refresh someone soon with a body and soul stopover at your expense and for God's pleasure.

JAN CARLBERG

The Hungry Heart

Now it happened one day that Elisha went to
Shunem, where there was a notable woman, and she
persuaded him to eat some food. So it was, as often
as he passed by, he would turn in there to eat some
food. And she said to her husband, "Look now, I
know that this is a holy man of God, who passes by
us regularly. Please, let us make a small upper room
on the wall; and let us put a bed for him there, and
a table and a chair and a lampstand; so it will be,
whenever he comes to us, he can turn in there."

2 KINGS 4:8—10

Be kindly affectionate to one another with brotherly
love, in honor giving preference to one another;
not lagging in diligence, fervent in spirit, serving
the Lord; rejoicing in hope, patient in tribulation,
continuing steadfastly in prayer; distributing to
the needs of the saints, given to hospitality.

ROMANS 12:10—13

Let brotherly love continue. Do not forget
to entertain strangers, for by so doing some
have unwittingly entertained angels.

HEBREWS 13:1—2

Embrace Truth and Find God's Grace

I know what it's like to have a past you'd just as soon forget. A past that you had no control over—your family of origin; your mother's choice of lifestyle; your family's battle with alcohol—as well as a past of misgivings made by your own free will. . . .

We all have "issues." We all carry burdens and regrets. And we all play a shell game of sorts, hoping to hide and deflect the broken places of our lives. But I say it's time to embrace truth.

So why not:

- Embrace the fact that you are a mess of magnificent proportions?
- Embrace the fact that you are not alone?
- Embrace the lavish reality of divine grace . . . that heals, restores, covers, forgives, renews, and abounds?

What true freedom!

JULIE ANN BARNHILL

Scandalous Grace

If we confess our sins, He is faithful and
just to forgive us our sins and to cleanse
us from all unrighteousness.

1 JOHN 1:9

The LORD is my shepherd;
I shall not want.
He makes me to lie down in green pastures;
He leads me beside the still waters.
He restores my soul.

PSALM 23:1—3

Have mercy upon me, O God,
According to Your lovingkindness;
According to the multitude
of Your tender mercies,
Blot out my transgressions.
Wash me thoroughly from my iniquity,
And cleanse me from my sin.
For I acknowledge my transgressions. . . .
Wash me, and I shall be whiter than snow.

PSALM 51:1—3, 7

. . . .

JULY 5

Independence Day

Life is full of starting-over days, days that often feel like a fresh taste of freedom. The choices and changes that are right around the corner seem sweet and exciting because the direction you choose to go is now solely up to you—and God.

Being dependent on God doesn't interfere with that newfound freedom. Relying on God for guidance, strength, comfort, wisdom, and countless other gifts allows you to risk throwing yourself wholeheartedly into the adventure of life. It's like having a partner belay your rope while rock climbing. It gives you the freedom and courage to tackle higher and harder climbs. The closer the partnership you have with God, the freer you'll find you are to reach your true potential.

Living God's Way

Evening

. . . .

"Fear not, for I am with you;
Be not dismayed, for I am your God.
I will strengthen you,
Yes, I will help you,
I will uphold you with My righteous right hand."

ISAIAH 41:10

Trust in the LORD with all your heart,
And lean not on your own understanding;
In all your ways acknowledge Him,
And He shall direct your paths.

PROVERBS 3:5—6

Even the youths shall faint and be weary,
And the young men shall utterly fall,
But those who wait on the LORD
Shall renew their strength;
They shall mount up with wings like eagles,
They shall run and not be weary,
They shall walk and not faint.

ISAIAH 40:30—31

What Is Love?

Fondly, dearly, and *devotedly*—think about the meanings of these words from love letters, and you might decide that they are hardly the most romantic ones that a person deeply in love would use to describe his or her tender feelings.

The Bible offers its own description of love. It says, "Love is patient, love is kind. It does not envy, it does not boast, it is not proud. It is not rude, it is not self-seeking, it is not easily angered, it keeps no record of wrongs. Love does not delight in evil but rejoices with the truth. It always protects, always trusts, always hopes, always perseveres" (1 Corinthians 13:4–7 NIV). These four scripture verses tell us exactly what true love is.

These then are the adverbs that God uses throughout His Word to describe how Christians should love one another: patiently, kindly, unselfishly, humbly, honorably, gently, truthfully, protectively, trustingly, hopefully, and eternally. Yet a single adverb describes how God loves us—*perfectly!* It is God's perfect love that is the source of our own love, and we should endeavor to love others in the same way that He loves us.

A Charles Dickens Devotional

He who does not love does not
know God, for God is love.

1 JOHN 4:8

By this we know love, because He laid
down His life for us. And we also ought to
lay down our lives for the brethren.

1 JOHN 3:16

No one has seen God at any time. If we
love one another, God abides in us, and
His love has been perfected in us.

1 JOHN 4:12

Now abide faith, hope, love, these three;
but the greatest of these is love.

1 CORINTHIANS 13:13

Our Work in the Battle

God has given us prayer to have a realistic "work" that can be done in prison, in a wheelchair, in bed, in a hospital or a hovel or a palace, on the march, in the midst of battle . . . , out on a Villars street as skiers are pushing and shoving past, or in the dark of a chalet when everyone else is asleep. We can have a practical, realistic part in the battle between God and Satan.

Astonishing? Unbelievable? But true. In Ephesians 6:10–20, the whole point is that the "armor of God" is needed to stand against, to wrestle against the "wiles of the devil." And it is there, in that context, that we are commanded to "pray always with all prayer and supplication in the Spirit." Prayer is not just icing on the cake of a so-called spiritual life; prayer is warm, close communication with the living God, and also a matter of doing an active work on His side of the battle.

EDITH SCHAEFFER

The Tapestry

You are of God, little children, and have
overcome them, because He who is in you
is greater than he who is in the world.

1 JOHN 4:4

Take the helmet of salvation, and the sword of
the Spirit, which is the word of God; praying
always with all prayer and supplication in
the Spirit, being watchful to this end with all
perseverance and supplication for all the saints.

EPHESIANS 6:17—18

Rejoice always, pray without ceasing, in
everything give thanks; for this is the
will of God in Christ Jesus for you.

1 THESSALONIANS 5:16—18

JULY 8

Learning to Rest

I'm so glad Jesus advocated rest for His followers. He doesn't guilt us into overdoing it even when it comes to ministry. Instead He teaches us (and modeled for us according to Mark 1:35 and Luke 4:42) to slow down and recuperate after giving our all for the sake of the gospel. To find a balance between *going out and doing* and *being still and knowing*. Resting—learning to weave practical Sabbaths into our schedules—isn't a punitive decree; it's God's generous endowment for our protection and perseverance. And I think Matthew narrated Jesus' words regarding this gift better than anyone else:

> Are you tired? Worn out? Burned out on religion? Come to me. Get away with me and you'll recover your life. I'll show you how to take a real rest. Walk with me and work with me—watch how I do it. Learn the unforced rhythms of grace. I won't lay anything heavy or ill-fitting on you. Keep company with me and you'll learn to live freely and lightly. (Matthew 11:28–30 MSG)

LISA HARPER

Stumbling into Grace

Evening

• • • • • • • • • •

In the morning, having risen a long while
before daylight, [Jesus] went out and departed
to a solitary place; and there He prayed.

MARK 1:35

When it was day, [Jesus] departed
and went into a deserted place.

LUKE 4:42

"You shall keep the Sabbath, therefore, for it is holy
to you. . . . Work shall be done for six days, but the
seventh is the Sabbath of rest, holy to the LORD."

EXODUS 31:14–15

Be a Hero

Heroism is not always about rushing into a burning building. Look around. Heroic moments are happening everywhere. Whether it's helping an elderly person pump gas, checking up on a neighbor, or helping an overtaxed waitress remember her order, you can be someone's hero. Anytime. Anywhere.

To be others-focused means to be conscious of the conversation in your head and to flip the switch from "me" and "mine" to "us" and "ours." Think in terms of generosity, sacrifice, connection, noticing, and giving.

More Than a Bucket List

Evening

· · · · · · · · · ·

Do nothing from selfishness or empty conceit,
but with humility of mind regard one another
as more important than yourselves; do
not merely look out for your own personal
interests, but also for the interests of others.

PHILIPPIANS 2:3–4 NASB

"Whoever desires to become great among you
shall be your servant. And whoever of you desires
to be first shall be slave of all. For even the Son
of Man did not come to be served, but to serve,
and to give His life a ransom for many."

MARK 10:43–45

Yet who knows whether you have come to
the kingdom for such a time as this?

ESTHER 4:14

393

The Beauty of Brokenness

The phrase *stained glass* conjures up not only the usefulness of brokenness, but also its potential beauty. . . . Even though the stained glass pieces are artistically designed, they still have been broken, sanded, and soldered. They didn't naturally fit the redemptive pattern without holy repairs. Also, stained glass art doesn't begin to show its beauty or its inspiration or release its story until light touches the dark. The light transforms an otherwise subtle picture into a brilliant, dimensional experience.

Isn't that how we are? Broken? Sharp edges? In need of repair? Longing to be, yet frightened of being, seen in the light? . . .

We have a Creator who knows where the scattered pieces of our achy-breaky hearts landed and how to fit them back together again. Not one splinter escapes his redemptive work.

PATSY CLAIRMONT
Stained Glass Hearts

"The LORD has anointed Me
To preach good tidings to the poor;
He has sent Me to heal the brokenhearted . . .
To comfort all who mourn . . .
To give them beauty for ashes."

ISAIAH 61:1—3

[The children of Israel] remembered that God was their rock,
And the Most High God their Redeemer.

PSALM 78:35

Your Maker is your husband,
The LORD of hosts is His name;
And your Redeemer is the Holy One of Israel;
He is called the God of the whole earth.

ISAIAH 54:5

The Secret Is the Salt

Last night, I telephoned the family farm back in Maryland to see how my sister Jay was doing. She was up to her elbows in pickles! Cucumbers are ripe off the vine from Jay's garden so she's spending her evenings boiling and blanching, straining and sealing. I love my sister's pickles, and I think her secret is . . . salt. She adds a lot of salt and tells me that it's the best way to preserve a pickle at its crunchiest, tastiest best.

Those words go well together—*salt* and *preserve*. As Christians, we act as a salty preservative in this world, infusing godly values into a life around us. We have the work of restraining evil and advancing good. And just as salt brings out flavor in food, we can "season to taste" our words when the world asks us the reason for the hope that is within us.

JONI EARECKSON TADA

Diamonds in the Dust

Evening

. . . .

"You are the salt of the earth; but if the salt loses
its flavor, how shall it be seasoned? It is then good
for nothing but to be thrown out and trampled
underfoot by men. You are the light of the world.
A city that is set on a hill cannot be hidden."

MATTHEW 5:13—14

Let your speech always be with grace,
seasoned with salt, that you may know
how you ought to answer each one.

COLOSSIANS 4:6

No spring yields both salt water and fresh.
Who is wise and understanding among you?
Let him show by good conduct that his works
are done in the meekness of wisdom.

JAMES 3:12—13

JULY 12

Linger with Your Lord

There are days we race through, as though God is an item to check off our "to do" lists. . . . Then there are times when those clamoring voices vying for attention will just have to wait; you want to spend time with your Maker. . . . You want nothing more than to be still in Him. So you linger, remaining there as long as possible because of the peace, the comfort, and the rest you feel. . . .

When you experience those moments, drink deeply. Receive Jesus, welcome Him, linger with Him. As in any good conversation, give Him time to speak and yourself time to listen. If your soul feels parched, ask Him to quench it in this way. When the day becomes busy, as it surely will, stay mindful that He remains with you. He is there and present.

This was Jesus' promise to the disciples and to us as He returned to the Father. We may not completely understand how He does this, but we can be certain that this is no hurdle for the One who conquered death.

MIRIAM DRENNAN

Devotions for the Beach

Evening

· · · · · · · · ·

"Surely I am with you always, to
the very end of the age."

MATTHEW 28:20 NIV

"Come to Me, all you who labor and are
heavy laden, and I will give you rest."

MATTHEW 11:28

[Jesus] said to them, "Come aside by yourselves
to a deserted place and rest a while."

MARK 6:31

JULY 13

Praise Makes a Difference

Without praise we experience an eroding that leads to bondage and death (Romans 1:21). . . . *With* praise, you and your circumstances can be changed, because it gives God entrance into every area of your life and allows Him to be enthroned there.

So any time you struggle with negative emotions—such as anger, unforgiveness, fear, hurt, oppression, depression, self-hatred, or worthlessness—thank God that He is bigger than all that. Thank Him that His plans and purposes for you are good. Thank Him that in any weak area of your life, He will be strong. Thank Him that He came to restore you. Remember the names of the Lord, and use them in your prayer. "I praise You, Lord, because You are my Deliverer and Redeemer." "Thank You, God, that You are my Healer and Provider." . . .

Praise lifts us powerfully into God's presence and aligns us with His purposes.

STORMIE OMARTIAN
Seven Prayers

Evening

· · · · · · · · · ·

Blessed be the name of the LORD
From this time forth and forevermore!
From the rising of the sun to its going down
The LORD's name is to be praised.

PSALM 113:2—3

Since the creation of the world [God's] invisible
attributes are clearly seen, being understood
by the things that are made, even His eternal
power and Godhead, so that [the ungodly] are
without excuse, because, although they knew
God, they did not glorify Him as God, nor were
thankful, but became futile in their thoughts.

ROMANS 1:20—21

I will extol You, my God, O King;
And I will bless Your name forever and ever.
Every day I will bless You,
And I will praise Your name forever and ever.
Great is the Lord, and greatly to be praised;
And His greatness is unsearchable.

PSALM 145:1—3

JULY 13

401

Let Your Dreams Take Wings

Why are swings so incredibly delightful? Remember the day when you suddenly realized you didn't have to be pushed to swing, that you could propel yourself through the air by pumping your legs? Ahh, what freedom!

Swings give a feeling of weightlessness—for a few moments you bypass the laws of gravity. For a few moments you fly!

Dreams do much the same thing. Dreams crash the confines of what is and what has been. As our minds dare to see the unseen, our imagination fuels our faith, and we begin to trust God for something more.

Some folks are afraid to dream. But connected to God, it is safe to dream. There is freedom to let faith take wings.

ALICIA BRITT CHOLE

Pure Joy

"What man is there among you who, if his son
asks for bread, will give him a stone? Or if he asks
for a fish, will he give him a serpent? If you then,
being evil, know how to give good gifts to your
children, how much more will your Father who is in
heaven give good things to those who ask Him!"

MATTHEW 7:9—11

Great is our Lord, and mighty in power;
His understanding is infinite.

PSALM 147:5

It will be recounted of the Lord to the next generation,
They will come and declare His
righteousness to a people who will be born.

PSALM 22:30—31

God Answers Prayer

I love ordering things from clothes catalogs. The order forms . . . are like crossword puzzles—but with all the answers provided. I feel really great, clever, and all that because I can fill them in!

The order is mailed and forgotten in the rush of more immediate things. Then *bang*, right in the middle of some activity totally unrelated to my catalog order, the parcel is delivered!

How like God. The specifics of my order are carefully tabulated and delivered in His time and with eternal efficiency. The answers are sent to prayers I prayed months, even years, ago—long after I have forgotten my requests. Sometimes it no longer really matters to me if the parcel even arrives! But my words are not allowed to fall to the ground. How good of God.

JILL BRISCOE
Quiet Times with God

Evening

· · · · · · · · ·

Let my prayer be set before You as incense,
The lifting up of my hands as the evening sacrifice.

PSALM 141:2

The LORD has heard the voice of my weeping.
The LORD has heard my supplication;
The LORD will receive my prayer.

PSALM 6:8—9

Christ who died, and furthermore is also
risen, . . . is even at the right hand of God,
who also makes intercession for us.

ROMANS 8:34

JULY 16

Empowered by God's Love

It's impossible to truly love until you have experienced God's love. I wish I had caught that earlier in life. But I'm so grateful to have caught it now.

The love of God our Father is the only love that eventually can heal the wounds in our hearts. The best example of that love is seen in the fierce love Jesus demonstrated on the cross. The best glimpse we will get of that love on this earth is the love we express toward each other. You want to live fully alive? In the words of an old song, "You gotta love somebody." And that love will be most fully expressed when we embrace the love of God and are empowered to love beyond ourselves.

Beyond friendship, beyond physical health, life itself depends on being loved and giving love. Those who do not know this vital connection do not know life. They are hollow shells of existence waiting to experience the real essence of living fully alive.

KEN DAVIS

Fully Alive

Evening

· · · · · · · · ·

When Jesus went out He saw a great multitude;
and He was moved with compassion
for them, and healed their sick.

MATTHEW 14:14

Beloved, let us love one another, for love is of God; and
everyone who loves is born of God and knows God. He
who does not love does not know God, for God is love.
In this the love of God was manifested toward us, that
God has sent His only begotten Son into the world,
that we might live through Him. In this is love, not
that we loved God, but that He loved us and sent His
Son to be the propitiation for our sins. Beloved, if
God so loved us, we also ought to love one another.

1 JOHN 4:7—11

Let us not love in word or in tongue,
but in deed and in truth.

1 JOHN 3:18

God's Love Letter

Over recent years I had turned from regarding the Bible as a boring history book, and started seeing it as an intimate love letter from God to me. The more I got into it, the more it got into me. I found that it was active and alive. It pierced me with its truths, and it had the power to actually change my life. . . .

When I just don't want to read God's Word, I pray for Him to give me that craving. I pray that He'll make me want to seek Him, because when we seek God, we can be sure of finding Him. . . .

I've found that the more I dig into the Bible as His love letter to me, the more I develop a passion for it, and for Him. When my heart is cold and unwilling, I ask Him to change it, and incredibly, He does. As my days unfold, I make sure to schedule uninterrupted time to read God's Word and pray. It's a discipline to do so . . . but when I do it, it fulfills my deepest desires.

DENISE JACKSON

It's All About Him

With my whole heart I have sought You;
Oh, let me not wander from Your commandments!
Your word I have hidden in my heart,
That I might not sin against You.
Blessed are You, O LORD!
Teach me Your statutes
PSALM 119:10—12

"It is written, 'Man shall not live by bread alone, but
by every word that proceeds from the mouth of God.'"
MATTHEW 4:4

Be diligent to present yourself approved
to God, a worker who does not need to be
ashamed, rightly dividing the word of truth.
2 TIMOTHY 2:15

Morning

. . . .

Fueled by God's Grace

When I am full of the knowledge of God, made clean by His forgiveness, and walking in the grace He has given to me, then I am a really cool mom. I am not Supermom, but in that full place, I know that I am loving my children as they were made to be loved.

When I am full, I'm not wishy-washy about my role as protector or provider. I overlook the small things. I major on my kids' hearts and look into their eyes and hear what's on the inside of them, trying to get out. I am not whiny or grumbling. I forgive them even as I'm giving out consequences. I dance with them more and take longer to brush their hair or watch a new skateboard trick. I am peaceful because I am living from the gift of God's peace to me. I know they can feel the difference. I am not empty, and they are the beneficiaries.

God's grace flows freely from my heart into theirs. And we are better. And life is brighter. And hope abounds.

ANGELA THOMAS

My Single Mom Life

If we love one another, God abides in us.

1 JOHN 4:12

Even the youths shall faint and be weary,
And the young men shall utterly fall,
But those who wait on the LORD
Shall renew their strength;
They shall mount up with wings like eagles,
They shall run and not be weary,
They shall walk and not faint.

ISAIAH 40:30 31

[God] said . . . "My grace is sufficient for you, for
My strength is made perfect in weakness."

2 CORINTHIANS 12:9

God's Provisions

A certain woman in Scripture is particularly interesting to me. . . . She was known as the bleeding woman. That twelve-year hemorrhage defined who she was. . . .

The woman had tried the conventional route to deal with her problem . . . but she was not going to be healed by the physicians. . . . This Gentile woman came to a point where she was willing to do something radical and scary. She would look for and she would find Jesus. If she could just get to Him surely she could be healed. She got only close enough to Him to touch the hem of His garment, but she was healed. . . .

If you are needy in any way, you need Jesus. Moreover, He is involved in everything that involves you. I think the point to be made here is that there is always the conventional way to do things, but that doesn't always work. It is what you try first, but when there are no answers, you can get radical—look for Jesus.

JAN SILVIOUS
Moving Beyond the Myths

Evening

· · · · · · · · ·

Now a certain woman had a flow of blood for twelve years, and had suffered many things from many physicians. She had spent all that she had and was no better, but rather grew worse. When she heard about Jesus, she came behind Him in the crowd and touched His garment. For she said, "If only I may touch His clothes, I shall be made well."

Immediately the fountain of her blood was dried up, and she felt in her body that she was healed of the affliction. And Jesus, immediately knowing in Himself that power had gone out of Him, turned around in the crowd and said, "Who touched My clothes?" . . .

And He looked around to see her who had done this thing. But the woman, fearing and trembling, knowing what had happened to her, came and fell down before Him and told Him the whole truth. And He said to her, "Daughter, your faith has made you well. Go in peace, and be healed of your affliction."

MARK 5:25–30, 32–34

Morning

. . . .

Most Important

Isn't it so easy to get preoccupied with our homes (and our lives) needing to be perfect or at least appearing that way? . . . This pursuit of impossible perfection can easily overshadow the things in life that should be more important, like our families and our faith. I have to remind myself (on many occasions) that there are more valuable pursuits than clutter-free counters, perfectly fluffed pillows, and spot-free slipcovers. It doesn't mean those things are wrong, but when that is the focus of my daily life, I've got a problem.

When we're striving for domestic perfection, we're missing the mark. If our highest priority is walking in faith and loving our families, we'll find joy in the sofa stains, the scratches on the dining room table, and the pile of shoes by the door. We'll be able to show love and grace when a child draws on the wall with a crayon or a husband leaves tools all over the counter. Most important, we will let the people in our lives know that we love them and that their mess doesn't take away from that.

MARIAN PARSONS

Inspired You

Evening

. . . .

"Seek first the kingdom of God
and His righteousness."

MATTHEW 6:33

"Teacher, which is the great commandment in the law?"
Jesus said to him, "'You shall love the LORD your
God with all your heart, with all your soul, and
with all your mind.' This is the first and great
commandment. And the second is like it: 'You
shall love your neighbor as yourself.'"

MATTHEW 22:36—39

When [Jesus] had called the people to Himself,
with His disciples also, He said to them, "Whoever
desires to come after Me, let him deny himself,
and take up his cross, and follow Me. For whoever
desires to save his life will lose it, but whoever
loses his life for My sake and the gospel's will
save it. For what will it profit a man if he gains
the whole world, and loses his own soul?"

MARK 8:34—36

What a Privilege!

Wisdom, power, and wealth—God warns us against pridefully finding glory in these. In Jeremiah 9:23–24, God calls us to glory in the fact that we know and understand Him. That is a rather mind-boggling reality—you have been invited to know and to be in relationship with the Creator, Sustainer, and sovereign Ruler of the universe. Knowing Him means seeing Him when others don't. You see His lovingkindness in the way He faithfully answers your prayers and provides for all your needs. You find hope and peace in the truth that He will one day exercise judgment against the immoral and ungodly. You see His righteousness in His commands, and you look forward to the ultimate victory when Jesus returns to reign in righteousness.

What a privilege to know the Lord! May your time spent reading God's Word, worshiping the Lord, and praying to Him bring you great joy day in and day out. Glory in the fact that you know the Lord!

100 Favorite Bible Verses

Evening

· · · · · · · · ·

"Let not the wise man glory in his wisdom,
Let not the mighty man glory in his might,
Nor let the rich man glory in his riches;
But let him who glories glory in this,
That he understands and knows Me,
That I am the LORD, exercising lovingkindness, judgment,
and righteousness in the earth.
For in these I delight," says the LORD.

JEREMIAH 9:23–24

All that is in the world—the lust of the flesh,
the lust of the eyes, and the pride of life—is
not of the Father but is of the world.

1 JOHN 2:16

Humble yourselves in the sight of the
Lord, and He will lift you up.

JAMES 4:10

Love and Marriage

Marriage is not something that can be improvised. You are both embarking on a long voyage, untrained, in a frail little boat headed, inevitably, for stormy waters. . . . There may be some days when you are safely anchored in the harbor, but that's not what boats are built for. They are built for sea travel.

Walter and I had a few safe harbor days, but most of the time it seemed we were out on the ocean, bailing water, pulling people from the ocean and into the boat, and trying to keep our own signals straight as husband and wife. During those times we needed our strong co-pilot, the Holy Spirit of God. And we needed the encouragement of fellow Christians who would cheer us on from their own boats nearby. . . .

Love is a decision, a judgment. It involves the intellect and the will. . . . I am reminded of a statement by Dr. Bovet: "First you choose the one you love and then you love the one you have chosen."

INGRID TROBISCH

The Hidden Strength

A threefold cord is not quickly broken.

ECCLESIASTES 4:12

"'A man shall leave his father and mother and be
joined to his wife, and the two shall become one
flesh'; so then they are no longer two, but one flesh."

MARK 10:7—8

Be filled with the Spirit . . . giving thanks always
for all things to God the Father in the name of
our Lord Jesus Christ, submitting to one another
in the fear of God. Wives, submit to your own
husbands, as to the Lord. For the husband is head
of the wife, as also Christ is head of the church . . .
Husbands, love your wives, just as Christ also
loved the church and gave Himself for her.

EPHESIANS 5:18, 20-22, 25

"Getting" God's Love

I think when we "get" God's love, really get it, so that we internalize it, our view of life changes. Circumstances don't necessarily change; yet suddenly, as if we just donned much-needed glasses, for the first time we see that hardships have purpose, we see why the moments of our days matter, we see ourselves on a directed path, and we see that people's impact on us is both neutralized *and* amplified for good. . . .

Faith is much more than feelings; yet feelings are certainly an integral part of our identities and therefore important to the One who designed us. But there is also a knowing that God's Spirit ignites within us that seems to solidify our confidence in his love. I believe God is ever present in his longing for our attention and affection. His love is ever wooing because of his constancy. And sometimes, rather than as a sudden breakthrough, our knowing comes as a gradual awakening, like a rose unfolding into full bloom. We grow into an understanding of how deeply he cares for us.

PATSY CLAIRMONT

Stained Glass Hearts

Evening

· · · · · · · · ·

May [Christ] dwell in your hearts through faith;
that you, being rooted and grounded in love, may be
able to comprehend with all the saints what is the
width and length and depth and height—to know
the love of Christ which passes knowledge; that
you may be filled with all the fullness of God.

EPHESIANS 3:17–19

I am persuaded that neither death nor life, nor angels
nor principalities nor powers, nor things present
nor things to come, nor height nor depth, nor any
other created thing, shall be able to separate us from
the love of God which is in Christ Jesus our Lord.

ROMANS 8:38–39

Behold what manner of love the Father has bestowed
on us, that we should be called children of God!

1 JOHN 3:1

Your Shepherd's Voice

The Eastern shepherd of Jesus' day raised his sheep primarily in the Judean uplands. The countryside was rocky, hilly, and filled with deep crevices and ravines. Patches of grass were sparse. So the shepherd had to establish a personal, working relationship with each sheep, developing its love and trust in him in order to lead it to where the path was the smoothest, the pasture was the greenest, the water was the cleanest, and the nights were the safest. The shepherd always *led* the sheep. He knew their names, and when he called them, they recognized his voice, following him like a swarm of little chicks follows the mother hen. When he stopped, the sheep huddled closely around him, pressing against his legs. Their personal relationship with him was based on his voice, which they knew and trusted.

Our Good Shepherd is Jesus, and the voice of the Good Shepherd is the Word of God. Our Shepherd speaks to us through the written words of our Bible, and His words are personal.

ANNE GRAHAM LOTZ
I Saw the Lord

Evening

. . . .

"I am the good shepherd; and I know My
sheep, and am known by My own. As the
Father knows Me, even so I know the Father;
and I lay down My life for the sheep."

JOHN 10:14—15

"The sheep hear [the shepherd's] voice; and he calls
his own sheep by name and leads them out. And when
he brings out his own sheep, he goes before them;
and the sheep follow him, for they know his voice."

JOHN 10:3—4

I will delight myself in Your commandments,
Which I love.

PSALM 119:47

Blessed to Be a Blessing

My grandmother never went out and purchased a new hat to combat the blahs. Money didn't grow on sassafras bushes; and, besides, she preferred a sunbonnet. But, oh yes, she had a cure. "Let's do something impulsive!" she used to say. "Let's go for a tramp in the woods. . . ."

When we'd come home we'd do an impulsive deed for a neighbor. Today, I looked back and tried to recall some of the things we did—because they're exactly what I plan to do!

- Write a letter when it's not your turn!
- Call somebody you haven't heard from in years;
- Make a batch of cookies and take them
  to a shut-in; and
- Go out and look for a stranger to smile at!

JUNE MASTERS BACHER

Quiet Moments for Women

Evening

. . . .

Remember the words of the Lord Jesus, that He said, "It is more blessed to give than to receive."

ACTS 20:35

Our mouth was filled with laughter,
And our tongue with singing.
Then they said among the nations,
"The LORD has done great things for them."

PSALM 126:2

I will bless you. . . .
And you shall be a blessing.

GENESIS 12:2

. . . .

Your Wonderful Uniqueness

When I was growing up and obsessing about the size of my nose (substantial), my grandmother used to tell me, "It gives you character." I distinctly recall thinking that I could've done with a little less "character." She would also remind me in my insecure moments that people were not thinking about me as much as I imagined they were. She said that they were all doing the same thing I was doing: wondering what others were thinking of *them*. If I could reclaim a chunk of lost time and wasted emotional energy, I would wish to have back all the moments I spent lost in those useless thoughts.

If beauty is in the eye of the beholder, your wonderful uniqueness is precisely what brings God pleasure. It gives you "character," and He's smitten with you. So don't just embrace your uniqueness; revel in it.

ANITA RENFROE
The Purse-Driven Life

Evening

· · · · · · · · ·

Your hands have made me and fashioned me;
Give me understanding,
that I may learn Your commandments.

PSALM 119:73

God has dealt to each one a measure of faith. For as we
have many members in one body, but all the members
do not have the same function, so we, being many,
are one body in Christ, and individually members of
one another. Having then gifts differing according
to the grace that is given to us, let us use them.

ROMANS 12:3—6

You are He who took Me out of the womb;
You made Me trust while on My mother's breasts.
I was cast upon You from birth.
From My mother's womb
You have been My God.

PSALM 22:9—10

427

We Are God's Pleasure

Ephesians 1:3–5 offers some of the richest words in the Bible for the believer in Jesus Christ. Every phrase is yeasty, making it rise off the page . . . edible in content. It's the universal church in a nutshell, chosen before the world was formed, whose recipients were destined to be children of God. If this isn't sovereignty to the max, I don't know what is.

When we read, "according to the good pleasure of His will" (Ephesians 1:5), that means God had us in mind before time began because He wanted to. It gave Him pleasure to think about us and pour out His grace on us.

We'll never understand this kind of love. It's a wonderful mystery, so I suggest we simply revel in it. We're accepted in God's beloved Son, and there's nothing we can do to change that. God did it. We believe it. It's a done deal. Enjoy it!

LUCI SWINDOLL
Women of Faith Devotional Bible

Blessed be the God and Father of our Lord Jesus
Christ, who has blessed us with every spiritual
blessing in the heavenly places in Christ, just
as He chose us in Him before the foundation of
the world, that we should be holy and without
blame before Him in love, having predestined us
to adoption as sons by Jesus Christ to Himself,
according to the good pleasure of His will.

EPHESIANS 1:3—5

If God is for us, who can be against us?

ROMANS 8:31

Transformation

Have you ever considered the humble beginnings of sea glass? All of it starts as glass that has been thrown away, discarded, and broken. Pieces of a former whole no longer serve their intended purpose, so they are cast away—then tossed about, taking some hard knocks, and finally emerging smooth, refined, beautiful.

Likewise, there are those days, even seasons, when we feel fragmented and useless. . . . Parts of a former whole, we find ourselves being tossed about, taking hard knocks, unsure of our direction or purpose.

The Father knows, and sometimes orchestrates, our seasons of refinement—it is part of a greater plan, His plan, which serves His purposes. Even when we're on the other side of that season, we may still not understand fully the *why* behind it, but we can be sure we have a Father who loves us, pursues us, and—once His hand is upon us—does not let go.

Trust that during these seasons, we are being refined and transformed into something useful. And ultimately, beautiful.

MIRIAM DRENNAN
Devotions for the Beach

You, O God, have tested us;
You have refined us as silver is refined.

PSALM 66:10

For I know the plans I have for you, declares
the LORD, plans for welfare and not for
evil, to give you a future and a hope.

JEREMIAH 29:11 ESV

"My sheep hear My voice, and I know them, and
they follow Me. And I give them eternal life, and
they shall never perish; neither shall anyone
snatch them out of My hand. My Father, who has
given them to Me, is greater than all; and no one
is able to snatch them out of My Father's hand."

JOHN 10:27—29

The Right Goal

Goals are a good thing. Focus in a particular direction helps you move forward. When you feel stuck or you're not quite reaching the goal you intended, it can present an opportunity. It can give you a chance to look at your goals and see if you're going after the right ones, the goals God designed for your life. You may be surprised. If your goal is truly the one God wants for you, then go for it. Be in it to win it! If your goal is not really part of His plan for you, then step back and take another look.

It always helps to seek the counsel of others when you're going after a goal. Who do you know right now who could mentor you or give you some wise advice? Pray, seek God's advice, and then head out with confidence to do the things you are truly meant to do today.

Your Promises from God Today

  Evening

     · · · · · · · · ·

I can of Myself do nothing. As I hear, I judge; and
My judgment is righteous, because I do not seek My
own will but the will of the Father who sent Me.

JOHN 5:30

Therefore, my beloved brethren, be steadfast,
immovable, always abounding in the work of the Lord,
knowing that your labor is not in vain in the Lord.

1 CORINTHIANS 15:58

But seek first the kingdom of God
and His righteousness, and all these
things shall be added to you.

MATTHEW 6:33

There are many plans in a man's heart,
Nevertheless the LORD's counsel—that will stand.

PROVERBS 19:21

When You Feel Like Job

If you've ever had a series of setbacks that occurred in your life at the same time, you may have wondered if you would survive it all. The biblical story of Job describes a man who did everything he could to please God, and yet calamity fell on him over and over again. He couldn't understand what was happening.

Some of our "Job" experiences happen for a few days and are gone, but other times, they take us on such a downward spiral that we wonder if recovery is possible. Worse yet, we wonder if God is going to help us get through it. We wonder if God is punishing us or if there is yet hope for the future.

In some very real ways, Job's story is our story. In the end, God gave him even more besides. In the end, He will do the same for us. We can't even imagine what good things He has in store for us in heaven, but we know He's already made plans for our good. Whatever you're going through, remember your Creator. He's the One who has planned a future where there are no tears.

Little Seeds of Hope

Evening

· · · · · · · ·

"Eye has not seen, nor ear heard,
Nor have entered into the heart of man
The things which God has prepared for those who love Him."

1 Corinthians 2:9

For the word of the LORD is right,
And all His work is done in truth.
He loves righteousness and justice;
The earth is full of the goodness of the LORD.

Psalm 33:4—5

God, who made the world and everything in it, since
He is Lord of heaven and earth, does not dwell in
temples made with hands. Nor is He worshiped
with men's hands, as though He needed anything,
since He gives to all life, breath, and all things.

Acts 17:24—25

435

Faith Takes Risks

Faith is taking the risk to put your life on the line for what you say you believe. . . .

Will it hurt? Occasionally. But it will be worth it. When your ultimate hope is in something bigger than death itself, then fear has to take a backseat to living. . . .

Banish fear from your life. God has promised to be with you. . . .

- Risk by reaching out to people who may reject you.
- Risk by trying things you have never tried before.
- Risk by giving until it hurts.
- Risk by following the steps of Christ no matter what the cost.
- Risk by forgiving when your heart prefers to clutch bitterness.
- Risk by taking the first step of faith by trusting Christ.
- Risk by tossing off all the stuff that hinders. . .
- Risk by looking for opportunity to serve.

KEN DAVIS
Fully Alive

[As] the feet of the priests who bore the ark dipped
in the edge of the water . . . the waters which came
down from upstream stood still, and rose in a heap
very far away. . . . So the waters . . . were cut off;
and the people crossed over opposite Jericho.

JOSHUA 3:15—16

Jesus went to [the disciples], walking on the sea. . . .
And Peter . . . said, "Lord, if it is You,
command me to come to You on the water."
So He said, "Come." And when Peter had come down
out of the boat, he walked on the water to go to Jesus.

MATTHEW 14:25, 28—29

Then Jesus said to His disciples, "If anyone
desires to come after Me, let him deny himself,
and take up his cross, and follow Me. For whoever
desires to save his life will lose it, but whoever
loses his life for My sake will find it."

MATTHEW 16:24—25

August

I will rejoice in the Lord,
I will joy in the God of my salvation.

HABAKKUK 3:18

Finish Strong!

Despite having almost twenty-six miles behind them, marathon runners find a boost of energy when the finish line comes into view. Despite the long hours of labor already behind her, the mother finds the ability to push one more time, and her baby is born. Joy in finishing a long race and achieving a goal can give much-needed strength in a grueling athletic event. Joy over finally being able to meet the child she already loves is a mother's source of strength in the hospital delivery room. Even more, joy in knowing the Lord is a sure source of strength for His people as they face the challenges, hurts, and disappointments of life.

You are undoubtedly bearing a cross of your own. After all, Jesus promised that His people would know trials and tribulations in this world. Yet the joy of the Lord truly can sustain you, whatever you're facing. Stay close to your heavenly Father and know joy despite life's circumstances.

100 Favorite Bible Verses

The joy of the LORD is your strength.

NEHEMIAH 8:10

Do you not know that those who run in a race
all run, but one receives the prize? Run in such
a way that you may obtain it. And everyone
who competes for the prize is temperate in all
things. Now they do it to obtain a perishable
crown, but we for an imperishable crown.

1 CORINTHIANS 9:24—25

Let all those rejoice who put their trust in You;
Let them ever shout for joy, because You defend them;
Let those also who love Your name
Be joyful in You.

PSALM 5:11

Be glad in the LORD and rejoice, you righteous;
And shout for joy, all you upright in heart!

PSALM 32:11

The Heavens Declare God's Glory

Deneb is one of the most luminous stars in the sky. Fully 60,000 times more luminous than the Sun, this star is estimated to be nearly sixteen hundred light-years away—that's 9.6 thousand trillion miles! . . .

These immense, intensely brilliant stars are so distant that they appear only as dim pinpricks of light. Equally amazing is that since light travels at a finite speed across the vast expanses of the galaxy, their starlight carries information about how things looked in the past, not the present. At sixteen hundred light-years away, Deneb's light left the star sixteen hundred years ago. . . .

The heavens declare God's glory. That is why He presents them to us. They show Him to be Lord over time and space. He is powerful, majestic, infinite, and creative beyond measure. The heavens declare these things better than anything else in all the created order. Contemplate the Maker of heaven and Earth today, and let His works ignite praise in your soul.

KEVIN HARTNETT

The Heavens

Evening

He counts the number of the stars;
He calls them all by name.
Great is our Lord, and mighty in power;
His understanding is infinite.

PSALM 147:4—5

The heavens declare the glory of God;
And the firmament shows His handiwork.

PSALM 19:1

Bless the LORD, O my soul;
And all that is within me, bless His holy name!
Bless the LORD, O my soul,
And forget not all His benefits.

PSALM 103:1—2

Give Yourself Away

My heart's desire is to find more opportunities to give myself away and teach my children the joy of service at the same time. One little problem: when?! A friend of mine once moaned, "There's just not enough of me to go around." Lots of us feel the same way and can't bear the thought of adding one more activity, one more "to do" item to our list, however worthy it may be.

For busy women like us, who don't know how we could manage the added role of volunteer, psychologist Virginia O'Leary offers a word of encouragement: "The more roles women have, the better off they are, and the less likely they are to be depressed or discouraged about their lives. When we have a lot to do, we complain that it's driving us crazy— but, in fact, it's what keeps us sane."

It's ironic that one of the best remedies for impending burnout is to give yourself away. To pick one time and place each week where you stretch out your hands for the pure joy of doing it.

LIZ CURTIS HIGGS

Only Angels Can Wing It

By this we know love, because He laid down His life for us. And we also ought to lay down our lives for the brethren. But whoever has this world's goods, and sees his brother in need, and shuts up his heart from him, how does the love of God abide in him?

1 JOHN 3:16–17

"Whoever receives one little child like this in My name receives Me."

MATTHEW 18:5

"'Lord, when did we see You hungry and feed You, or thirsty and give You drink? When did we see You a stranger and take You in, or naked and clothe You? Or when did we see You sick, or in prison, and come to You?' And the King will answer and say to them, 'Assuredly, I say to you, inasmuch as you did it to one of the least of these My brethren, you did it to Me.'"

MATTHEW 25:37–40

Our Redeemer God

Life experience has shown me this truth . . . verified by social scientists: our childhood sets the stage for how we act out the rest of our lives.

What we experienced as children determines the props on the stage of our lives. . . . We can change the props . . . paint them, reupholster them, or change their position in the room—but they remain onstage with us. . . .

Each experience we have had—regardless of how embarrassing, sad, shameful, or even seemingly insignificant—has the potential to be used redemptively by God in the people whose paths cross ours. If the people who came to a Galilean hillside with their meager and simple food had refused to relinquish it to the disciples, we wouldn't have the marvelous miracle of Jesus feeding a multitude. Sometimes I imagine the people on that hillside coming to us and encouraging us by saying, "Give your stories away and get ready for God to use them beyond your wildest hopes and dreams!"

CHRISTINE WOOD

Character Witness

446

Evening

I will restore to you the years that the
swarming locust has eaten,
The crawling locust,
The consuming locust,
And the chewing locust. . . .
You shall eat in plenty and be satisfied,
And praise the name of the LORD your God,
Who has dealt wondrously with you;
And My people shall never be put to shame.

JOEL 2:25–26

He has sent redemption to His people;
He has commanded His covenant forever:
Holy and awesome is His name.

PSALM 111:9

All have sinned and fall short of the glory of
God, being justified freely by His grace through
the redemption that is in Christ Jesus.

ROMANS 3:23–24

Morning

. . . .

What Does God See?

When I met my husband, Dave, I liked him. As I spent time with him, I got to know him more and more. We talked, laughed, and even cried together, and I realized my "like" had turned into love, and I couldn't get enough of him.

When God surveys our love for Him, I wonder what He sees. Does He find us being in "like" with Him only? Is He sorrowful for what He knows our relationship could be but isn't because of the absence of time together? Is He sad when we talk and laugh and cry only with others? Does He weep when we let the fire of our love grow cold?

Falling in love with God happens through time spent. The more time we spend with Him, the more we fall in love. It's that simple. It's that joyous. It's that wonderful.

LYNDA HUNTER BJORKLUND

Women of Faith Devotional Bible

Evening

· · · · · · · · ·

What does the LORD your God require of you,
but to fear the LORD your God, to walk in all His
ways and to love Him, to serve the LORD your God
with all your heart and with all your soul?

DEUTERONOMY 10:12

I am persuaded that neither death nor life, nor angels
nor principalities nor powers, nor things present
nor things to come, nor height nor depth, nor any
other created thing, shall be able to separate us from
the love of God which is in Christ Jesus our Lord.

ROMANS 8:38—39

We love Him because He first loved us.

1 JOHN 4:19

Roller Coasters

For each of us, life can feel like a roller coaster. One minute you're heading toward the top of the highest peak, somewhat apprehensive but excited. The next minute you're heading downward faster than you ever thought you'd go, and you're not sure if you're screaming with sheer terror or joy. What do you do? You hold on! You hold on to the hope that God always has for you.

Your roller-coaster experience may be about crashing financial pictures, or about the unexpected death of someone you love, or about your spouse being deployed to a volatile part of the world. Personal tragedies abound, and somehow between the ones we experience ourselves and the ones we hear about from our friends, we're overwhelmed with those tragedies. We can hardly catch our breath before another one hits us. It's definitely not an easy ride.

How do we smooth things out and hold on? We find an anchor. God gave us His Son and His Spirit to comfort us and strengthen us. He knows we'll hit hard times along with the good times, and so He never leaves us alone.

Little Seeds of Hope

Evening

. . . .

For You are my hope, O Lord GOD;
You are my trust from my youth.
By You I have been upheld from birth;
You are He who took me out of my mother's womb.
My praise shall be continually of You.

PSALM 71:5—6

God is our refuge and strength,
A very present help in trouble.
Therefore we will not fear,
Even though the earth be removed,
And though the mountains be carried into the midst of the sea;
Though its waters roar and be troubled,
Though the mountains shake with its swelling.

PSALM 46:1—3

Now may the God of hope fill you with all joy
and peace in believing, that you may abound
in hope by the power of the Holy Spirit.

ROMANS 15:13

AUGUST 7

Hope in the Lord, Not Man

Be sure that your future hope is firmly rooted *only* in the one true God.

Loving fellowship with people and placing trust in them is a relational gift ordained by God, but it should never replace our need for God. On this point the apostle Paul wrote, "We . . . comfort those who are in any affliction, with the comfort with which we ourselves are comforted by God" (2 Corinthians 1:4–5). It is helpful to remember that when friends let you down—and it will happen, at some point, to everyone—you will find it easier to forgive and move forward if your trust is secure in the immovable, unchangeable love of the Savior.

While You can't know for certain that your friends will be faithful and loyal when you need them most, you *can* know that God will fill that expectation! Resolve today to be a friend who loves with a Christlike love, but seek your deepest soul-comfort in the one true Source. *He* will never let you down.

A Jane Austen Devotional

Evening

. . . .

Oh, taste and see that the LORD is good;
Blessed is the man who trusts in Him!

PSALM 34:8

Through the LORD's mercies we are not consumed,
Because His compassions fail not.
They are new every morning;
Great is Your faithfulness.

LAMENTATIONS 3:22—23

He Himself has said, "I will never leave
you nor forsake you."

HEBREWS 13:5

453

Prompted to Praise

I vividly remember the first times I felt my babies move.... Some women describe those first movements like popcorn popping, butterflies fluttering, or goldfish swimming.... It's undoubtedly one of the strangest and most wondrous things about pregnancy, feeling a little life moving within. The wonder of those little flutters (and later karate chops) is something that never gets old.

In some ways the movement of the Spirit of God is similar. Jesus likened the Spirit's movement to the wind: we can see the wind's effects, but we can't see the wind and we definitely can't control it. Likewise, we can feel our babies, but we can't see them. And as any mama who's had Baby keep her up late can tell you, we can't control when that movement starts and stops. Seeing the Spirit move in our lives, like feeling our babies move, is one of those wonders that should never get old. Let them both nudge you to praise.

CATHERINE CLAIRE LARSON
Waiting in Wonder

You formed my inward parts;
you knitted me together in my mother's womb.
I praise you, for I am fearfully and wonderfully made.

PSALM 139:13—14 ESV

"It is to your advantage that I go away; for if I do
not go away, the Helper will not come to you; but
if I depart, I will send Him to you. And when He
has come, He will convict the world of sin, and of
righteousness, and of judgment. . . . When He, the
Spirit of truth, has come, He will guide you into all
truth; for He will not speak on His own authority,
but whatever He hears He will speak; and He will
tell you things to come. He will glorify Me, for He
will take of what is Mine and declare it to you.

JOHN 16:7—8, 13—14

"Unless one is born of water and the Spirit,
he cannot enter the kingdom of God. That
which is born of the flesh is flesh, and that
which is born of the Spirit is spirit."

JOHN 3:5—6

Following God

I once saw a bumper sticker that said "God is my co-pilot." That sounds spiritual, but it isn't true. The truth is that on our faith journey, God is the Pilot, and we must follow, not co-lead.

We are not in charge of the journey. We are called to restfully follow. Our Pilot is completely trustworthy. There's no need for us to fret, for He is capable of navigating us through all the turbulence of the journey. We can rest in the very situation where He has lovingly placed us. And when we do, we'll find the fabulous freedom of following.

JENNIFER ROTHSCHILD
Lessons I Learned in the Dark

Evening

· · · · · · · · ·

I have taught you in the way of wisdom;
I have led you in right paths.

<small>PROVERBS 4:11</small>

Your word is a lamp to my feet
And a light to my path.

<small>PSALM 119:105</small>

Ponder the path of your feet,
And let all your ways be established.

<small>PROVERBS 4:26</small>

There are many plans in a man's heart,
Nevertheless the LORD's counsel—that will stand.

<small>PROVERBS 19:21</small>

AUGUST 10

Friends for All Seasons

If family is the way we establish our roots on earth's soil, then friends are the fertilizer. Friends are the sunshine and the rain, the ones who help us grow to be better and stronger than we'd be on our own. In that regard we cultivate a variety of types of friends.

Some friends are part of our work environment, and they bring us insight into the projects at hand or the opportunities around us. They nurture our desires to become better at the things we do. They encourage our growth along the path of our career choices.

If we're truly blessed, there's a friend or two who creates a space for us like no one else can do. They help us to dig deeper into who we are and what we want out of life. They nourish our spirits with laughter and warm conversations each time we meet. They are the gifts that truly strengthen our growth and help us become beautiful.

These friends are with you when hope is thin, the ones who remind you brighter days are just ahead and that God is with you. This kind of friendship is rooted in love.

Little Seeds of Hope

Evening

· · · · · · · ·

A friend loves at all times,
And a brother is born for adversity.

PROVERBS 17:17

A man who has friends must himself be friendly,
But there is a friend who sticks closer than a brother.

PROVERBS 18:24

Do not forsake your own friend or your father's friend.

PROVERBS 27:10

Put Off Procrastination

Do you have pet procrastinations? Maybe you want to lose five pounds but you keep putting off that daily three-mile walk you pledged to yourself in order to help that happen. Maybe you want to go back to college, but you always find it too difficult to get the application filled out. Timing is everything, and so if you're missing the boat too often, you may want to rethink your priorities and let God help you set some new goals.

You know you're willing to put off things that don't really appeal to you. You've been planning to read the Bible more or to pray more regularly. What if today was all you had left? Do the things today that would mean the most to you, and discover what to make a priority.

Give yourself credit today for each choice you make to complete something you started, stick to a plan you created, or not give yourself an out to put something off. Give God thanks for this day and the opportunity you have to start again to do things right.

Your Promises from God Today

Evening

· · · · · · · · · ·

He who observes the wind will not sow,
And he who regards the clouds will not reap.

ECCLESIASTES 11:4

To everything there is a season,
A time for every purpose under heaven:
A time to be born,
And a time to die;
A time to plant,
And a time to pluck what is planted;
A time to kill,
And a time to heal;
A time to break down,
And a time to build up.

ECCLESIASTES 3:1—3

The LORD will perfect that which concerns me;
Your mercy, O LORD, endures forever;
Do not forsake the works of Your hands.

PSALM 138:8

AUGUST 12

Set Free from Sin

Why does our hair do that? You know, how it frizzes, frays, and frustrates as it flies around in the salty breeze. . . .

Salt-air hair can remind us of this truth [from today's verse]: there are just some things that are out of our control . . . and . . . cannot succeed against God. . . .

Times when evil seems to win: . . . our best friend is making a wrong decision, we give in to an addiction we think we've long ago conquered . . . We want to retaliate. . . . Since God instructs us to let Him take care of these matters, our own schemes really won't work. In due time, either now or in the final tally, those who have wronged us will have to answer to God as well. He is fair like that.

So celebrate this truth. . . . Let your hair fly free as a reminder that your soul already does.

MIRIAM DRENNAN

Devotions for the Beach

Evening

· · · · · · · · ·

There is no wisdom, no insight, no plan
that can succeed against the LORD.

PROVERBS 21:30 NIV

A man's heart plans his way,
But the LORD directs his steps.

PROVERBS 16:9

Now having been set free from sin, and having
become slaves of God, you have your fruit to
holiness, and the end, everlasting life. For
the wages of sin is death, but the gift of God
is eternal life in Christ Jesus our Lord.

ROMANS 6:22—23

Divine Appointments

About a year ago we had a second phone line installed in our home that was only one digit off from the long distance information line in a certain region of South Carolina. At first I was so frustrated with the influx of callers wanting phone numbers to Bud's Seafood and Bessie's Best Bathing Suit Shop. Just as I was about to call the phone company and demand they fix the problem immediately, God reminded me of my commitment to make the most of every evangelism opportunity He gives me.

So the "God line" was born. I started proudly answering the phone, "God-line information. We don't have all the answers but we know the One who does. How may I help you?" Most of the time I get a bewildered "Huh?" on the other line, but every now and then God uses this wrong number to set divine appointments with Him.

LYSA TERKEURST

Living Life on Purpose

Evening

. . . .

May the Lord repay every man
for his righteousness and his faithfulness.

1 SAMUEL 26:23

My eyes shall be on the faithful of the land,
That they may dwell with me;
He who walks in a perfect way,
He shall serve me.

PSALM 101:6

"His lord said to him, 'Well done, good and
faithful servant; you were faithful over a
few things, I will make you ruler over many
things. Enter into the joy of your lord.'"

MATTHEW 25:21

Morning

. . . .

Opening the Door of Hospitality

Everything I needed to know about being hospitable I learned from Lois the first evening she invited me to dinner in her home. . . . When I arrived, she opened the door and warmly invited me in. I followed her to the kitchen where, to be frank, I expected to see the preparation of an elaborate meal. Lois's husband was a doctor and, to be perfectly honest, that raised my expectations. I saw nothing. I smelled nothing. As I began to wonder about this meal, she opened the refrigerator door and casually asked, "Let's see, what shall we have for dinner?" She wasn't kidding! Before long I had joined her search for food and her creative approach to preparation. Then we began cooking it together. Inwardly I breathed a big sigh of relief. Even I can do this, I thought.

After experiencing this comfortable approach, not only did I know I could do this, but my heart desired to do it. When our hospitality emphasizes pleasing people rather than elaborately preparing for them, much of the stress evaporates.

CHRISTINE WOOD

Character Witness

Above all things have fervent love for one another,
for "love will cover a multitude of sins." Be hospitable
to one another without grumbling. As each one
has received a gift, minister it to one another, as
good stewards of the manifold grace of God.

1 PETER 4:8—10

"The righteous will answer Him, saying, 'Lord, when
did we see You hungry and feed You, or thirsty and
give You drink? When did we see You a stranger and
take You in, or naked and clothe You? Or when did
we see You sick, or in prison, and come to You?' And
the King will answer and say to them, 'Assuredly,
I say to you, inasmuch as you did it to one of the
least of these My brethren, you did it to Me.'"

MATTHEW 25:37—40

Be kindly affectionate to one another with
brotherly love, in honor giving preference to
one another; . . . distributing to the needs
of the saints, given to hospitality.

ROMANS 12:10, 13

Morning

. . . .

A Sharper Focus

Years ago, if I had a free hour in the afternoon, I would have read a magazine or played tennis or perhaps eaten cheesecake. . . . Now, though I still love tennis, reading, and cheesecake (not necessarily in that order), I'm drawn like a magnet to spend even more time with God. . . .

Throughout the day, in whatever moments I have, I "turn my eyes" onto Jesus by reading the Bible, listening to sermons or uplifting music on CDs, and connecting with friends who share the same passion. The more I focus on Jesus, the more I can fill up with His love and pass that love on to others. . . .

Bible reading and prayer are the ways to really connect with Jesus . . . It's grafting into *His* strength, like branches of a tree drawing life from the vitality of the trunk and the roots.

This kind of relationship with Jesus isn't dull duty. It's a fun, unpredictable adventure. It's also a paradox: when we're rooted in God, we really begin to go places, places we couldn't have imagined otherwise!

DENISE JACKSON

It's All About Him

Evening

· · · · · · · · ·

"I am the vine, you are the branches. He who abides
in Me, and I in him, bears much fruit; for without Me
you can do nothing. . . . If you abide in Me, and My
words abide in you, you will ask what you desire, and
it shall be done for you. By this My Father is glorified,
that you bear much fruit; so you will be My disciples."

JOHN 15:5, 7–8

"Whoever comes to Me, and hears My sayings and
does them, I will show you whom he is like: He is like
a man building a house, who dug deep and laid the
foundation on the rock. And when the flood arose,
the stream beat vehemently against that house, and
could not shake it, for it was founded on the rock."

LUKE 6:47–48

Rejoice always, pray without ceasing, in
everything give thanks; for this is the
will of God in Christ Jesus for you.

1 THESSALONIANS 5:16–18

Being Faithful

The great benefit of good spiritual habits is that they enable us to practice the presence of God objectively—by reading His Word, spending time in prayer, worshiping, observing the Sabbath—even when positive subjective feelings are not there.

I am so grateful to my parents for instilling in me from earliest childhood the habits of regular worship and tithing. The result is that I never even have to ask myself on a Sunday morning whether I feel like going to worship or at the beginning of a month whether I feel like giving God a certain percentage of my income. Feelings never even enter the picture, and I don't ever have to waste time trying to make a choice.

MARVA DAWN

Morning by Morning

Evening

By this we know that we know Him, if we keep
His commandments. . . . Whoever keeps His
word, truly the love of God is perfected in him.

1 JOHN 2:3, 5

Having been justified by faith, we have peace with
God through our Lord Jesus Christ, through whom
also we have access by faith into this grace in which
we stand, and rejoice in hope of the glory of God.
And not only that, but we also glory in tribulations,
knowing that tribulation produces perseverance;
and perseverance, character; and character, hope.

ROMANS 5:1–4

Be strong in the Lord and in the power of His
might. Put on the whole armor of God, that you may
be able to stand against the wiles of the devil.

EPHESIANS 6:10–11

Morning

. . . .

Time to Rest

Times change, but our basic needs remain stable. We need rest. You should see my neighbor. While I rush through one job with my mind on the next in line, she just drops down on the grass, idly chewing a pepperwood stem. "I'm unable to finish all that needs doing today, so what's the rush?" [and] "I accomplish more if I sit a spell—not working—just thinking and appreciating." . . .

Somewhere there's a recipe for people like me who try to do a year's work in one day—and rob themselves of "thinking time." My friend reads "so I can know the hopes and dreams in a world before my time," she says. My friend listens to music "so I can enlarge my heart and mind." My friend prays "so I can enlarge my soul." Her philosophy is contagious.

JUNE MASTERS BACHER

Quiet Moments for Women

In Your presence is fullness of joy;
At Your right hand are pleasures forevermore.

PSALM 16:11

The eyes of the LORD are on the righteous,
And His ears are open to their prayers.

1 PETER 3:12

I set my face toward the Lord God to make
request by prayer. . . . I prayed to the LORD my
God, and made confession, and said, "O Lord,
great and awesome God, who keeps His covenant
and mercy with those who love Him, and with
those who keep His commandments."

DANIEL 9:3–4

The Freedom of Forgiving

Leftovers . . . again? How much of that dish did we make?!!! . . .

No, this is not about . . . Cousin Harry's triple-fried chicken or our own energy-producing five-bean chili. This addictive leftover is the ultimate classic: Have you ever served yourself *rehash of the past*?

Somewhere, somehow, someone hurt us, and we have kept that wound in our active memory, pressing rewind and play in the theatre of our minds. With each rehearsal, we see it all and feel it all and digest it all over again. . . .

Jesus tells us that this leftover is lethal: "If you do not forgive men their sins, neither will your Father forgive your sins" (Matthew 6:15). . . .

Forgiving means we stop pressing rewind and play. Forgiving means we refuse to let our minds house the moldy leftovers of other's sins against us.

ALICIA BRITT CHOLE
Sitting in God's Sunshine

Evening

. . . .

"If your brother sins against you, rebuke him; and if
he repents, forgive him. And if he sins against you
seven times in a day, and seven times in a day returns
to you, saying, 'I repent,' you shall forgive him."

LUKE 17:3—4

"Forgive us our debts,
As we forgive our debtors."

MATTHEW 6:12

Not that we are sufficient of ourselves to
think of anything as being from ourselves,
but our sufficiency is from God.

2 CORINTHIANS 3:5

AUGUST 19

Be Yourself!

We are the most appealing to others, and the happiest within, when we are completely ourselves. But it is a constant struggle because, as Scripture teaches, the world is always trying to press us into its mold. The mold of the world is the mold of the synthetic, the mold of the artificial, the mold of the celluloid—the "Plastic Person."

The world cries, "You've got to be young and you've got to be tan. You've got to be thin and you've got to be rich. You've got to be great." But Scripture says, "You don't have to be any of those things. You simply have to be yourself—at any age—as God made you, available to Him so that He can work in and through you to bring about His kingdom and His glory." Now relax. Trust Him and be yourself!

LUCI SWINDOLL
You Bring the Confetti

Present your bodies a living sacrifice, holy,
acceptable to God. . . . And do not be conformed
to this world, but be transformed by the renewing
of your mind, that you may prove what is that
good and acceptable and perfect will of God.

ROMANS 12:1—2

He has shown you, O man, what is good;
And what does the LORD require of you
But to do justly,
To love mercy,
And to walk humbly with your God?

MICAH 6:8

Behold what manner of love the Father has bestowed
on us, that we should be called children of God!

1 JOHN 3:1

Morning

. . . .

Giving God's Love

Most of us grew up hearing the golden rule: "Do unto others as you would have them do unto you." God pushes His children beyond their personal backyards to a global golden rule. Linked by satellites, [Internet, smart phones,] and jet travel, we know of worlds beyond our small one. But with knowledge comes responsibility. Personal, national, and global costs skyrocket when we knowingly do wrong or purposely withhold our help. To obey God's global golden rule is to love as God loves. Giving God's love never harms the giver or the recipient.

You make a world of difference as you obey God's global golden rule.

JAN CARLBERG

The Hungry Heart

Evening

· · · · · · · · · ·

"Give, and it will be given to you. Good measure,
pressed down, shaken together, running over,
will be put into your lap. For with the measure
you use it will be measured back to you."

LUKE 6:38 ESV

He who gives to the poor will not lack,
But he who hides his eyes will have many curses.

PROVERBS 28:27

Defend the poor and fatherless;
Do justice to the afflicted and needy.
Deliver the poor and needy;
Free them from the hand of the wicked.

PSALM 82:3—4

Choose to Love

Love is an act of will: listening to someone when we are bored, keeping that perfectly couched comeback to ourselves, letting old Mrs. Jones win the argument over something unimportant, biting our tongues instead of reminding others of our triumphs, hearing out our spouse one more time on the same old saw (and hoping he . . . will return the favor). Love is not waiting to feel good before plunging into these and other unselfish acts, but rather love is the decision to behave a certain way even when we feel like Ms. or Mrs. Grump.

LESLIE WILLIAMS
Seduction of the Lesser Gods

Evening

· · · · · · · · ·

"Greater love has no one than this, than
to lay down one's life for his friends."

JOHN 15:13

Let all that you do be done with love.

1 CORINTHIANS 16:14

Let us love one another, for love is of God. . . . No one
has seen God at any time. If we love one another, God
abides in us, and His love has been perfected in us.

1 JOHN 4:7, 12

AUGUST 22

A Disciplined Prayer Life

The value of time spent in prayer cannot be overestimated.

Jesus offered a striking example of regular prayer. Throughout His ministry, Jesus would "withdraw to desolate places and pray" (Luke 5:16). Jesus' apostles followed His lead, and now, as Christ followers twenty centuries later, we are encouraged to do the same. The many benefits of prayer include communing with God, learning to listen for His voice, and letting His words and thoughts guide our lives. Think of that! *We have a direct means of communicating with God.* When we pray, we speak the unique language of our relationship with Him.

If you desire to be a true disciple of Christ—if you want to become like Him—there is no better place to start than with consistent times of devoted prayer.

A Jane Austen Devotional

Evening

· · · · · · · · · ·

Now it came to pass, as He was praying in a
certain place, when He ceased, that one of
His disciples said to Him, "Lord, teach us to
pray, as John also taught his disciples."

LUKE 11:1

Now when Daniel knew that the writing [that forbade
worship of anyone other than the king] was signed,
he went home. And in his upper room, with his
windows open toward Jerusalem, he knelt down on
his knees three times that day, and prayed and gave
thanks before his God, as was his custom since early
days. Then these men assembled and found Daniel
praying and making supplication before his God.

DANIEL 6:10—11

Self-Confidence

Self-confidence is defined by Merriam-Webster's dictionary as "confidence in oneself and in one's powers and abilities." But how confident can we be when we rely only on ourselves? The Bible says, "For the LORD will be your confidence" (Proverbs 3:26), and "Such confidence as this is ours through Christ before God. Not that we are competent in ourselves to claim anything for ourselves, but our competence comes from God" (2 Corinthians 3:4–5 NIV).

In 1 Samuel 17, we find the story of David, a slight, young man courageously fighting Goliath, a bullish, nine-foot-tall warrior from Gath. David found his confidence in trusting in the Lord, and armed with just a slingshot and stones, he defeated the giant soldier. Could David have done this by himself? No!

Our own powers and abilities sometimes fail us, but there is One who never fails. The story of David illustrates that true self-confidence is dependent upon a solid trust in God. When we rely on God, His confidence flows through us.

A Charles Dickens Devotional

Evening

· · · · · · · · · ·

Blessed is the one who trusts in the LORD,
whose confidence is in him.

JEREMIAH 17:7 NIV

"Whoever hears these sayings of Mine, and does
them, I will liken him to a wise man who built his
house on the rock: and the rain descended, the floods
came, and the winds blew and beat on that house;
and it did not fall, for it was founded on the rock."

MATTHEW 7:24—25

Trust in the LORD with all your heart,
And lean not on your own understanding;
In all your ways acknowledge Him,
And He shall direct your paths.

PROVERBS 3:5—6

Purposeful Pain

Wander by an old dock or around some boat slips, and you'll hear the muffled, rhythmic moans of ropes, indicative of pain, of tension, of the purposeful intent to hang on. . . .

Now move in closer and study those ropes. You'll notice that time and tension also contributed to their frayed, discolored appearance. Ironically, however, these alleged blemishes make them more pliable, more useful, and even stronger. . . .

How many days do you experience something similar? You are quietly straining, moaning, painfully trying to keep it together for the sake of others, and maybe unsure that you can. . . . You bear the marks of time and experience, but don't seem to gain the wisdom and strength.

Quite often, our pain has purpose, but just as often, we don't see it. Instead, we focus on the fear of what might happen if our grip should slip.

The difference is, however, that even if we let go, God hasn't let go of us. He doesn't. And He won't.

MIRIAM DRENNAN
Devotions for the Beach

Evening

· · · · · · · · ·

The pain turned you to God.

2 CORINTHIANS 7:9 TLB

In this you greatly rejoice, though now for a little
while, if need be, you have been grieved by various
trials, that the genuineness of your faith, being
much more precious than gold that perishes,
though it is tested by fire, may be found to praise,
honor, and glory at the revelation of Jesus Christ.

1 PETER 1:6—7

Count it all joy when you fall into various trials,
knowing that the testing of your faith produces
patience. But let patience have its perfect work, that
you may be perfect and complete, lacking nothing.

JAMES 1:2—4

487

Choosing to Trust

In reading the book of Job . . . I [am] comforted that Job could not simply settle for the long-accepted religious answers when they did not make sense with his experience. When the atrocities of his physical condition worsened and the taunting of his comforters seemed never-ending, he chose to take both his experience and his questions and argue them before God. Even in the midst of his pain and confusion and despair, even under the silence of heaven, Job never trifled with the hopelessness of shutting God out. For whatever he did not understand about what was happening to him and why God had let it happen, he still trusted God enough to say, "Though he slay me, yet will I hope in him" (Job 13:15).

VERDELL DAVIS

Riches Stored in Secret Places

Job arose, tore his robe, and shaved his head; and
he fell to the ground and worshiped. And he said:
"Naked I came from my mother's womb,
And naked shall I return there.
The LORD gave, and the LORD has taken away;
Blessed be the name of the LORD."
In all this Job did not sin nor charge God with wrong.

JOB 1:20–22

We do not have a High Priest who cannot sympathize
with our weaknesses, but was in all points tempted
as we are, yet without sin. Let us therefore come
boldly to the throne of grace, that we may obtain
mercy and find grace to help in time of need.

HEBREWS 4:15—16

I know the thoughts that I think toward you, says the
LORD, thoughts of peace and not of evil, to give you a
future and a hope. Then you will call upon Me. . . . ,
and I will listen to you. And you will seek Me and
find Me, when you search for Me with all your heart.

JEREMIAH 29:11—13

Morning

. . . .

Run with Endurance

During my four years of high school, I ran track and cross-country. I trained three hours per day. I trained to win. When race day came, I was ready. Standing on the starting line, gun ready to fire, adrenaline pumping, I occasionally wondered, *Can I really do this?* Then I would look up and see the crowds and my teammates ready to cheer me on.

In Christ we've been called to run a wonderful race—a race to pursue His presence and His purposes. Sin keeps us from being able to run that race the way God intended. Let us follow Christ's example and turn away from any vice that keeps us from running well. Dear saint, do not give up! Run, run, run! Jesus Himself sits among the great crowd cheering you on!

HEATHER MERCER

Women of Faith Devotional Bible

Evening

· · · · · · · ·

Since we are surrounded by so great a cloud of
witnesses, let us lay aside every weight, and the sin
which so easily ensnares us, and let us run with
endurance the race that is set before us, looking
unto Jesus, the author and finisher of our faith.

HEBREWS 12:1–2

Those who wait on the LORD
Shall renew their strength;
They shall mount up with wings like eagles,
They shall run and not be weary,
They shall walk and not faint.

ISAIAH 40:31

I can do all things through
Christ who strengthens me.

PHILIPPIANS 4:13

Great Expectations

The Bible tells of a man who put God at the center of his expectations.

David expected to become king of Israel, but his expectation was hindered when King Saul threatened to kill him. Instead of becoming king, David found himself running from a murderer. David wrote in one of his psalms, "My soul, wait silently for God alone, for my expectation is from Him" (Psalm 62:5). David's hope stayed firm in the Lord. He expected God to lead him to the throne in His own time and way.

When we put God at the center of our expectations, He often gives us more than we anticipate and in ways that we cannot imagine. Ephesians 3:20 says that God "is able to do exceedingly abundantly above all that we ask or think." Because God was at the center of David's expectations, David became Israel's greatest king who brought unity and godly rule to the nation. Indeed, when our plans and dreams are rooted in God, we all can have great expectations—and, by God's grace, experience His blessing.

A Charles Dickens Devotional

Evening

· · · · · · · · ·

A man's heart plans his way,
But the LORD directs his steps.

PROVERBS 16:9

The eyes of all look expectantly to You,
And You give them their food in due season.
You open Your hand
And satisfy the desire of every living thing.

PSALM 145:15—16

"Seek first the kingdom of God and
His righteousness, and all these
things shall be added to you."

MATTHEW 6:33

Morning

. . . .

Loving with God's Love

Jennifer Rothschild is a beautiful woman and a gifted speaker and communicator. She is also blind. . . . She said at a Women of Faith conference that since she couldn't see herself in the earthly mirror, she had to learn to see herself in the mirror of God's love and grace.

Wow. I need to do the same thing. . . .

I began to realize that one of the reasons I'm so comfortable around Jennifer is, well, she can't *see* me, so it's easy to believe she loves the real me, authentic and unlayered, because she doesn't know what I look like.

While that subconscious thought made me feel especially comfortable around Jennifer, it was actually a sad revelation about my feelings for myself. I want to move through life with the same attitude toward myself that I perceive Jennifer has about me. I want to be so comfortable with myself that whether my weight is up or down, I know with all my heart that I'm God's princess.

SANDI PATTY

Layers

The LORD said to Samuel, "Do not look at his appearance or at his physical stature, because I have refused him. For the LORD does not see as man sees; for man looks at the outward appearance, but the LORD looks at the heart."

1 SAMUEL 16:7

Do not let your adornment be merely outward— arranging the hair, wearing gold, or putting on fine apparel—rather let it be the hidden person of the heart, with the incorruptible beauty of a gentle and quiet spirit, which is very precious in the sight of God.

1 PETER 3:3—4

The fruit of the Spirit is love, joy, peace, longsuffering, kindness, goodness, faithfulness, gentleness, self-control.

GALATIANS 5:22—23

Seeds of Joy

It's human nature to notice red lights, lines that are moving faster than yours, and dogs that behave better than yours. This tendency doesn't make it easy to find joy in the day-to-day aspects of life. It instead keeps us focused on ourselves and on how unfair life can be.

But we don't have to live like that. We can learn to obey the command of Philippians 4:4, "Rejoice in the Lord always. Again I will say, rejoice!" We can learn to rejoice—always! Note that Paul didn't say to rejoice about your circumstances. He didn't call us to celebrate hurtful relationships or painful losses. Speaking on God's behalf, Paul instead commanded us to rejoice in the Lord—in His sovereign power, His unwavering goodness, and His unfailing love.

So train yourself to look for evidence of God's presence and activity in your life. Let people know when [you are] very aware of God being at work in your life.

Be warned! These seeds of joy that you sow will bear the fruit of more joy!

100 Favorite Bible Verses

Evening

· · · · · · · · ·

Most of all, friends, always rejoice in the
Lord! I never tire of saying it: Rejoice!

PHILIPPIANS 4:4 THE VOICE

Be glad in the LORD and rejoice, you righteous;
And shout for joy, all you upright in heart!

PSALM 32:11

Your mercy, O LORD, is in the heavens;
Your faithfulness reaches to the clouds.

PSALM 36:5

Forever, O LORD,
Your word is settled in heaven.
Your faithfulness endures to all generations.

PSALM 119:89—90

Praise God!

The wisdom and doctrine of Scripture teach that the experience of celebrating God is the core of worship. It is the quintessence of praise and thanksgiving—the most perfect manifestation of a heart that gratefully fellowships with the One who provides life and all the gifts of living. In fact, a grateful heart is not only the greatest virtue; it is the seedbed for all other virtues.

When we are caught up in the celebration of God, there is neither room nor time for the invasion of negative living. As we rejoice before the Lord, as we serve Him in the area of our calling, as we enter into the love that surrounds our days, as we give thanks to Him for His kindness and faithfulness, we celebrate God.

LUCI SWINDOLL
You Bring the Confetti

Evening

· · · · · · · · ·

Sing to the LORD a new song,
And His praise in the assembly of saints.

PSALM 149:1

Praise the LORD!
Oh, give thanks to the LORD, for He is good!
For His mercy endures forever.
Who can utter the mighty acts of the LORD?
Who can declare all His praise?

PSALM 106:1—2

From the rising of the sun to its going down
The LORD's name is to be praised.

PSALM 113:3

AUGUST 31

Stand in There

I've often heard it said, in an effort to comfort someone, "It will be alright. You just hang in there." Although those words do offer encouragement, I'd like to look at it another way. To "hang in there" paints a picture of dangling out of control, of being vulnerable and exposed. I have child-hood visions of sheets and pillowcases flapping wildly on the clothesline in my mother's backyard. At the threat of a strong summer-afternoon rainstorm, we'd rush to remove the fresh laundry before it was ruined by dust or a family pet running for cover.

I choose to encourage others by saying, "It will be alright. You just stand there." Because Christ was hung up for our hang-ups, we can stand up with confidence, knowing that our foundation is secure. Why "hang in there" when you can stand still and watch God work a miracle on your behalf?

BABBIE MASON

Women of Faith Devotional Bible

Evening

· · · · · · · · · ·

Do not be afraid. Stand still, and see the salvation of
the Lord, which He will accomplish for you today.

EXODUS 14:13

Put on the whole armor of God, that you may
be able to stand against the wiles of the devil.
For we do not wrestle against flesh and blood,
but against principalities, against powers,
against the rulers of the darkness of this
age, against spiritual hosts of wickedness in the
heavenly places. Therefore take up the whole
armor of God, that you may be able to withstand
in the evil day, and having done all, to stand.

EPHESIANS 6:11—13

September

The fruit of the Spirit is love, joy, peace, longsuttering, kindness, goodness, faithfulness, gentleness, self-control.

GALATIANS 5:22–23

Morning

. . . .

Making a Big "To Do" Out of Life

Sometimes I wonder if I've become so busy scheduling every moment of my life for success that I miss the one thing I long for most: time to live.

Time to walk hand in hand with my wife . . .

Time to lie on my back and watch the clouds . . .

Time to write about the stirrings of my heart.

Time to visit with those people across the street I've never met.

Time to pray—not during scheduled prayer time, but simply because I'm overcome with gratitude, weariness or joy.

Time to simply talk to God.

God had a plan, but His plan was about relationships, not achievements. He designed time for being more than for doing. My job requires a hunk of my time for doing. My calling is to find time in the midst of it all—just for being.

The stuff of real life is not on your "To Do" list.

KEN DAVIS

Lighten Up!

Evening

· · · · · · · · ·

This is the day the LORD has made;
We will rejoice and be glad in it.

PSALM 118:24

To everything there is a season,
A time for every purpose under heaven.

ECCLESIASTES 3:1

Jesus made His disciples get into the boat
and go before Him to the other side, while
He sent the multitudes away. And when He
had sent the multitudes away, He went up
on the mountain by Himself to pray.

MATTHEW 14:22—23

SEPTEMBER 1

505

Morning

. . . .

Your Circumstances Won't Win

Maybe this morning you woke up in your ordinary bed and . . . walked into your ordinary bathroom and stared at that ordinary woman with the ordinary puffiness underneath her ordinary eyes. You put on your ordinary clothes and made an ordinary breakfast. . . . Hurried to your ordinary desk at your ordinary job with those ordinary people and their ordinary excuses. Then looked up to heaven and heard your broken heart cry, *What in the world will God ever do with an ordinary woman like me?*

Maybe, right this minute, you need to hear God's voice saying to you, *Hey, you with the heavy load. Lay it down. Just put it all right here in front of Me. All your dreams and your insecurities and your pain. . . . All your worry. . . . The disappointment over how life turned out. Your weakness and your weariness and your aching body. The constant needs that never go away. . . . Lay it down and come to Me. . . . I do extraordinary work with ordinary women like you. These circumstances will not win. Love has the final say.*

ANGELA THOMAS

My Single Mom Life

Evening

. . . .

"Come to Me, all you who labor and are heavy
laden, and I will give you rest. Take My yoke upon
you and learn from Me, for I am gentle and lowly
in heart, and you will find rest for your souls."

MATTHEW 11:28—29

I heard the voice of the Lord, saying:
"Whom shall I send,
And who will go for Us?"
Then I said, "Here am I! Send me."

ISAIAH 6:8

"Seek first the kingdom of God and His
righteousness, and all these things shall be added
to you. Therefore do not worry about tomorrow,
for tomorrow will worry about its own things.
Sufficient for the day is its own trouble."

MATTHEW 6:33—34

507

Morning

. . . .

Asking for God's Advice

When you're faced with a tough decision, it's only natural to go to a friend for advice. Chatting openly with someone who knows you and your situation well can help you put the pros and cons of your options into clearer perspective. So, what could make more sense than spending time talking things over with the One who knows you better than anyone else?

God cares about the direction in which your life is headed. The decisions you make each day help determine that direction. Weighing your decisions by what's written in the Bible and using the wisdom that God provides for the asking will not only help you determine right from wrong, but better from best.

Living God's Way

Evening

· · · · · · · · ·

If any of you lacks wisdom, let him ask of
God, who gives to all liberally and without
reproach, and it will be given to him.

JAMES 1:5

"Seek first the kingdom of God
and His righteousness."

MATTHEW 6:33

The wisdom that is from above is first pure, then
peaceable, gentle, willing to yield, full of mercy and
good fruits, without partiality and without hypocrisy.

JAMES 3:17

It's Never Too Late

I smiled when I read the poster in the window of the mall beauty salon: "It's never too late to be what you might have been." It was surrounded by pictures of the latest hairstyles and colors. I guess that was supposed to be the message: It's never too late to be a blonde if that's what you know you are deep inside! . . .

I think it's a wonderful statement and a spiritual truth. In God it's never too late to be what you might have been. So many people walk through life with regret. That seems like such a wasted, draining emotion to me. We are not powerless in our lives to make a change, to start over again, to learn to do better next time.

There is so much in life that is wonderful, and it's not too late to grab hold of it.

SHEILA WALSH

The Best Devotions of Sheila Walsh

Evening

. . . .

One thing I do, forgetting those things which
are behind and reaching forward to those things
which are ahead, I press toward the goal for the
prize of the upward call of God in Christ Jesus.

PHILIPPIANS 3:13—14

If anyone is in Christ, he is a new creation; old things
have passed away; behold, all things have become new.

2 CORINTHIANS 5:17

Now to Him who is able to keep you from stumbling,
And to present you faultless
Before the presence of His glory with exceeding joy,
To God our Savior,
Who alone is wise,
Be glory and majesty,
Dominion and power,
Both now and forever.
Amen.

JUDE VV. 24—25

511

His Calling,
His Presence

"God, with all due respect, You either have the wrong person or Your timing is way off," we whisper, shaking our heads in disbelief. But His will keeps pressing on our hearts, calling us to dream with Him again, calling us to do the impossible.

"Maybe in the past or in the future . . . perhaps if I had more experience or fewer birthdays . . . possibly if I possessed greater gifts or lighter responsibilities or . . ." Our excuses are endless.

But God does not expect us to evaluate the unknown future and calmly conclude that it is manageable. He is not asking us to place our abilities on one side of the scale and His calling on the other and declare that they balance. They do not balance and they never will!

So if not in a sober, reasonable, accurate estimation of our aptitude, what does God expect us to hold on to in order to risk following Him into the unknown? . . .

His presence! His calling always includes His presence.

ALICIA BRITT CHOLE
Sitting in God's Sunshine

Evening

· · · · · · · · · ·

Then Moses answered [the LORD] and said,
"But suppose they will not believe me or
listen to my voice; suppose they say, 'The
LORD has not appeared to you.'" . . .
Then Moses said to the LORD, "O my Lord, I am
not eloquent, neither before nor since You have
spoken to Your servant; but I am slow of speech
and slow of tongue. . . . O my Lord, please send
by the hand of whomever else You may send."

EXODUS 4:1, 10, 13

"I am with you always, even to the end of the age."

MATTHEW 28:20

The way of the LORD is strength for the upright.

PROVERBS 10:29

513

Morning

. . . .

Come to the Waters

Have you ever offered to give someone something they needed, but instead of graciously receiving your gift, they insisted on paying you for it? It is hard to receive without wanting to "make things even" with the one who is giving.

Perhaps that is why the divine call of Isaiah 55:1 has been a stumbling block to so many. "Surely, I must do something to receive this salvation. It cannot be free." But free it is! God does not sell His living water. Because He knows our inclination to want to pay, He says, "This is the way you buy—without money and without price."

Everyone is at liberty to respond to this gracious invitation to eternal refreshment and joy.

CYNTHIA HEALD
Women of Faith Devotional Bible

For what man knows the things of a man except the
spirit of the man which is in him? Even so no one
knows the things of God except the Spirit of God.
Now we have received, not the spirit of the world,
but the Spirit who is from God, that we might know
the things that have been freely given to us by God.

1 CORINTHIANS 2:11—12

"As you go, preach, saying, 'The kingdom
of heaven is at hand.' Heal the sick, cleanse
the lepers, raise the dead, cast out demons.
Freely you have received, freely give."

MATTHEW 10:7—8

The Spirit and the bride say, "Come!" And let him
who hears say, "Come!" And let him who thirsts come.
Whoever desires, let him take the water of life freely.

REVELATION 22:17

Worship Makes a Difference

On the days I arrived [at church] in plenty of time to get a seat before the service started and was a full participant through the entire worship time, I found I was open to receive the message as if God were speaking directly to me. My heart was made soft and receptive to what the Holy Spirit wanted to teach me because of the twenty or thirty minutes I had spent praising God. Negative attitudes I had come in with were melted away and replaced with ones more in alignment with what God desired. I was made ready and open to receive from God.

Worship invites God's presence, and that's where deliverance happens. Two men in prison were singing praises to God when suddenly the prison doors flew open and their chains fell off (Acts 16:26). In the spirit realm when we praise the Lord, the prison doors of our lives are opened, our bonds are broken, and we are set free. Praising God opens you to experience His love, and it will liberate you.

STORMIE OMARTIAN

Seven Prayers

I will praise You with my whole heart. . . .
For Your lovingkindness and Your truth.

PSALM 138:1—2

The multitude rose up together against [Paul and
Silas]; and the magistrates . . . threw them into
prison . . . and fastened their feet in the stocks.
But at midnight Paul and Silas were praying and
singing hymns to God, and the prisoners were
listening to them. Suddenly there was a great
earthquake, so that the foundations of the prison
were shaken; and immediately all the doors were
opened and everyone's chains were loosed. . . .
[The keeper of the prison] called for a light,
ran in, and fell down trembling before Paul
and Silas. And he brought them out and
said, "Sirs, what must I do to be saved?"
So they said, "Believe on the Lord Jesus Christ,
and you will be saved, you and your household."

ACTS 16:22-26, 29—31

517

Morning

. . . .

Obstacle or Opportunity?

Opportunities come in all shapes and sizes. What if those things you see now as obstacles could be seen instead as *gold bricks*? Bricks can be used to build a wall or as paving stones for your road to success. You can follow the yellow brick road to where you want to be, or you can remain stymied by that big wall that seals off any progress you want to make. It all depends on how you look at the obstacles. . . .

The point is that perspective is all about how we choose to see things. Because we look as much with our mind as with our eyes, we tend to "see" what we expect to see or want to see. Changing our perspective calls for a willingness to see things differently. That's the key to developing a positive attitude regardless of what happens to us.

BARBARA JOHNSON
Mama, Get the Hammer!

Evening

• • • • • • • • •

In the fear of the Lord there is strong confidence,
And His children will have a place of refuge.
The fear of the Lord is a fountain of life,
To turn one away from the snares of death.

PROVERBS 14:26—27

"My thoughts are not your thoughts,
Nor are your ways My ways," says the Lord.
"For as the heavens are higher than the earth,
So are My ways higher than your ways,
And My thoughts than your thoughts."

ISAIAH 55:8—9

For the Lord God is a sun and shield;
The Lord will give grace and glory;
No good thing will He withhold
From those who walk uprightly.

PSALM 84:11

· · · · · · · · ·

The By-Product of Praise

The Bible tells us that when we pray, it is important that we praise God. What is praise? First, what it's not: praise is not flattery. Flattery is when we say something good about another person just because we want him to do something for us. It may or may not be true. But praise is very different. It simply acknowledges, with no self-serving desires, the good qualities in another.

Jesus teaches us to praise God. We want to acknowledge the fact that there is a difference between God's character and our sinfulness. Praise simply affirms who He is and reminds us what we're not.

But there's also a wonderful by-product of praising God. Praise helps us focus on the greatness of God. This lifts us above our troubles. You see, when we begin to focus on how great God really is, we realize that no matter what trial, what difficulty, what hardship we are facing, God is bigger than all of that. When we remember that God is big, our troubles begin to seem small.

BRYANT WRIGHT

Right from the Heart

Evening

· · · · · · · · · ·

Holy, holy, holy,
Lord God Almighty,
Who was and is and is to come! . . .
You are worthy, O Lord,
To receive glory and honor and power;
For You created all things,
And by Your will they exist and were created.

REVELATION 4:8, 11

The LORD is my rock and my fortress and my deliverer;
My God, my strength, in whom I will trust;
My shield and the horn of my salvation, my stronghold.
I will call upon the LORD, who is worthy to be praised.

PSALM 18:2—3

So [Jesus] said to [His disciples], "When you pray, say:
Our Father in heaven,
Hallowed be Your name.
Your kingdom come.
Your will be done
On earth as it is in heaven."

LUKE 11:2

Morning

. . . .

God Hears—
and Acts

Hagar the homeless and her son Ishmael present a stark portrait of despair and futility. They wandered in a desert, out of water and worse, out of hope. Who would hear the sobs and notice one little homeless family? "God heard the boy crying, and the angel of God called to Hagar . . . 'Do not be afraid. . . .' Then God opened her eyes and she saw a well of water" (Genesis 21:17–19). This was no mirage; this was a miracle handled by ministering angels of our loving Father God. They drank, and "God was with the boy as he grew up" (v. 20).

What is your desert of despair, your place of parched hopelessness? The God of Hagar and Ishmael sees and hears you in your desert. He waits to sustain and refresh you today with living water.

JAN CARLBERG

The Hungry Heart

Evening

· · · · · · · · ·

[Hagar] departed and wandered about
in the wilderness of Beersheba.
When the water in the skin was used up, she left
the boy [Ishmael] under one of the bushes. . . . sat
opposite him, and lifted up her voice and wept. God
heard the lad crying; and the angel of God called
to Hagar from heaven and said to her, "What is the
matter with you, Hagar? Do not fear, for God has
heard the voice of the lad where he is. Arise, lift up
the lad, and hold him by the hand, for I will make
a great nation of him." Then God opened her eyes
and she saw a well of water; and she went and filled
the skin with water and gave the lad a drink.

GENESIS 21:14–19 NASB

The LORD will comfort Zion,
He will comfort all her waste places;
He will make her wilderness like Eden,
And her desert like the garden of the LORD;
Joy and gladness will be found in it,
Thanksgiving and the voice of melody.

ISAIAH 51:3

Morning

. . . .

Joy *In* and *Despite* Life's Trials

"Count it all joy" (James 1:2) is a tough assignment. It was for first-century Christ-followers just as it is for us today. God is very aware of our trials and very present in them. God allows trials to test and strengthen your faith in Him and to grow in you greater patience for life's tough times.

Of course those growth pains hurt, yet God enables us to count these tough times "all joy." He has, for instance, graciously revealed Himself to be faithful, wise, and loving. Also, we know from His Word that He can and does redeem the most difficult life experiences. We also know the ultimate security: we will spend eternity with Him. The promise of eternity can help us remember that there's more to life than what this world has for us.

So choose to rejoice not *for* life's trials, but *in* and *despite* those trials. After all, God is with you on the journey, He will not let you go, and He has reserved a place for you in heaven for eternity.

100 Favorite Bible Verses

Evening

• • • • • • • • •

"In the world you will have tribulation; but be
of good cheer, I have overcome the world."

JOHN 16:33

Count it all joy when you fall into various trials,
knowing that the testing of your faith produces
patience. But let patience have its perfect work, that
you may be perfect and complete, lacking nothing.

JAMES 1:2—4

"In My Father's house are many mansions;
if it were not so, I would have told you.
I go to prepare a place for you."

JOHN 14:2

Morning

. . . .

Human Origami

It's hard to come in second. . . .

While painful at the time, I can see now, many years later when I look in the rearview mirror of my life, evidence of God's tremendous love and unfolding adventure for me. I've received many letters . . . in my life that started out "Dear Bob." Some were letters so thick they had to be folded several times to fit in the envelope. They left me feeling as folded as when I read their words with shattering disappointment. Still, whatever follows my "Dear Bobs" is often another reminder that God's grace comes in all shapes, sizes, and circumstances as God continues to unfold something magnificent in me.

And when each of us looks back at all the turns and folds God has allowed in our lives, I don't think it looks like a series of folded-over mistakes and do-overs that have shaped our lives. Instead, I think we'll conclude in the end that maybe we're all a little like human origami and the more creases we have, the better.

BOB GOFF

Love Does

Evening

· · · · · · · · ·

Humble yourselves under the mighty hand of
God, that He may exalt you in due time, casting
all your care upon Him, for He cares for you.
Be sober, be vigilant; because your adversary the
devil walks about like a roaring lion, seeking whom
he may devour. Resist him, steadfast in the faith,
knowing that the same sufferings are experienced
by your brotherhood in the world. But may the
God of all grace, who called us to His eternal glory
by Christ Jesus, after you have suffered a while,
perfect, establish, strengthen, and settle you.

1 PETER 5:6—10

I consider that the sufferings of this present
time are not worthy to be compared with
the glory which shall be revealed in us.

ROMANS 8:18

We all, with unveiled face, beholding as in
a mirror the glory of the Lord, are being
transformed into the same image from glory
to glory, just as by the Spirit of the Lord.

2 CORINTHIANS 3:18

527

Morning

. . . .

The Right Medicine

Church . . . is one of God's many gracious provisions for human frailty. He knows we are prone to wander and need to be reminded of His goodness and faithfulness. So our Creator provided a divine pit stop . . . wherein we can have our souls refueled by worshiping Him and hanging out with other limping, like-minded disciples. It was never meant to be a prescribed time and place for us to obsess about doing the appropriate thing at the appropriate moment all while wearing an appropriate outfit. . . .

I think when believers gather it would be more God-honoring if we functioned as a medical center instead of a country club. Wouldn't it be awesome if everybody wore hospital gowns, complete with the requisite gap in the back, and had to choose either a wheelchair or crutches as our mode of transportation before entering the sanctuary? It might just help us remember that we're all sick and in desperate need of the medicine only Jesus provides.

LISA HARPER

Stumbling into Grace

Evening

- - - - - - - - - -

[The] scribes and the Pharisees complained
against His disciples, saying, "Why do You eat
and drink with tax collectors and sinners?"
Jesus answered and said to them, "Those
who are well have no need of a physician, but
those who are sick. I have not come to call the
righteous, but sinners, to repentance."

LUKE 5:30—32

All have sinned and fall short of the glory of
God. . . . The wages of sin is death, but the gift of
God is eternal life in Christ Jesus our Lord.

ROMANS 3:23; 6:23

God anointed Jesus of Nazareth with the Holy
Spirit and with power, who went about doing
good and healing all who were oppressed
by the devil, for God was with Him.

ACTS 10:38

Morning

. . . .

The Best News

In the book of Isaiah, the prophet foretold the coming salvation of Israel through the Messiah. While the Messiah had not yet come, God had assured Isaiah of the reality of this coming salvation. It was so certain that he could shout it from the mountaintops and tell it everywhere.

Being on the other side of the cross, we have the luxury of spreading the good news of Christ with a fuller picture of what that salvation means. The gospel is not simply good news; it is the best news. Christ has come. He lived a perfect life and carried the full weight of our sin to the cross, satisfying the wrath of a just God, that we might live at peace and know the fullness of life with Him. That's news worth shouting!

CATHERINE CLAIRE LARSON

Waiting in Wonder

Evening

· · · · · · · · ·

Sing to the LORD a new song,
And His praise from the ends of the earth,
You who go down to the sea, and all that is in it,
You coastlands and you inhabitants of them!
Let the wilderness and its cities lift up their voice. . . .
Let them shout from the top of the mountains.
Let them give glory to the LORD,
And declare His praise in the coastlands.

ISAIAH 42:10—12

God demonstrates His own love toward us, in that
while we were still sinners, Christ died for us.

ROMANS 5:8

If you confess with your mouth the Lord Jesus
and believe in your heart that God has raised
Him from the dead, you will be saved.

ROMANS 10:9

531

Morning

. . . .

Messengers of Truth

In Jesus' day, a king's envoys would go before him, making the way safe and announcing his coming. Before Jesus began His public ministry, John the Baptist went before Him, announcing His coming with a call to repentance and baptism. After four hundred years of God's silence—of no prophetic voice speaking on the Lord's behalf—the people of Israel were eager to hear God's message spoken by John, the self-proclaimed fulfillment of Malachi's prophecy.

Like John, you and I can testify to the coming of Jesus—His first coming to defeat sin and death and His Second Coming to establish His eternal kingdom. You and I can be messengers of this truth, of this good news, or gospel. As Saint Francis of Assisi said to believers, "Preach the gospel at all times. If necessary use words."

JACK COUNTRYMAN
The Hope of Christmas

Evening

· · · · · · · · ·

"Behold, I send My messenger,
And he will prepare the way before Me.
And the Lord, whom you seek,
Will suddenly come to His temple,
Even the Messenger of the covenant,
In whom you delight.
Behold, He is coming,"
Says the LORD of hosts

MALACHI 3:1

John answered, saying to all, "I indeed baptize
you with water; but One mightier than I is coming,
whose sandal strap I am not worthy to loose. He
will baptize you with the Holy Spirit and fire."

LUKE 3:16

533

Morning

· · · · · · · ·

Coping with a Crisis

The apostle Paul exhort[ed] us (Philippians 4:6, AMPLI-FIED) to pray about everything, to pour our hearts out to the heavenly Father with "definite requests."

My problem is that having done this, having laid my concern before the Father, I get the feeling that if I do not frequently return to it in my mind and keep "worrying" it, much as a dog would a bone, then there certainly can be no chance of solving it. . . .

God seems to point out chapter four in Philippians as a blueprint for handling crises His way:

- Rejoice in the Lord always.
- Do not fret about anything.
- Pray about everything.
- Be content with our earthly lot, whatever it is.
- Guard our thoughts; think only positive things.

CATHERINE MARSHALL

A Closer Walk

Rejoice in the Lord always. Again I will say, rejoice!

PHILIPPIANS 4:4

Be anxious for nothing, but in everything by prayer
and supplication, with thanksgiving, let your
requests be made known to God; and the peace of
God, which surpasses all understanding, will guard
your hearts and minds through Christ Jesus.

PHILIPPIANS 4:6—7

I have learned in whatever state I am, to
be content: I know how to be abased, and I
know how to abound. Everywhere and in all
things I have learned both to be full and to be
hungry, both to abound and to suffer need.

PHILIPPIANS 4:11—12

Morning
· · · · · · · · ·

Godly Habits, Godly Living

Some people continuously act on impulse, grabbing at whatever seems attractive at the moment. Now some spontaneity is healthy, but when we face all of life with a senseless striving to satisfy our impulses, we defeat ourselves.

Sometimes we do what we do to escape what we perceive to be more threatening, demanding, or painful. We may put up with a dirty house because it is unpleasant to wash the kitchen floor, or we may avoid working out conflicts because it is painful to face our weaknesses.

We need to make conscious decisions in order to change. Our aim is to develop godly habits that result in godly living.

KATHY BABBITT

Habits of the Heart

Evening

· · · · · · · · ·

Serve the LORD with gladness.

PSALM 100:2

Our Lord . . . has saved us and called us with a
holy calling, not according to our works, but
according to His own purpose and grace which was
given to us in Christ Jesus before time began.

2 TIMOTHY 1:0   9

We have known and believed the love that
God has for us. God is love, and he who abides
in love abides in God, and God in him.

1 JOHN 4:16

Morning

· · · · · · · ·

Cloaked in Mystery

I shouldn't be surprised that God is cloaked in mystery because he is pure spirit. I'm not. He is absolute in His holiness. I'm not. He is blameless. I'm not (except in Christ). He is love. I'm ornery by nature. He is mysterious. I'm a complicated puzzle to myself and to those who know me, but to God I'm an easy read, an open book, a known story. . . .

I'm committed by faith to Christ, in whom I believe, but I ponder with uncertainty many of the particulars. Mrs. She-Who-Thinks-She-Has-the-Answers has learned instead to take shelter under the marvel of his mystery. For there I don't have to know answers; I'm just asked to trust. God doesn't ask me to defend his reputation or to debate with others doctrinally, but he does make it clear I'm to love.

We are temporarily confined to this planet in a leaky earth suit. One day that will change, and then we will see what we can't imagine, and we will understand what we can't comprehend.

PATSY CLAIRMONT

Stained Glass Hearts

Now we see in a mirror, dimly, but then
face to face. Now I know in part, but then
I shall know just as I also am known.

1 CORINTHIANS 13:12

The message of the cross is foolishness to those
who are perishing, but to us who are being
saved it is the power of God. For it is written:
"I will destroy the wisdom of the wise,
And bring to nothing the understanding
of the prudent." . . .
The foolishness of God is wiser than men, and
the weakness of God is stronger than men.

1 CORINTHIANS 1:18—19, 25

If you seek [wisdom] as silver,
And search for her as for hidden treasures;
Then you will understand the fear of the LORD,
And find the knowledge of God.
For the LORD gives wisdom;
From His mouth come knowledge and understanding.

PROVERBS 2:4—6

Morning

· · · · · · · · ·

Let Jesus In

Jesus existed to please His Father. His Father met every need He had for wisdom, direction, purpose, love, relationship, and hope. There is something infectious about the way they interact, the sheer delight that Christ has done all that His Father has asked, the joy and love and submission Christ has for His Father.

"We love Him because He first loved us" (1 John 4:19).

When we don't love or feel joy or peace or passion, it's because we do not know His love or His joy or peace or passion. He is a person, not a magic pill you take when your life or your soul is broken. He is a person. He is a person you talk to and listen to and love and respect. He's someone you decide to spend time with and dream with, whom you follow and learn from and hurt with, and to whom you ask things—someone you choose over anybody else, over anything else. He is a person—the person who defines my life, sweeps in and changes me. When I let Him in.

JENNIE ALLEN

Anything

Evening

. . . .

"As the Father knows Me, even so I know the
Father; and I lay down My life for the sheep. . . .
Therefore My Father loves Me, because I lay down
My life that I may take it again. No one takes it
from Me, but I lay it down of Myself. I have power
to lay it down, and I have power to take it again.
This command I have received from My Father."

JOHN 10:15, 17—18

"I do not pray for these alone, but also for those who
will believe in Me through their word; that they
all may be one, as You, Father, are in Me, and I in
You; that they also may be one in Us, that the world
may believe that You sent Me. And the glory which
You gave Me I have given them, that they may be
one just as We are one: I in them, and You in Me;
that they may be made perfect in one, and that the
world may know that You have sent Me, and have
loved them as You have loved Me. . . . I have declared
to them Your name . . . that the love with which
You loved Me may be in them, and I in them."

JOHN 17:20—23, 26

About Friendship

The Bible contains many interesting stories about friendship. The most well-known is that of David and Jonathan in 1 Samuel 20. Their relationship held no jealousy. They were loyal friends, supportive and protective of one another. They were so committed to each other that they pledged to be friends for life. Even after Jonathan was killed, David honored their friendship by looking after members of Jonathan's family.

Such solid friendships are a gift from God, but His greatest gift of friendship is our friendship with Jesus Christ, the One who loved us so much that He gave His life for our salvation. This is what Jesus said to His disciples: "You are my friends if you do what I command. I no longer call you servants, because a servant does not know his master's business. Instead, I have called you friends, for everything that I learned from my Father I have made known to you. You did not choose me, but I chose you" (John 15:14–16 NIV). When we choose to believe in Him, Jesus chooses to be our Friend—our very best Friend.

A Charles Dickens Devotional

"Greater love has no one than this, than
to lay down one's life for his friends."

JOHN 15:13

A friend loves at all times.

PROVERBS 17:17

The Scripture was fulfilled which says, "Abraham
believed God, and it was accounted to him for
righteousness." And he was called the friend of God.

JAMES 2:23

"As the Father loved Me, I also have loved you;
abide in My love. If you keep My commandments,
you will abide in My love, just as I have kept My
Father's commandments and abide in His love."

JOHN 15:9-10

Morning

. . . .

The Joy of My Heart

When my children were young, they would head straight for the kitchen after walking in the door from school. The work and stress of the day seemed to melt away with one glance at a plate of cookies waiting on the counter.

Jeremiah wrote about similar appetites. He also headed to the "kitchen" to eat—to consume or devour—God's Word. We, too, will know we are walking closely with Him when we find childlike joy in feasting daily, not only on Scripture but also on the knowledge that Someone knows and loves us so much that He leaves us plates of goodies.

LYNDA HUNTER BJORKLUND

Women of Faith Devotional Bible

Evening

· · · · · · · · ·

Your words were found, and I ate them,
And Your word was to me the joy and rejoicing of my heart;
For I am called by Your name,
O LORD God of hosts.

JEREMIAH 15:16

[Jesus] answered and said, "It is written, 'Man
shall not live by bread alone, but by every word
that proceeds from the mouth of God.'"

MATTHEW 4:4

"I say to you, whoever does not receive the kingdom
of God as a little child will by no means enter it."

MARK 10:15

545

Get Off the Emotional Roller Coaster

Can you even begin to think of the time, energy, and emotions you've wasted on the uncontrollable things in your life? I've certainly done my share of wishing, fretting, complaining, and trying to manipulate uncontrollable things and people. When I do that, I use up immense quantities of emotional energy for nothing when it could have been expended in a productive way. . . .

Remember this: When the uncontrollable things or people in our lives are making us miserable, it is because we allow them to do that to us. They can't keep us on that roller coaster if we decide to get off. How do you get off? By choice, by a decision of your will, by much prayer, and by the power of God's Spirit within you. It takes determination on your part, but if you don't let God supply the power, you're not likely to be able to do it.

MARY WHELCHEL
How to Thrive from 9 to 5

Evening

. . . .

Choose for yourselves this day whom you will serve . . .
As for me and my house, we will serve the LORD.

JOSHUA 24:15

God has not given us a spirit of fear, but of
power and of love and of a sound mind.

2 TIMOTHY 1.7

[Pray] always with all prayer and supplication
in the Spirit, being watchful to this end with all
perseverance and supplication for all the saints.

EPHESIANS 6:18

Morning

· · · · · · · · ·

Celebrate Success!

Isn't *victory* a wonderful word? Especially when it applies in your own life? *Victory* has been defined as "achievement in a struggle against odds or difficulties." It means winning. Look for a minute at some of the occasions in your past where you've been victorious in a pursuit or struggle, and you celebrated when it was over (or should have [celebrated] if you didn't):

- Job promotions
- Graduation from school
- Losing weight
- Paying off a debt
- Starting a business
- Writing a book

There are dozens more victories in your life that you can name, too. Didn't you feel relieved and ecstatic at the same time once that specific goal was attained? You're a winner, a success, a victor!

LUCI SWINDOLL
You Bring the Confetti

I can do all things through Christ
who strengthens me.

PHILIPPIANS 4:13

"Well done, good and faithful servant;
you have been faithful."

MATTHEW 25:23

"Do not lay up for yourselves treasures on earth,
where moth and rust destroy and where thieves break
in and steal; but lay up for yourselves treasures in
heaven, where neither moth nor rust destroys and
where thieves do not break in and steal. For where
your treasure is, there your heart will be also."

MATTHEW 6:19—21

Morning

. . . .

Choosing to Worship

Before Hannah knew she was going to have a baby, she promised God that if she had a son, she would give him to the Lord. It is one thing to make a promise when you are empty. It is quite another matter to keep your promise when full. Mothering made the years slip by quickly, and soon Samuel was weaned and ready to be brought to the temple. Hannah faced a tough challenge of faith as she prepared to permanently drop off her son at Eli's Day and Night Care Center. Eli's wicked sons had marred his reputation as a father. How could she leave her precious Samuel with such a family?

The answer was in God! God would tend to her son. She had promised her son to God, not to Eli. She must have left Samuel's ears ringing with the sounds of his mother worshiping, not weeping.

JAN CARLBERG

The Hungry Heart

Evening

· · · · · · · · ·

Hannah had no children. . . . and prayed to the LORD
and wept in anguish. Then she made a vow and
said, "O LORD of hosts, if You will indeed look on
the affliction of Your maidservant and remember
me, and not forget Your maidservant, but will
give Your maidservant a male child, then I will
give him to the LORD all the days of his life." . . .

So it came to pass in the process of time
that Hannah conceived and bore a son, and
called his name Samuel, saying, "Because I
have asked for him from the LORD." . . .
Now when she had weaned him, she took him up with
her . . . to the house of the LORD in Shiloh. And the
child was young. . . . And she said, "O my lord! As
your soul lives, my lord, I am the woman who stood by
you here, praying to the LORD. For this child I prayed,
and the LORD has granted me my petition which I
asked of Him. Therefore I also have lent him to the
LORD; as long as he lives he shall be lent to the LORD."

1 SAMUEL 1:2, 10—11, 20, 24—28

Morning

· · · · · · · · ·

Quite the Family Tree

Writing to a primarily Jewish audience, Matthew outlined Jesus' ancestry. The gospel writer wanted his Hebrew audience to clearly see that Jesus was indeed the long-awaited King of Israel, in the line of David, who would set God's people free from captivity to sin and its consequences.

Yet Matthew did something unusual as he outlined the family tree. He named five *women*: Tamar, a Canaanite; Rahab, a Gentile; Ruth, a Moabite; Bathsheba, King David's wife; and Mary, the teenage mother of Jesus. Why? Because their stories demonstrate that God's grace is available to all, regardless of gender, race, or personal history. In fact, even today God seems to delight in welcoming into His family those we might never expect.

JACK COUNTRYMAN
The Hope of Christmas

You are a holy people to the LORD your God; the
LORD your God has chosen you to be a people for
Himself, a special treasure above all the peoples
on the face of the earth. The LORD did not set His
love on you nor choose you because you were more
in number than any other people, for you were the
least of all peoples; but because the LORD loves you.

DEUTERONOMY 7:6–8

The book of the genealogy of Jesus Christ, the
Son of David, the Son of Abraham. . . . So all the
generations from Abraham to David are fourteen
generations, from David until the captivity in Babylon
are fourteen generations, and from the captivity in
Babylon until the Christ are fourteen generations.

MATTHEW 1:1, 17

There is neither Jew nor Greek, there is neither
slave nor free, there is neither male nor
female; for you are all one in Christ Jesus.

GALATIANS 3:28

Morning

. . . .

Fix Your Eyes on Jesus

Do you think anything concerning you right now is too small?

Your house or apartment? Your personal reputation? Your influence? Your job?

Your family (you want to add a spouse or children)? Your circle of friends? Your salary? Your life?

Until I paid attention to Psalm 131, I chafed. Then I discovered that God's leash wasn't too tight—my heart was too proud! I thought I "deserved" more; my self-image had greater expectations, and that attitude was the very grease on which I slid into self-pity, discontent, ungratefulness, misery.

Then I fixed my eyes on Jesus—and in my own eyes I became smaller and smaller. What was my stature, my purity, my power, my excellence compared with His?

ANNE ORTLUND

Fix Your Eyes on Jesus

Evening

· · · · · · · · ·

By pride comes nothing but strife.

PROVERBS 13:10

The poor shall eat and be satisfied;
Those who seek Him will praise the LORD.

PSALM 22:26

Do not overwork to be rich;
Because of your own understanding, cease!
Will you set your eyes on that which is not?
For riches certainly make themselves wings;
They fly away like an eagle toward heaven.

PROVERBS 23:4—5

LORD, my heart is not haughty,
Nor my eyes lofty.
Neither do I concern myself with great matters,
Nor with things too profound for me.

PSALM 131:1

Morning

. . . .

Savor What Is

To experience happiness we must train ourselves to live in this moment, to savor it for what it is, not running ahead in anticipation of some future date nor lagging behind in the paralysis of the past. With wholeness and sensitivity we must live in the here and now. "But what if I don't like the here and now?" you ask. "What if my present moment is one of disappointment or impairment or heartache? How then do I savor that moment?" Good questions. And the answers reside in the first and most profound principle for the art of savoring life: pleasure lies in the heart, not in the happenstance. Our circumstances may be dreadful and riddled with reasons for discouragement or sorrow, but that doesn't mean those moments are utterly devoid of happiness. . . . Those special savored moments of fun, reflection, happiness, and pleasure give us a tiny taste of what eternity with Christ will one day be like.

LUCI SWINDOLL

You Bring the Confetti

Evening

. . . .

"Do not worry about tomorrow, for tomorrow
will worry about its own things. Sufficient
for the day is its own trouble."

MATTHEW 6:34

Our light affliction, which is but for a moment, is
working for us a far more exceeding and eternal
weight of glory, while we do not look at the things
which are seen, but at the things which are not
seen. For the things which are seen are temporary,
but the things which are not seen are eternal.

2 CORINTHIANS 4:17–18

Oh, taste and see that the LORD is good;
Blessed is the man who trusts in Him! . . .
The young lions lack and suffer hunger;
But those who seek the LORD shall not lack any good thing.

PSALM 34:8, 10

Morning

. . . .

God Sees Us Through

Shipwrecked, beaten, imprisoned, stoned, run out of town, hungry, thirsty, cold, naked, threatened by Gentiles and fellow Jews, facing danger in cities, in the sea, and in the wilderness—Paul experienced all this and more as he served his Lord and Savior. And who saw him through? His Lord and Savior. Each step of the way.

Perhaps metaphorically you're dealing with a ship-wrecked relationship or a beating in your place of employment. Maybe you feel imprisoned by past sin, unpaid bills, or a meaningless job. The end of a significant relationship may have left you feeling cold and alone. A cross-country move may have left you hungry and thirsty for friends, fellowship, and a church to call home. Life can be very difficult, but hear again the confident statement of the apostle Paul: "I can do everything through Christ, who gives me strength."

Jesus is indeed an unwavering source of strength for us. He will show Himself to be sufficient to meet your every need. Give Him the opportunity to do just that.

100 Favorite Bible Verses

Evening

· · · · · · · · ·

From the Jews five times I received forty stripes minus one. Three times I was beaten with rods; once I was stoned; three times I was shipwrecked; . . . in perils of robbers, in perils of my own countrymen, in perils of the Gentiles, in perils in the city, in perils in the wilderness, in perils in the sea, in perils among false brethren; in weariness and toil, in sleeplessness often, in hunger and thirst, in fastings often, in cold and nakedness.

2 CORINTHIANS 11:24–27

I can do everything through Christ,
who gives me strength.

PHILIPPIANS 4:13 NLT

I have fought the good fight, I have finished
the race, I have kept the faith.

2 TIMOTHY 4:7

559

Morning

"Made Himself Nothing"

It is fascinating to ponder the fact that two thousand years ago God Himself chose to live . . . outside of His own enormity and entered into our smallness.

Jesus certainly could have opted for the spiritual power play. He could have come swooping into our world in a lightning-driven chariot. He could have zapped entire cities with the snap of His fingers. Instead, He arrived in one of the most fragile and vulnerable packages in the world, the body of a newborn baby. He grew up in a middle-class family, learned a trade, went to temple like other Jewish boys, and didn't even begin His formal ministry until He was thirty years old. Then He set out on foot to cover a relatively small corner of the world. He spoke to a few thousand people (often one at a time), discipled a handful of followers, and died the death of a common criminal. Still, He was pleased enough with the results of His small-scope ministry to say from the cross, "It is finished."

CLAIRE CLONINGER
When God Shines Through

Evening

· · · · · · · · ·

Have the same mindset as Christ Jesus: Who, being in
very nature God, did not consider equality with God
something to be used to his own advantage; rather, he
made himself nothing by taking the very nature of a
servant, being made in human likeness. And being
found in appearance as a man, he humbled himself by
becoming obedient to death—even death on a cross!

PHILIPPIANS 2:5—8 NIV

Oh, the depth of the riches both of the wisdom
and knowledge of God! How unscarchable are
His judgments and His ways past finding out!

ROMANS 11:33

He has no form or comeliness;
And when we see Him,
There is no beauty that we should desire Him.
He is despised and rejected by men,
A Man of sorrows and acquainted with grief.

ISAIAH 53:2—3

Choose Joy

Everywhere I turn today, something tries to steal my joy. If I can't rejoice and be glad today, I will never rejoice and be glad. I will waste the joyous opportunities of today waiting for tomorrows that may or may not ever come. If I wait until life slows down, the sun comes back, the kids are older and less demanding, I lose some weight, my husband gets that raise, then I'll spend my life waiting rather than living and being glad.

The joys of life are found in and amongst life itself. Yes, life is full of frustrations, disappointments, pain, and suffering; but no matter what we are facing, having an attitude of joy will allow us to find the good that God promises us is there. If an oyster can make a pearl out of an irritating grain of sand, just think what you could do if in every situation you chose to rejoice!

LYSA TERKEURST

Living Life on Purpose

Evening

Oh, satisfy us early with Your mercy,
That we may rejoice and be glad all our days!

PSALM 90:14

Let the righteous be glad;
Let them rejoice before God.

PSALM 68:3

I have trusted in Your mercy;
My heart shall rejoice in Your salvation.

PSALM 13:5

Let all those rejoice who put their trust in You;
Let them ever shout for joy, because You defend them;
Let those also who love Your name
Be joyful in You.

PSALM 5:11

563

October

You will show me the path of life;
In Your presence is fullness of joy;
At Your right hand are pleasures forevermore.

PSALM 16:11

OCTOBER 1

Holding on to Hope

Hope is the perfect life preserver in the midst of any storm. It helps keep your head above water, enabling you to fight off feelings of discouragement and despair. As you catch an occasional glimpse of what lies beyond the waves, it aids in reminding you that help is on the way, even if you can't quite see it yet. Hope helps you survive.

When storm clouds are gathering on the horizon, or if a torrential downpour has caught you by surprise, hold fast to hope. Remember how God came through time and time again for people in the Bible. Think about how He's come through for you. Then meditate on His steadfast promises, your greatest source of hope. Help is on its way.

Living God's Way

If we hope for what we do not see, we
eagerly wait for it with perseverance.

ROMANS 8:25

Oh, love the LORD, all you His saints!
For the LORD preserves the faithful,
And fully repays the proud person.
Be of good courage,
And He shall strengthen your heart,
All you who hope in the LORD.

PSALM 31:23—24

Now faith is the substance of things hoped
for, the evidence of things not seen.

HEBREWS 11:1

OCTOBER 1

How to Move a Mountain

Have you ever felt your faith in God slipping away? If so, you are not alone. Every life—including yours—is a series of successes and failures, celebrations and disappointments, joys and sorrows. But even when we feel very distant from God, God is never distant from us.

Jesus taught His disciples that if they had faith, they could move mountains. You can too. When you place your faith, your trust, and even your whole life in the hands of Jesus, you'll be amazed at the marvelous things He can do with you and through you. So strengthen your faith through praise, through worship, through Bible study, and through prayer. And trust God's plans. He stands ready to open a world of possibilities for you if you have faith.

Living God's Way

Evening

· · · · · · · · ·

Jesus said to [the boy's father], "If you can believe, all things are possible to him who believes."

MARK 9:23

"If you have faith as a mustard seed, you will say to this mountain, 'Move from here to there,' and it will move; and nothing will be impossible for you."

MATTHEW 17:20

"Go therefore and make disciples of all the nations, baptizing them in the name of the Father and of the Son and of the Holy Spirit, teaching them to observe all things that I have commanded you; and lo, I am with you always, even to the end of the age."

MATTHEW 28:19—20

569

The Art of Waiting

Arguably one of the most difficult concepts in life for us to grasp is the art of waiting patiently. . . . But sometimes what we learn and who we become in the process of waiting is even more important than what we're waiting on. . . .

We're all waiting for something. An answer. A response. A reaction. A second chance. An e-mail. . . . If you're still waiting for it, it means you're not yet ready for it . . . whatever "it" is, so stop looking at waiting as a punishment and start looking at it as preparation! . . .

Sometimes the moments spent waiting for something are even more important than the moment the something actually happens. And not all wishes are meant to come true. Some wishes are only there to teach us how to wait. These wishes . . . bring us not an instant blessing but a lifelong lesson.

During those seasons of waiting, remember this: The stretching of your faith is immediate pain that results in ultimate gain. It is in the waiting that we become who we are meant to be.

MANDY HALE

The Single Woman

Evening

· · · · · · · · ·

I wait for the LORD, my soul waits,
And in His word I do hope.
My soul waits for the Lord
More than those who watch for the morning—
Yes, more than those who watch for the morning.

PSALM 130:5—6

My soul, wait silently for God alone,
For my expectation is from Him.
He only is my rock and my salvation;
He is my defense;
I shall not be moved.

PSALM 62:5—6

Wait on the LORD;
Be of good courage,
And He shall strengthen your heart;
Wait, I say, on the LORD!

PSALM 27:14

Morning

. . . .

A Season of Sadness

A fellow-learner in a class I taught shared thoughts about the tendency of many women to fight depression in the fall of the year. She reminded us that Psalm 1 suggests that we are all to be like trees planted by a stream—trees which bear fruit "in . . . season."

Her insight? That even trees don't flower and bear fruit all the time—only in season. But men and women alike seem to think that we should be bearing fruit all the time; we punish ourselves when we're not. She was teaching us the beauty of personal dormancy: we must allow for it and accept it joyfully. . . . A time of inner strength-gathering for a better bloom later.

GAIL MACDONALD
High Call, High Privilege

Jesus said to them, "My time has not yet come."

JOHN 7:6

Blessed is the man
Who walks not in the counsel of the ungodly,
Nor stands in the path of sinners,
Nor sits in the seat of the scornful;
But his delight is in the law of the LORD,
And in His law he meditates day and night.
He shall be like a tree
Planted by the rivers of water,
That brings forth its fruit in its season.

PSALM 1:1—3

To everything there is a season,
A time for every purpose under heaven . . .
A time to plant,
And a time to pluck what is planted . . .
A time to break down,
And a time to build up;
A time to weep,
And a time to laugh.

ECCLESIASTES 3:1—4

Studying God's Ways

As a child, my favorite part about visiting the beach was going to the boardwalk. After a day in the ocean, we'd shower, dress, and run up to the boardwalk for ice cream cones. My sisters and I would sit on a bench, lick our cones, and watch all the people stroll by. Kids with cotton candy. Lovers ambling arm-in-arm. Older ladies in flowered dresses with parasols. People-watching was the neatest part.

I still enjoy looking at people, thinking about where they live, wondering where they work, and if they're happy. Studying people, for me, is a habit.

Wouldn't it be great if we were as conscious about studying God as we were people? Watching Him, wondering about Him, looking closely at what makes Him who He is, and just . . . enjoying Him.

JONI EARECKSON TADA

Diamonds in the Dust

Evening

· · · · · · · · ·

Teach me Your way, O LORD;
I will walk in Your truth;
Unite my heart to fear Your name.

PSALM 86:11

As for God, His way is perfect;
The word of the LORD is proven;
He is a shield to all who trust in Him.

PSALM 18:30

Show me Your ways, O LORD;
Teach me Your paths.

PSALM 25:4

OCTOBER 5

575

"Wings Like Eagles"

Eagles have a seven-foot wingspan, and they are able to carry well over their body weight. Their strength is also evident when they appear to be motionless in hurricane-force winds. Eagles can reach speeds of more than one hundred fifty miles per hour and dive at the speed of two hundred miles per hour. These amazing birds can soar half a mile above the earth and glide at altitudes of more than 2,500 feet. And as eagles perform these amazing feats, they appear to do so effortlessly.

With these facts in mind, consider again the promise in Isaiah. . . . You will grow weary—physically, emotionally, mentally, and spiritually—as you journey through life, but you don't have to stay at that low point. Turn to God; wait on Him. Open His Word and remind yourself of His strength, power, and love. Find time to worship Him. Think back over God's great faithfulness to you. Kneel and pray. Let God know what He already knows, that you are feeling overwhelmed, vulnerable, weak. Let Him lift you up.

100 Favorite Bible Verses

Evening

· · · · · · · · ·

Those who wait on the LORD
Shall renew their strength;
They shall mount up with wings like eagles,
They shall run and not be weary,
They shall walk and not faint.

ISAIAH 40:31

"Come to Me, all you who labor and are
heavy laden, and I will give you rest."

MATTHEW 11:28

Suddenly a great tempest arose on the
sea, so that the boat was covered with
the waves. But [Jesus] was asleep.

MATTHEW 8:24

OCTOBER 6

Morning

. . . .

Be a True Contender

You'd be hard-pressed to find anywhere in the Bible where God directs believers to argue, quarrel, or squabble with others over the doctrines of the Christian faith. It's easy to fall in to the trap of spending more time defending our faith to fellow believers than we do contending for the faith.

What does it mean to be a contender? It means to know what you believe, know why you believe it, and be able to articulate it humbly, thoughtfully, and biblically to another person. It means expressing your faith in everyday acts of love, service, and faithfulness. Sometimes it means being silent, just as Jesus modeled under fire.

When we "set apart Christ as Lord," as Peter instructed in 1 Peter 3:15, we willingly enter into communion with Him. Communion with Jesus is a sanctuary that exists within you—a place to go for fellowship, insight, love, and power that will allow you to step into the world each day as a worthy, mighty contender.

More Than a Bucket List

Be ready to speak up and tell anyone who
asks why you're living the way you are,
and always with the utmost courtesy.

1 PETER 3:15 MSG

May [we] no longer be children, tossed to and
fro by the waves and carried about by every wind
of doctrine, by human cunning, by craftiness
in deceitful schemes. Rather, speaking the
truth in love, we are to grow up in every way
into him who is the head, into Christ.

EPHESIANS 4:14-15 ESV

Walk worthy of the calling with which you were called,
with all lowliness and gentleness, with longsuffering,
bearing with one another in love, endeavoring to
keep the unity of the Spirit in the bond of peace.

EPHESIANS 4:1—3

Get Obsessed

We obsess about work, our kids, our house, and the future. We obsess about our weight, our relationships, and our 401(k) plans. But what would happen if we flipped that obsession to the things of God? What would your life look like? What if we cheered for God the way we cheer for the New York Giants or for our firstborn as he rounds third base? What if our eyes popped open each morning because we were exhilarated about how God is moving in our life?

Jesus was obsessed. He was preoccupied and fixed on one thing only—the message and miracle of salvation (John 17:3). His earthly life culminated in three years of public ministry. He had a precious window of time in which to lay out the feast of heaven before a famished, sin-filled, skeptical world.

The dictionary defines obsession as "the domination of one's thoughts or feelings by a persistent idea, image, or desire." May Christ dominate our thoughts, may the idea of holiness own our hearts, and may the persistent image before us always be the grace and miracle of the cross. Now that's an obsession I'd be happy to indulge in!

More Than a Bucket List

Evening

· · · · · · · · ·

"Love the LORD your God with all your
heart, with all your soul, with all your
mind, and with all your strength."

MARK 12:30

I have fought the good fight, I have finished
the race, I have kept the faith.

2 TIMOTHY 4:7

Whatever things are true, whatever things are noble,
whatever things are just, whatever things are pure,
whatever things are lovely, whatever things are of
good report, if there is any virtue and if there
is anything praiseworthy—meditate on these things.

PHILIPPIANS 4:8

One Step, Then Another

God can make a way for you where nothing has seemed possible. . . . I wish I could take you by the hand and walk you to the nearest field to point you toward the horizon. To whisper, "Can you see that? Your whole life is still in front of you. Can you see God there, calling you toward the plans He has for you . . . ? Can you hear Him saying your name and directing your steps?" . . .

I don't know everything about this journey, but I am positive that every time God is involved, we are supposed to live with passion and purpose. I just see too many of us waiting to live. . . .

Don't let your circumstances mislead you. . . . Live like everything God has promised is true. God is here. He is ready to heal and restore and make your life new. Turn and see.

One turn.

Eyes raised, squinting toward the horizon.

Deep breath.

One step. Then another . . .

Until you run.

ANGELA THOMAS
My Single Mom Life

Evening

· · · · · · · ·

"I know the plans I have for you," declares the
Lord, "plans to prosper you and not to harm
you, plans to give you hope and a future."

JEREMIAH 29:11 NIV

A man's heart plans his way,
But the Lord directs his steps.

PROVERBS 16:9

Direct my steps by Your word,
And let no iniquity have dominion over me.

PSALM 119:133

The Lord is gracious and full of compassion,
Slow to anger and great in mercy.
The Lord is good to all,
And His tender mercies are over all His works.

PSALM 145:8—9

Morning

. . . .

"A Very Present Help"

The Truth is, life is hard. We live in a fallen world. Even those who have been redeemed live in earthly bodies and have to deal with the realities of temptation, sin (both our own and others'), disease, loss, pain, and death. Becoming a Christian . . . does not wrap us up in some sort of celestial cocoon where we are immune to pain. . . . There will be tears, sorrows, pressures, and problems.

But—and here's the good news—God is not removed or detached from our problems. He doesn't just sit up in heaven and watch to see if we will manage to survive. No, the God of the Bible is "a very present help in trouble" (Psalm 46:1). . . . He uses pressures and problems to mold and shape our lives and to make us like His Son Jesus. . . .

We want God to fix all our problems. God says instead, "I have a purpose for your problems. I want to use your problems to change you and to reveal My grace and power to the world." That is the Truth—and the Truth will set you free.

NANCY LEIGH DEMOSS

Lies Women Believe

Evening

. . . .

God is our refuge and strength,
A very present help in trouble.

PSALM 46:1

"If you abide in My word, you are My disciples
indeed. And you shall know the truth,
and the truth shall make you free."

JOHN 8:31–32

"In the world you will have tribulation; but be
of good cheer, I have overcome the world."

JOHN 16:33

We All Have Faith

I always smile when someone tells me he or she has no faith. . . . Everyone lives by faith to a certain extent. When you go to a doctor, you need faith to trust his diagnosis. When the pharmacy fills your prescription, you have faith that you'll receive the appropriate medicine. When you eat at a restaurant, you trust that the people serving you have not contaminated or poisoned the food. (Some restaurants require more faith than others.) Every day is a walk of faith on some level. . . .

We choose what we will believe in. Some people choose to believe in themselves, some in government, some in evil, some in science . . . some in God. The only person I've ever known who didn't believe in anything ended up in a mental hospital because it drove her crazy. Faith is something we can't live without.

Faith is something we can't die without either. Our faith determines what happens to us after we leave this world. If you have faith in Jesus, you know that your eternal future is secure.

STORMIE OMARTIAN
The Power of a Praying Wife

God so loved the world that He gave His only
begotten Son, that whoever believes in Him
should not perish but have everlasting life.

JOHN 3:16

Faith is the substance of things hoped
for, the evidence of things not seen.

HEBREWS 11:1

"If you have faith as a mustard seed, you
will say to this mountain, 'Move from
here to there,' and it will move."

MATTHEW 17:20

Count it all joy when you fall into
various trials, knowing that the testing
of your faith produces patience.

JAMES 1:2—3

Morning

· · · · · · · ·

Celebrate More

How many times do you let a birthday, anniversary, or special accomplishment simply slip away with little revelry? Go overboard for a friend's birthday. Commemorate your anniversary with real fireworks. Surprise your staff with a "small wins" celebration: take time to call out ten successes over the past month. Take your friend to lunch to celebrate a promotion or an answered prayer. When we celebrate the big and the little things, we live out God's blessings in 3-D and honor the joys taking place all around us.

This month, choose one big and one little thing to celebrate—and be creative!

More Than a Bucket List

Evening

· · · · · · · · ·

This is the day the LORD has made;
We will rejoice and be glad in it.

PSALM 118:24

Every good gift and every perfect gift is from above.

JAMES 1:17

It is good to give thanks to the LORD,
And to sing praises to Your name, O Most High.

PSALM 92:1

[Give] thanks always for all things to God the
Father in the name of our Lord Jesus Christ.

EPHESIANS 5:20

Morning

. . . .

Making the Right Choices

The other day, I was driving down a busy road when I came upon a traffic light that was both green and red at the same time. I slowed, unsure of what I should do, as did the other cars coming from all directions. It was confusing and dangerous. Some people stopped, others ran right through the light, and still others pulled off to the side of the intersection.

I finally made it through the intersection and thought about this unusual happening. It was as if God were showing me a visual picture of what it's like when a person is indecisive in her obedience to Him. We can't seek to follow God wholeheartedly if part of our heart is being pulled in a different direction. We can't pursue the radically obedient life and still continue to flirt with disobedience in certain areas of our life. We can't be both red and green toward God at the same time. It gets us nowhere. It's confusing. It's dangerous.

LYSA TERKEURST

Radically Obedient, Radically Blessed

Evening

· · · · · · · · ·

I have set before you life and death, blessing
and cursing; therefore choose life, that both
you and your descendants may live.

DEUTERONOMY 30:19

"No one can serve two masters; for either he
will hate the one and love the other, or else he
will be loyal to the one and despise the other.
You cannot serve God and mammon."

MATTHEW 6:24–27

The wisdom of this world is foolishness with God.

1 CORINTHIANS 3:19

OCTOBER 13

Making Emotions Our Allies

Emotions. Can you imagine a life without them? Sure, it may be easier, it may be less complicated, and it may be more efficient. But how dull, how colorless, how unexciting! Emotions are a gift from God. To refuse to recognize them severs us from living with the fullness that can be ours through Jesus Christ. . . .

Gaining self-discipline over our emotions does not mean repressing or ignoring them. Our emotions can be strong allies if we recognize them, work through what they mean to us, and then choose to act a certain way to bring about positive and healthy changes in our lives.

KATHY BABBITT

Habits of the Heart

"'You shall love the LORD your God with all your heart, with all your soul, with all your strength, and with all your mind,' and 'your neighbor as yourself.'"

LUKE 10:27

"Be angry, and do not sin"; do not let the sun go down on your wrath, nor give place to the devil.

EPHESIANS 4:26—27

Oh, sing to the LORD a new song!
For He has done marvelous things . . .
Shout joyfully to the LORD, all the earth;
Break forth in song, rejoice, and sing praises.

PSALM 98:1, 4

Morning

. . . .

Living Only for God

Before she met Jesus, Mary Magdalene was full of demons and sickness . . . unclean and unfit to be in decent company. Jesus didn't care what man thought of her. God had created her . . . and He was not about to give up on her. . . . She became His devoted follower and one of several women who travelled with Him and the apostles . . . [helping] them and [taking] care of them. It may not have seemed particularly appropriate for a single woman to be traveling with a group of men, but she didn't care what people thought. She lived only to serve God.

Mary Magdalene was the only woman at the cross who was not a member of Jesus' family. She witnessed His burial and was the first to see the resurrected Jesus. . . .

None of us is ever a lost cause to Jesus. If we seek Him with all our hearts, we will find Him. Even if our lives are so tangled and knotted that it seems nothing can undo all the craziness, God will take our lives . . . [and] give back our abundant lives full of purpose and meaning.

MICHELLE CLARK JENKINS

She Speaks

"I have come that they may have life, and
that they may have it more abundantly."

JOHN 10:10

"Do not worry, saying, 'What shall we eat?' or 'What
shall we drink?' or 'What shall we wear?' . . . But seek
first the kingdom of God and His righteousness,
and all these things shall be added to you."

MATTHEW 6:31—33

"Enter by the narrow gate; for wide is the gate
and broad is the way that leads to destruction,
and there are many who go in by it. Because
narrow is the gate and difficult is the way which
leads to life, and there are few who find it."

MATTHEW 7:13—14

Morning

. . . .

Your Beautiful Story

God longs to take the ashes from your life and turn them into beauty (Isaiah 61:3). He wants to help you embrace your story and grow from it. The only way you can do that is by letting Him have the master pen. With God writing your story, I can guarantee your life on earth won't turn out exactly as you planned, but there is no doubt you will have a heavenly "happily ever after."

If you already see beauty in your relationships and in yourself, God wants to make your story even more beautiful. Don't count yourself out of this!

So how does God create beautiful endings? First, He waits for us to hand Him the pen and then to ask Him to change the way our story is going. When we invite God to be our first and most important Dad, He edits the way we look at our problems. He edits the way we act in our relationships, the way we think of ourselves, and the way we think of Him. He makes our story beautiful.

JENNA LUCADO BISHOP

Redefining Beautiful

Evening

Let us run with endurance the race that
is set before us, looking unto Jesus, the
author and finisher of our faith.

HEBREWS 12:1—2

Trust in the LORD with all your heart,
And lean not on your own understanding;
In all your ways acknowledge Him,
And He shall direct your paths.

PROVERBS 3:5—6

A man's heart plans his way,
But the LORD directs his steps.

PROVERBS 16:9

Morning

. . . .

Trust God—and Get Busy!

Sometimes it's hard to explain hope—just what is hope, anyway? The cutest illustration of hope I've found is about a little boy who was standing at the foot of the escalator in a big department store, intently watching the handrail. He never took his eyes off the handrail as the escalator kept going around and around. A salesperson saw him and finally asked him if he was lost. The little fellow replied, "Nope. I'm just waiting for my chewing gum to come back."

If your face is in the dust, if you are in a wringer situation, be like the little boy waiting for his chewing gum to come back. Stand firm, be patient, and trust God. Then get busy with your life . . . there is work to do.

BARBARA JOHNSON

Stick a Geranium in Your Hat and Be Happy

Evening

· · · · · · · · ·

My brethren, count it all joy when you fall into various
trials, knowing that the testing of your faith produces
patience. But let patience have its perfect work, that
you may be perfect and complete, lacking nothing.

JAMES 1:2—4

My soul waits for the Lord
more than those who watch for the morning—
Yes, more than those who watch for the morning.

PSALM 130:6

Be patient, brethren, until the coming of the Lord.
See how the farmer waits for the precious fruit of
the earth, waiting patiently for it until it receives
the early and latter rain. You also be patient.

JAMES 5:7—8

Morning

. . . .

Good Days Ahead

You've been waiting for months for the release of the sequel to your favorite movie. Finally the time has come. You've waited in line, purchased your ticket, and found yourself a seat. You have an idea of what lies ahead, but you don't know exactly what's going to happen. All you know is that it's bound to be great.

That's the kind of expectation you can have about the life God has planned for you. He is more creative than any filmmaker, more amazing than any special effect, and more wonderful than any cinematic hero. You may not fully understand your story's beauty until you've reached the finale, but God promises every detail of the plot has been chosen for your ultimate good.

Living God's Way

Evening

. . . .

Now to Him who is able to do exceedingly
abundantly above all that we ask or think,
according to the power that works in us.

 EPHESIANS 3:20

I know the thoughts that I think toward you,
says the LORD, thoughts of peace and not of
evil, to give you a future and a hope.

JEREMIAH 29:11

In Your book they all were written,
The days fashioned for me,
When as yet there were none of them.

PSALM 139:16

The Joy of God's Plan for Your Life

No banners or bands welcomed Ruth when she arrived in Bethlehem. She had forsaken her familiar gods for the true God of Israel while living in Moab. . . . Yet, as a newcomer to faith and to fields of barley, Ruth found no manna or quail to feed her hunger, only fields to comb for small pickings. But Ruth did not glean unnoticed in a barley field in Bethlehem. God noticed her fresh faith in Him, her committed love for Naomi, and her willingness to glean instead of grumble, so He touched the heart of Boaz, who owned the field. How Boaz must have encouraged Ruth with his kindness and keen observations! God's wings—place of refuge for Ruth—hovered over Bethlehem, stirring up a harvest of blessings for an old and a young believer.

Will you believe that God sees you in your barley field, your place of difficult duty? God's blessings crop up even in barley fields!

JAN CARLBERG

The Hungry Heart

Evening

. . . .

[Naomi] arose with her daughters-in-law that
she might return from the country of Moab, for
she had heard . . . that the LORD had visited His
people by giving them bread. . . . Naomi said to
her two daughters-in-law, "Go, return each to her
mother's house. The LORD deal kindly with you, as
you have dealt with the dead and with me. . . ."
Ruth clung to [Naomi]. . . . Ruth said:
"Entreat me not to leave you,
Or to turn back from following after you;
For wherever you go, I will go;
And wherever you lodge, I will lodge;
Your people shall be my people,
And your God, my God."

RUTH 1:6, 8, 14–16

Whatever you do, do it heartily, as
to the Lord and not to men.

COLOSSIANS 3:23

Morning

. . . .

Freedom
Part 1

Once we have tasted [God's] grace, we are compelled to give our lives away because of it. Because God was that good to love us despite our sin. He was that merciful to give everything to make us right with Him. . . . And we long to follow a God like that. A God who is offering life and peace to those who obey Him. . . . He is even offering the means to obey and live a life for Him, through the Holy Spirit.

Obedience turns into a response to the love of our God rather than a duty to perform for Him.

We move from focusing on our need to fixing our eyes on the face of God. . . . [Nineteenth-century pastor] Andrew Murray . . . defines *humility* as being "fully occupied with God." We must move our eyes from our sin to God or we will stay stuck in our sin. His grace is why we can confess our sin and find freedom. We live in His grace and then we give His grace to everyone we encounter.

JENNIE ALLEN

Stuck

Evening

· · · · · · · · ·

God demonstrates His own love toward us, in that
while we were still sinners, Christ died for us.

ROMANS 5:8

By grace you have been saved through faith,
and that not of yourselves; it is the gift of God,
not of works, lest anyone should boast.

EPHESIANS 2:8—9

You shall love the LORD your God, and keep
His charge, His statutes, His judgments,
and His commandments always.

DEUTERONOMY 11:1

Morning

. . . .

Freedom
Part 2

Whatever attack or injustice I might perceive, . . . looking past my offender and at my God, is radical but the most powerful path to freedom.

Freedom is found in:

- allowing God to defend me, even if that means I don't see it until heaven; . . .
- embracing my faults, rather than proving my point;
- releasing others' perceptions and understandings of me, and holding on to God's, since He knows my heart; . . .
- embracing the death of my rights and desires, and receiving His will for me. . . .

Every one of our rights is a little cross that [Jesus] calls us to die on. . . . Why would I choose to die? Because life is not about me, because this world is not my home. . . .

And somehow, even though it feels like death, in laying down my rights I find freedom.

JENNIE ALLEN

Stuck

Let nothing be done through selfish ambition or
conceit, but in lowliness of mind let each esteem
others better than himself. Let each of you look
out not only for his own interests, but also for the
interests of others. Let this mind be in you which was
also in Christ Jesus, who, being in the form of God,
did not consider it robbery to be equal with God, but
made Himself of no reputation, taking the form of a
bondservant, and coming in the likeness of men.

PHILIPPIANS 2:3—7

Jesus said to His disciples, "If anyone desires to
come after Me, let him deny himself, and take up
his cross, and follow Me. For whoever desires to save
his life will lose it, but whoever loses his life for My
sake will find it. For what profit is it to a man if he
gains the whole world, and loses his own soul?"

MATTHEW 16:24—26

Our citizenship is in heaven.

PHILIPPIANS 3:20

Morning

. . . .

The Hope of Heaven

I know a place where there will be no more wars.

I know a place where there will never be another broken heart. . . .

I know a place where all our longings, all our desires, our all will be fulfilled and found in The One. . . .

If you asked me why I believe in God, in Jesus, and in the hope of a place called Heaven, it would be for this reason alone: God always wraps up what He started. From Adam and Eve to that final tear wiped from its beloved owner's face, God wraps up what He started. . . .

Can you imagine what it will be like to see the face of The One who has lavished us with His grace, rescued us with His Cross, and purposed us to live forever and forever with Him?

JULIE ANN BARNHILL

Exquisite Hope

Evening

· · · · · · · · ·

OCTOBER 22

"Rejoice because your names are written in heaven."

LUKE 10:20

Blessed be the God and Father of our Lord Jesus
Christ, who according to His abundant mercy has
begotten us again to a living hope through the
resurrection of Jesus Christ from the dead, to an
inheritance incorruptible and undefiled and that
does not fade away, reserved in heaven for you.

1 PETER 1:3—4

"In My Father's house are many mansions; if it
were not so, I would have told you. I go to prepare
a place for you. And if I go and prepare a place for
you, I will come again and receive you to Myself;
that where I am, there you may be also."

JOHN 14:2—3

609

In the Ring

It sure can feel like you're in the boxing ring of life sometimes. The bell goes off, and you go in swinging with all your might, doing the best you can, fighting the good fight. Then you receive a blow from out of nowhere. You're stunned! You can hardly breathe, and you aren't sure you'll ever rise again.

Well, whether you've lost a job, been diagnosed with an illness, or found yourself in some other difficult situation, God is there with you. In fact, He got into the ring the moment you did. He is right there ready to help you get back on your feet.

Isn't it great to know you're not out there taking on the world all by yourself? No matter how many blows the world delivers, God is with you—always and in all ways!

Your Promises from God Today

Evening

· · · · · · · · ·

The LORD preserves all who love Him,
But all the wicked He will destroy.

PSALM 145:20

Fear not, for I am with you;
Be not dismayed, for I am your God.
I will strengthen you,
Yes, I will help you,
I will uphold you with My righteous right hand.

ISAIAH 41:10

We are hard-pressed on every side, yet
not crushed; we are perplexed, but not
in despair; persecuted, but not forsaken;
struck down, but not destroyed.

2 CORINTHIANS 4:8—9

611

Identifying Goals

Whether we are sizing up our lives in total or confronting a specific decision, our important first questions must be, "Where do I want to go?" "What are my objectives?" "What, ultimately, do I want to accomplish?"

Identifying our objectives can be a complex task. Often there is more than one objective. For the Christian, the ultimate objective might be to best serve God with our abilities and talents, or to become more like Jesus. These are long range objectives, and they are of prime importance. Added to them may be other, short-term goals: to house or care for our families, to be good stewards of our finances, to finish a specific project or to mend a broken relationship. . . .

We human beings can be very clever at conning ourselves. We can rationalize—even spiritualize—almost anything. But, in the final analysis, what we think is most important is what we will choose, no matter what we tell ourselves or other people.

GLORIA GAITHER

Decisions

Evening

· · · · · · · · ·

Who can discern their own errors?
Forgive my hidden faults.
Keep your servant also from willful sins;
may they not rule over me.
Then I will be blameless,
innocent of great transgression.

PSALM 19:12–13 NIV

The humble He guides in justice,
And the humble He teaches His way.

PSALM 25:9

Commit your way to the LORD,
Trust also in Him.

PSALM 37:5

613

Paring Down Our Schedules

God is interested in the texture of our days. One thing I've come to accept is that some days are busier than others; if we choose to participate in life, we cannot avoid this ebb and flow. On the busy days, when urgency drives us and we lurch (late) from one event to the next, we can pray for time . . . and God will give us little corners to cut so we don't have to be so breathless. It also helps on the busy days to know that ebb days will return and that if we pray and pare down our schedules, we will not ultimately drown.

LESLIE WILLIAMS

Seduction of the Lesser Gods

Evening

. . . .

"Come to Me, all you who labor and are heavy
laden, and I will give you rest. Take My yoke upon
you and learn from Me, for I am gentle and lowly
in heart, and you will find rest for your souls."

MATTHEW 11:28–29

"Do not worry, saying, 'What shall we eat?' or 'What
shall we drink?' or 'What shall we wear?' For after
all these things the Gentiles seek. For your heavenly
Father knows that you need all these things. But seek
first the kingdom of God and His righteousness,
and all these things shall be added to you."

MATTHEW 6:31–33

"The Sabbath was made for man."

MARK 2:27

God's Purposes and Intentions

You ought to see how many half-finished drawings and paintings I have in my art studio. They are piled everywhere. I get an idea, render a few quick sketches, and then my attention gets diverted—perhaps a different art project was overdue or I was up against some other deadline. Occasionally, I get back to those sketches but, more than likely, they get thrown onto a pile in the corner.

Half-finished pastels. Almost-completed paintings. Not-quite-done watercolors. I have an idea I'll never place any of them back up on my art easel.

I am so relieved my Creator doesn't approach things as I do. God always finishes what He begins. He completes every purpose. He fulfills every intention. God has a long way to go in my life, and I'm grateful that He hasn't finished with me yet.

JONI EARECKSON TADA

Diamonds in the Dust

Evening

. . . .

Job answered the LORD and said: "I know that
You can do everything, and that no purpose
of Yours can be withheld from You."

JOB 42:1–2

The LORD of hosts has sworn, saying,
"Surely, as I have thought, so it shall come to pass,
And as I have purposed, so it shall stand."

ISAIAH 14:24

The LORD of hosts has purposed,
And who will annul it?
His hand is stretched out,
And who will turn it back?

ISAIAH 14:27

Morning

. . . .

God's Power for Us

A man from Australia bought a Rolls Royce in England and took it home with him. However, he neglected to find out the horsepower. He wrote to the manufacturer but received only the terse British reply, "Adequate!" The British firm believed that was all the owner of the car needed to know.

We don't need to know how God's power works; we only need to know that His power in us is available and wholly "adequate." Use it to its full advantage for God's kingdom!

JILL BRISCOE

Quiet Times with God

Evening

. . . .

He rules by His power forever; . . .
Oh, bless our God, you peoples!

PSALM 66:7–8

Be exalted, O LORD, in Your own strength!
We will sing and praise Your power.

PSALM 21:13

He has made the earth by His power;
He has established the world by His wisdom,
And stretched out the heaven by His understanding.

JEREMIAH 51:15

"Not by might nor by power, but by My Spirit,"
Says the LORD of hosts.

ZECHARIAH 4:6

OCTOBER 27

619

God Is Our Refuge

I once had an accident in my hometown. The police helped me and took me away by car. Whenever a policeman in Holland does anything, a report has to be submitted. So out came his notebook, and he asked my name. "Corrie ten Boom." He looked up in surprise and asked, "Are you a member of the Ten Boom family we arrested during the war?" "Yes, I am." During that time many good policemen were forced to work for the German Gestapo; they stayed in their positions to help political prisoners. The man said, "I'll never forget that night. I was on duty when the whole Ten Boom family and about forty friends were arrested because they had helped Jews. There was an atmosphere of celebration in our police station rather than a gathering of prisoners likely to die in prison and concentration camps. I often still tell of how your father took out his Bible and read Psalm 91 and then prayed so calmly."

Ten years later the policeman still remembered which psalm my father had read: "He is my refuge and my fortress" (Psalm 91:2 NIV).

CORRIE TEN BOOM

Messages of God's Abundance

Evening

· · · · · · · · ·

He who dwells in the secret place of the Most High
Shall abide under the shadow of the Almighty.
I will say of the LORD,
"He is my refuge and my fortress;
My God, in Him I will trust."

PSALM 91:1–2

The LORD also will be a refuge for the oppressed,
A refuge in times of trouble.

PSALM 9:9

In the shadow of Your wings I will make my refuge,
Until these calamities have passed by.

PSALM 57:1

621

God Has Your Back

What can people actually do to us? They can stain our reputations, but God fully knows all hearts. They can stand in the way of opportunity, but God opens doors that no man can close. They can steal our earthly goods, but God is our true treasure. They can restrict our physical freedom, but God's Spirit is unchained. They can hinder or take our jobs, but God is our Provider. They can even kill our body, but they cannot touch our souls.

So the next time we feel threatened by someone's words or ways, let us resist the fear of people by remembering these two truths:

1. The person that stands before us is human.
2. The One that stands behind us is God.

ALICIA BRITT CHOLE
Sitting in God's Sunshine

Evening

· · · · · · · ·

Help us, O God of our salvation,
For the glory of Your name;
And deliver us, and provide atonement for our sins,
For Your name's sake!

PSALM 79:9

Who provides food for the raven,
When its young ones cry to God,
And wander about for lack of food?

JOB 38:41

May He who supplies seed to the sower, and bread
for food, supply and multiply the seed you have sown
and increase the fruits of your righteousness.

2 CORINTHIANS 9:10

God's Might

First, imagine all the raindrops in the world. Then add all the snowflakes and hailstones, the fog and mists. Next, bring in all the creeks and ponds and puddles. Finally, add all the glaciers and snow packs, the streams and rivers, the wells and underground springs, and even all the lakes and the mammoth oceans. All the waters of the earth, added together—and God holds them in a single handful! Inconceivable!

Even if we limited our picture to just one of these bodies of water . . . the image is mind-boggling. . . .

We can't even begin to imagine what God is like: all our pictures are shockingly dazzling, and yet they don't even scratch the surface of the unutterable wonder of His inexpressible infinity. Why are we such blind fools in our presumptions that we do not trust this God who exercises His might on our behalf?

MARVA DAWN

To Walk and Not Faint

Evening

. . . .

Who has measured the waters
in the hollow of His hand,
Measured heaven with a span
And calculated the dust of the earth in a measure?

ISAIAH 40:12

Great is our Lord, and mighty in power;
His understanding is infinite.

PSALM 147:5

He gives power to the weak,
And to those who have no might He increases strength.

ISAIAH 40:29

Halloween Grace
Part 1

The last few verses of Genesis 3 have had a profound impact on my life. I used to read them as judgment, but now I see them as full of grace from a God who loves us fiercely. . . . I used to view brokenness as the bad news, but now because of the outrageous grace of God, I see it as a profound, breathtaking gift. . . .

Do you see grace in [Genesis 3:22–24]?

Can you imagine what would have happened if God had allowed our fallen First Parents to stay in the garden and eat from the Tree of Life? Yes, they would have lived forever—but forever broken. Eternally miserable. Wracked with guilt. Fearful. And empty—oh, so very empty. Their eternal "life" would become eternal hell, full of guilt and shame and bitterness and regret. . . .

Physical death, a gift of grace? Oh my, yes! . . .

I call this kind of grace "Halloween grace," because it wears an unanticipated costume.

SHEILA WALSH

God Loves Broken People

Evening

Then the LORD God said, "Behold, the man has
become like one of us in knowing good and evil.
Now, lest he reach out his hand and take also of the
tree of life and eat, and live forever—" therefore the
LORD God sent him out from the garden of Eden to
work the ground from which he was taken. He drove
out the man, and at the east of the garden of Eden
he placed the cherubim and a flaming sword that
turned every way to guard the way to the tree of life.

GENESIS 3:22—24 ESV

The LORD God is a sun and shield;
The LORD will give grace and glory;
No good thing will He withhold
From those who walk uprightly.
O LORD of hosts,
Blessed is the man who trusts in You!

PSALM 84:11—12

627

November

Make a joyful shout to the Lord, all you lands!
Serve the Lord with gladness;
Come before His presence with singing.

PSALM 100:1-2

Halloween Grace
Part 2

Not all grace looks like what we expected.

The apostle John said Jesus came to us from the Father, "full of grace and truth" (John 1:14, NIV). . . . [Jesus] always tells the truth. And He always comes with grace.

But the grace He brings can look *very* different from situation to situation. . . .

What does Halloween grace look like? . . . I can give you a few biblical examples:

- When God put Jacob's hip out of joint and left him with a permanent, painful limp . . .
- When Jesus caused a minor panic among the disciples by telling them to feed a hungry crowd . . .
- When three times the Lord refused Paul's request for healing

I don't know what sort of Halloween grace the Lord might have working in your life right now. But if you have placed your faith in Jesus, then Jesus lives within you—which means that grace and truth live there too.

SHEILA WALSH

God Loves Broken People

Evening

. . . .

As each one has received a gift, minister
it to one another, as good stewards
of the manifold grace of God.

1 PETER 4:10

A thorn in the flesh was given to me, a messenger
of Satan to buffet me, lest I be exalted above
measure. Concerning this thing I pleaded with
the Lord three times that it might depart from
me. And He said to me, "My grace is sufficient for
you, for My strength is made perfect in weakness."

2 CORINTHIANS 12:7—9

"For My thoughts are not your thoughts,
Nor are your ways My ways," says the LORD.
"For as the heavens are higher than the earth,
So are My ways higher than your ways,
And My thoughts than your thoughts."

ISAIAH 55:8—9

A Thankful Heart

You don't need a turkey to celebrate Thanksgiving. All you need is a reason. And God has given you more reasons to be thankful than He's created stars in the sky, so why wait?

Start with what you see—the clothes you're wearing, the food in the fridge, the beauty of a summer day. Then think about the people you love and how they've touched your life. Next, consider what God has given you that can't be held in your hands—things like hope, forgiveness, and your future home in heaven. Sit quietly as God brings to mind even more reasons to say thank you.

Stopping to say thanks will remind you of how big God is and how good your life is, no matter what kind of day you're having.

Living God's Way

Evening

· · · · · · · · ·

In everything give thanks; for this is the
will of God in Christ Jesus for you.

1 THESSALONIANS 5:18

Blessing and glory and wisdom,
Thanksgiving and honor and power and might,
Be to our God forever and ever.
Amen.

REVELATION 7:12

I will praise the name of God with a song,
And will magnify Him with thanksgiving.

PSALM 69:30

Morning

· · · · · · · · ·

God Is at Work

Read what God says to us through the prophet Isaiah:

"Forget about what's happened; don't keep going over old history. Be alert, be present. I'm about to do something brand-new. It's bursting out! Don't you see it? There it is! I'm making a road through the desert, rivers in the badlands." (43:18–19 MSG)

Today, what if you decided to turn and see God? What if you could see that everywhere God is, there is the fullness of His character and that He promises you a love that is big and deep and wide and high? He is doing a new thing with your future. He makes brand-new roads through the desert of your circumstances. His plans for you include more than you could ever imagine or hope for. The day has come for you to stop going over "old history." The future is bursting out in front of you. Turn and see. There has been a long, dark valley, but we are walking toward the mountain of God.

ANGELA THOMAS

My Single Mom Life

Evening

· · · · · · · · ·

May [you] be able to comprehend with all the saints
what is the width and length and depth and height—to
know the love of Christ which passes knowledge;
that you may be filled with all the fullness of God.
Now to [God] who is able to do exceedingly
abundantly above all that we ask or think,
according to the power that works in us, to
Him be glory in the church by Christ Jesus to
all generations, forever and ever. Amen.

EPHESIANS 3:18—21

"Prepare the way of the LORD;
Make straight in the desert
A highway for our God.
Every valley shall be exalted
And every mountain and hill brought low;
The crooked places shall be made straight
And the rough places smooth;
The glory of the LORD shall be revealed,
And all flesh shall see it together;
For the mouth of the LORD has spoken."

ISAIAH 40:3—5

NOVEMBER 3

Just for Today

Each day, a seed embraces the task placed before it. Today it might have to embrace the dark soil it has been pushed into. Tomorrow, it might be not resisting the water that makes it literally disintegrate and fall apart. And then in a week or two, a green shoot pushes up and out of the deep, dark, messy place. Eventually, the seed sprouts and reveals exactly what it was always meant to be. The seed's potential is unlocked and its purpose is revealed through embracing each and every circumstance God brought its way. . . .

So, just for today I will live this way. . . . I will not let the subtle influences of pride and thinking I know what is best for me overshadow my desire for more of God in my life. Today, I will believe with absolute certainty. Today, I will obey with complete surrender. Today, I will seek with complete abandon. For doing this is fulfilling the purpose for which I was created . . . not to bring myself glory by some great accomplishment but to bring God glory by making Him my greatest heart's desire.

LYSA TERKEURST

Becoming More Than a Good Bible Study Girl

This is the day the LORD has made;
We will rejoice and be glad in it.

PSALM 118:24

Do you not know that your body is the temple
of the Holy Spirit who is in you, whom you have
from God, and you are not your own? For you
were bought at a price; therefore glorify God in
your body and in your spirit, which are God's.

1 CORINTHIANS 6:19—20

Beware, brethren, lest there be in any of you an
evil heart of unbelief in departing from the living
God; but exhort one another daily, while it is
called "Today," lest any of you be hardened through
the deceitfulness of sin. For we have become
partakers of Christ if we hold the beginning of our
confidence steadfast to the end, while it is said:
"Today, if you will hear His voice,
Do not harden your hearts as in the rebellion."

HEBREWS 3:12—15

NOVEMBER 5

Deep Roots

In north Georgia where my family and I live, the landscape displays tall Georgia pine trees. While the stately tree is beautiful, during even the mildest storm our yards and streets are littered with tree limbs.

The landscape in south Georgia is different, though. Along the balmy coast stands the stately palm tree. This tree is not the least bit moved by the threat of strong winds. You see, the palm tree's trunk and deep root system allow it to bend but not break. It possesses great resistance and resilience, even in the fiercest storm.

When the Word of God is in you, you don't have to worry about life's storms. You can even lie down at night and rest peacefully, knowing that God is in control. Your heavenly Father will be up all night, so you, my friend, might as well get some sleep.

BABBIE MASON

Women of Faith Devotional Bible

Evening

· · · · · · · · · ·

I will both lie down in peace, and sleep;
For You alone, O LORD, make me dwell in safety.

PSALM 4:8

The LORD bless you and keep you;
The LORD make His face shine upon you,
And be gracious to you;
The LORD lift up His countenance upon you,
And give you peace.

NUMBERS 6:24—26

The LORD is my shepherd;
I shall not want.
He makes me to lie down in green pastures;
He leads me beside the still waters.
He restores my soul.

PSALM 23:1—3

Everlasting Hope

The Bible tells us, "Surely there is a future, and your hope will not be cut off" (Proverbs 23:18 NASB). Jesus reminds us, "Everything is possible for one who believes" (Mark 9:23 NIV). There are many stories in the Gospels of people putting their hope in the Lord Jesus Christ. First Timothy 4:10 (NIV) says, "That is why we labor and strive, because we have put our hope in the living God, who is the Savior of all people, and especially of those who believe."

God is our everlasting hope. When we feel as if we are drowning in a sea of despair, we know that we can call on Him, and He hears us. His answer might not be what we expect, but, when we hope in God, we know that He will faithfully provide exactly what we need.

A Charles Dickens Devotional

Through the LORD's mercies we are not consumed,

Because His compassions fail not.

They are new every morning;

Great is Your faithfulness.

"The LORD is my portion," says my soul,

"Therefore I hope in Him!"

LAMENTATIONS 3:22—24

Happy is he who has the God of Jacob for his help,

Whose hope is in the LORD his God,

Who made heaven and earth,

The sea, and all that is in them.

PSALM 146:5—6

Blessed be the God and Father of our Lord Jesus Christ, who according to His abundant mercy has begotten us again to a living hope through the resurrection of Jesus Christ from the dead, to an inheritance incorruptible and undefiled and that does not fade away, reserved in heaven for you.

1 PETER 1:3—4

Morning

. . . .

Say, "Thank You!"

The beach is a perfect setting to reignite our love for God—or, for some, to discover it for the first time.

How often do we say, "I love You" to the Lord? We know we love Him. We know He loves us. But how often do we say it with full and grateful hearts? As we're absorbing His creation . . . do we take a moment to snap a mental picture and remember to let Him know how much we love Him? . . .

God pursues. He listens. He understands. He reassures us. He keeps His promises. He provides. He gives good gifts. If any human being were to do this much for us, we'd most certainly let that person know.

So why not say "thank You" to the One who breathed us into existence?

MIRIAM DRENNAN
Devotions for the Beach

Evening

· · · · · · · · · ·

You shall love the LORD your God with all your heart,
with all your soul, and with all your strength.

DEUTERONOMY 6:5

I will love You, O LORD, my strength.
The LORD is my rock and my fortress and my deliverer;
My God, my strength, in whom I will trust.

PSALM 18:1—2

I will extol You, my God, O King;
And I will bless Your name forever and ever.
Every day I will bless You,
And I will praise Your name forever and ever.
Great is the LORD, and greatly to be praised;
And His greatness is unsearchable.

PSALM 145:1—3

Morning

. . . .

Calming a Noisy Head

It can get pretty noisy inside your head. When you start to realize how noisy it is and toss some worries on top of the pile you've already created there, it becomes overwhelming, practically deafening. What would it take for you to turn down the noise or change the station? God can help you find a more soothing serenade anytime you ask Him to do so.

It may not be surprising that you can't absorb all the noise and clamor that comes into your head. You're surrounded. Everywhere you turn, the world bombards you with endless noise. God reminds you that He has already overcome the noise of the world. He can bring you true peace.

Your Promises from God Today

Finally, brethren, whatever things are true,
whatever things are noble, whatever things are
just, whatever things are pure, whatever
things are lovely, whatever things are of good
report, if there is any virtue and if there is anything
praiseworthy—meditate on these things.

PHILIPPIANS 4:8

And do not be conformed to this world, but be
transformed by the renewing of your mind, that you
may prove what is that good and acceptable and perfect
will of God. For I say, through the grace given to me, to
everyone who is among you, not to think of himself more
highly than he ought to think, but to think soberly,
as God has dealt to each one a measure of faith.

ROMANS 12:2—3

"For My thoughts are not your thoughts,
Nor are your ways My ways," says the LORD.
"For as the heavens are higher than the earth,
So are My ways higher than your ways,
And My thoughts than your thoughts."

ISAIAH 55:8—9

645

Morning

. . . .

Contentment
Part 1

It's our nature to see things and desire them. People have been struggling with it since God created the world. If we continue to crave the next best thing, though, we'll never find contentment. If we find ourselves constantly wishing for and wanting more, perhaps we need to close the catalog and focus on all the things we have to be thankful for. There's no better way to readjust our perspective and move to a place where "I want that!" is referring to kindness, love, humility, and contentment.

When our focus is on being thankful, earthly treasures start to lose their importance. Suddenly our wish lists shrink, and we're a lot more appreciative of what we have. That doesn't mean we all move into cardboard boxes and start wearing potato sacks. The problem isn't in what we own or how much of it we have but in how we view those possessions. . . .

To be able to say that we are content no matter the circumstance is definitely a treasure that has great worth.

MARIAN PARSONS

Inspired You

Evening

· · · · · · · · ·

I have learned in whatever state I am, to be content.

PHILIPPIANS 4:11

"You shall not covet your neighbor's house; you
shall not covet your neighbor's wife, nor his male
servant, nor his female servant, nor his ox, nor his
donkey, nor anything that is your neighbor's."

EXODUS 20:17

"Do not lay up for yourselves treasures on earth,
where moth and rust destroy and where thieves
break in and steal; but lay up for yourselves treasures
in heaven, where neither moth nor rust destroys
and where thieves do not break in and steal."

MATTHEW 6:19—20

Morning

. . . .

Contentment
Part 2

What are some practical ways we can find contentment in our lives and in our homes?

- Be Thankful—Be thankful for everything in your life, even trials. We often grow the most in times of want and hardship. Turn complaints into gratitude—"I'm so thankful that pipe burst in my bathroom. It's giving me a perfect opportunity to practice patience and self-control." (Easier said than done, I know!)

- Serve—You can serve those less fortunate who are in your own backyard. Serving others brings joy that far outlasts any high attained from retail therapy.

- Give Generously—Someone, somewhere, always has less than you do. Sharing what you have with others is a great way to combat selfishness. Remember that giving isn't always about writing a check. You can give your time, gifts, talents, and resources as well.

MARIAN PARSONS

Inspired You

Evening

· · · · · · · · ·

Rejoice always, pray without ceasing, in
everything give thanks; for this is the
will of God in Christ Jesus for you.

1 THESSALONIANS 5:16—18

"Then the righteous will answer Him, saying,
'Lord, when did we see You hungry and feed You, or
thirsty and give You drink?' . . . And the King
will answer and say to them, 'Assuredly, I say
to you, inasmuch as you did it to one of the least
of these My brethren, you did it to Me.'"

MATTHEW 25:37, 40

He who has a generous eye will be blessed,
For he gives of his bread to the poor.

PROVERBS 22:9

Morning

. . . .

No Matter the Circumstances

No matter what our circumstances, you and I have a God-given reason to rejoice. . . . The God of the universe, who spoke everything into being and who created each of us, has called us to Himself. We are given purpose through our identification as His sons and daughters; we know that God is in control. Our primary job is to trust, believe, and follow Him closely, even when life does not feel rewarding, pleasant, or productive. Thanks to the nature and the character of God, growing closer and closer to Him will produce the natural response of worship.

Look for ways in your life to express joy and thankfulness, even amid trials, determine not to get bogged down by your present situation. God chooses to love us; we can, in turn, choose to be grateful with our hearts and our lips. Remember, we are saved for eternity. That is reason enough to rejoice!

A Jane Austen Devotional

Evening

· · · · · · · · · ·

Let all those rejoice who put their trust in You;
Let them ever shout for joy, because You defend them;
Let those also who love Your name
Be joyful in You.

PSALM 5:11

Oh, taste and see that the LORD is good;
Blessed is the man who trusts in Him!
Oh, fear the LORD, you His saints!
There is no want to those who fear Him.

PSALM 34:8—9

God has given us eternal life, and this life is in
His Son. He who has the Son has life; he who does
not have the Son of God does not have life.

1 JOHN 5:11—12

Morning

. . . .

Refreshed by Simplicity

There is something about baking bread that brings me back to earth from all the stresses of everyday modern life. Maybe it's kneading the dough, in all its simplicity and physicalness, that helps the most in relaxing me. Maybe it's the time required to let the bread rise that forces me temporarily to slow down. But whatever it is, these "back to earth days" and baking bread in general have become for me a safety zone where I can take some time and gain a perspective on what I'm doing. It is as though my feet get firmly placed again on earth, and the problems of yesterday begin to look solvable. Afterwards, that which looked hopeless no longer seems so impossible, and that which seemed complex appears less so in the light of a new day.

ELIZABETH SKOGLUND

Safety Zones

Evening

. . . .

The LORD your God in your midst,
The Mighty One, will save;
He will rejoice over you with gladness,
He will quiet you with His love,
He will rejoice over you with singing.

ZEPHANIAH 3:17

The LORD was not in the wind; and after the wind an
earthquake, but the LORD was not in the earthquake;
and after the earthquake a fire, but the LORD was not
in the fire; and after the fire a still small voice.

1 KINGS 19:11–12

Ask for the old paths, where the good way is,
And walk in it;
Then you will find rest for your souls.

JEREMIAH 6:16

653

Something Is Happening in Heaven

I know with all my heart that when I sing praises to God, something is happening in heaven, because my spirit gets relief, my emotions change from negative to positive, my mind feels inspired to think more wisely, my heart is guarded from the pain I might otherwise experience, my physical body relaxes, and I'm drawn into God's presence knowing His loving arms are wrapped around me in His safe and secure protection. . . .

Make a habit of praising God throughout your day and just see it if doesn't soothe your spirit's dryness with the oil of joy. Don't make it a one-time morning or bedtime deal. And don't wait until you get an answer to your prayers or a blessing from God before you praise Him. God is good all the time, and we need to praise Him all the time—whether or not we feel like it.

THELMA WELLS

Listen Up, Honey

Evening

. . . .

Those who sow in tears
Shall reap in joy.

PSALM 126:5

Though now you do not see Him, yet believing, you
rejoice with joy inexpressible and full of glory.

1 PETER 1:8

Praise the LORD!
Praise God in His sanctuary;
Praise Him in His mighty firmament!
Praise Him for His mighty acts;
Praise Him according to His excellent greatness!
Praise Him with the sound of the trumpet;
Praise Him with the lute and harp!
Praise Him with the timbrel and dance;
Praise Him with stringed instruments and flutes!
Praise Him with loud cymbals;
Praise Him with clashing cymbals!
Let everything that has breath praise the LORD.
Praise the LORD!

PSALM 150

Thirty People, Thirty Days

Choose thirty people in your life, and on each of the next thirty days, tell one of those listed that you love him or her and why. Don't overthink the task. You can call, e-mail, post to a Facebook page, or send a handwritten note. Pray for the people you choose before you connect with them, and allow God to reveal Scripture, thoughts, or ways you might bless them. You'll be surprised by how expressing your thanks and love will strengthen your relationships and immediately enrich the quality of your life.

More Than a Bucket List

Therefore I exhort first of all that supplications,
prayers, intercessions, and giving of
thanks be made for all men.

1 TIMOTHY 2:1

As each one has received a gift, minister
it to one another, as good stewards
of the manifold grace of God.

1 PETER 4:10

Be kindly affectionate to one another with brotherly
love, in honor giving preference to one another.

ROMANS 12:10

Morning

· · · · · · · ·

Holy Actions

On his second missionary journey, Paul along with Silas had several "waits" before they were led by the Spirit—in a very roundabout way—to go to Philippi. . . . I wonder what his expectations were. A city-wide evangelistic crusade? Media coverage? . . .

We would no doubt be safe in assuming there were some *disappointments* upon arrival. Instead of an impressive crowd . . . they met a handful of women by a river and shared their faith. Then a slave girl followed them. Paul cast a demon out of her in Jesus' name, . . . and the rest is history. Paul and Silas were jailed, stripped, and severely beaten, with their feet fastened in stocks.

If I had been there, my deepest longing would have been to escape and leave! Not Paul. His longing was a deep yearning to preach the gospel and lead people to Jesus Christ. . . . Thus, his action of praying and singing hymns to God in the middle of his imprisonment led to another holy action. Instead of escaping after the earthquake, he stayed and led the jailer to Christ.

CAROL KENT

Secret Longings of the Heart

Evening

. . . .

My heart is steadfast, O God,
My heart is steadfast;
I will sing and give praise.

PSALM 57:7

I will sing praise to Your name forever.

PSALM 61:8

In everything give thanks; for this is the
will of God in Christ Jesus for you.

1 THESSALONIANS 5:18

Morning

. . . .

Sit Still

Often in life we get so caught up in what we don't have that we forget to be grateful for what we do have. We get so busy asking and seeking and begging and pursuing that we never take time out simply to be. To sit still and contemplate just how marvelous life really is, and how blessed we are to be a part of it. Wherever you are in your journey, take a minute to stop and give thanks for life. For love. For family. For faith. For friends. For another day. For the chance to get it right, no matter how many times you've gotten it wrong before. No matter what you think you're lacking today, there is so much to be thankful for . . . so much beauty and hope and magic and opportunity and life right in front of you. Don't let another second pass you by without pausing to appreciate it.

MANDY HALE

The Single Woman

Evening

. . . .

One of [the ten lepers], when he saw that he was
healed, returned, and with a loud voice glorified
God, and fell down on his face at [Jesus'] feet,
giving Him thanks. And he was a Samaritan.
So Jesus answered and said, "Were there
not ten cleansed? But where are the nine?
Were there not any found who returned to
give glory to God except this foreigner?"

LUKE 17:15—18

Every good gift and every perfect gift is from
above, and comes down from the Father of lights.

JAMES 1:17

Be still, and know that I am God. . . .
The LORD of hosts is with us;
The God of Jacob is our refuge.

PSALM 46:10—11

661

Grace: Getting What We Don't Deserve

One of my dear friends, Elizabeth, came from an exceptionally broken and destructive family—a family whose experience included prison, abuse, and suicide. At sixteen years old, Elizabeth cried in anger to her mentor, "This is not fair! I don't deserve this family, this life!"

Most of us would agree with this outcry from a sweet teenage girl subjected to such a life. But Elizabeth's mentor knew Jesus, and . . . replied, "You're right. You don't deserve this life. You deserve hell and death, and so do I. But God's gracious love for us provided a Savior who took our sins and died for them. He didn't deserve death, and we don't deserve life. It is God's grace that we have life at all."

And with that simple word God moved Elizabeth's perspective from disappointment to hope. Her view of her life shifted from anger to gratitude. Elizabeth found freedom from the bitterness that was beginning to mark her life. Today, Elizabeth is one of the most joyful and encouraging people I know.

JENNIE ALLEN

Stuck

Evening

· · · · · · · · ·

Have mercy upon me, O God,

According to Your lovingkindness;

According to the multitude of Your tender mercies,

Blot out my transgressions.

Wash me thoroughly from my iniquity,

And cleanse me from my sin.

For I acknowledge my transgressions,

And my sin is always before me.

PSALM 51:1–3

The wages of sin is death, but the gift of

God is eternal life in Christ Jesus our Lord.

ROMANS 6:23

Shall we indeed accept good from God,

and shall we not accept adversity?

JOB 2:10

For Your name's sake, O LORD,

Pardon my iniquity, for it is great.

PSALM 25:11

A Heart of Praise

For every action there is an equal but opposite reaction. This is Sir Isaac Newton's Third Law of Motion and a basic principle of physics. Does it apply in the spiritual realm?

God freely gives us His mercy: an *action*. And what is our *reaction* to this action? Praise—and may it be equal to the weight of His mercy in our lives!

It is God's very nature to give His children mercy and grace—but not because we deserve it. "His mercy endures forever"—and forever is a long time. There is no expiration date. Why does God do this for us? Simply because He loves us.

God sends a sunrise every morning, He listens when we talk, and He gave us His only Son. . . . How can we react to God's infinitely gracious actions? With our praises. By worshiping Him with all our heart, soul, mind, and strength. No, that reaction can never equal God's generosity; thankfully, He is more concerned about our hearts than about the laws of physics.

JACK COUNTRYMAN
The Hope of Christmas

Evening

. . . .

Praise the LORD!
Oh, give thanks to the LORD, for He is good!
For His mercy endures forever.
Who can utter the mighty acts of the LORD?
Who can declare all His praise?
Blessed are those who keep justice,
And he who does righteousness at all times!

PSALM 106:1–3

I will extol You, my God, O King;
And I will bless Your name forever and ever.
Every day I will bless You,
And I will praise Your name forever and ever.
Great is the LORD, and greatly to be praised;
And His greatness is unsearchable.
One generation shall praise Your works to another,
And shall declare Your mighty acts.

PSALM 145:1—4

Morning

. . . .

Live a Life
That Sings

Oliver Wendell Holmes observed that the average person goes to his grave with his music still in him. Maybe that silent song in you is clamoring to get out. Perhaps you have a heart for adoption or a whole new career in mind. Perhaps you dream of performing, fixing your marriage, or mustering up the courage to found a nonprofit.

What's the song that your heart quietly hums? What's the passion that's filling your spirit? What's keeping you quiet?

Write down five things you need to do today to take that song from inside your heart and out into the world.

More Than a Bucket List

Evening

· · · · · · · ·

Shout joyfully to the LORD, all the earth;
Break forth in song, rejoice, and sing praises.

PSALM 98:4

Behold, I will do a new thing,
Now it shall spring forth;
Shall you not know it?

ISAIAH 43:19

Oh come, let us sing to the LORD!
Let us shout joyfully to the Rock of our salvation.

PSALM 95:1

Morning

. . . .

Keeping Your Heart Soft Toward God

How do we maintain a green-tree heart, especially through a blustery winter? . . .

Choose gratitude. . . . [W]e can in the midst of [our losses] thank God for who he is. . . .

Learn to be content not to have all our questions answered. . . .

Choose gratitude. Actively being grateful is a conscious choice at first, then with ongoing attentiveness, a habit.

Avoid giving easy answers to hard questions that the hurting ask. . . . It's okay to admit you don't know what God is up to. . . . When I'm hurting, I'd rather have a friend who stands and weeps with me . . . than one who rattles off his or her thin take on the universe.

Choose gratitude. Yes, I know I'm repeating myself, but in the midst of hardship, gratitude is the first thing we discard and the first thing we need to recover . . .

Ask God to give you a new song. . . . [And] choose gratitude. Yes, I said it again.

PATSY CLAIRMONT

Stained Glass Hearts

Rejoice with those who rejoice, and
weep with those who weep.

ROMANS 12:15

Oh, the depth of the riches both of the wisdom
and knowledge of God! How unsearchable are His
judgments and His ways past finding out!

ROMANS 11:33

I waited patiently for the LORD;
And He inclined to me,
And heard my cry.
He also brought me up out of a horrible pit,
Out of the miry clay,
And set my feet upon a rock,
And established my steps.
He has put a new song in my mouth—
Praise to our God;
Many will see it and fear,
And will trust in the LORD.

PSALM 40:1—3

New Every Morning

God's Word assures us that His mercies are new every morning. This is a wonderful promise, but only because we know tomorrow is but hours away. . . . Because of its slow rotation and rapid movement around the Sun, the interval between one sunrise and the next on Mercury is 176 Earth days! . . . The strangest place for calendars and clocks in the solar system is on the planet Venus. The Venusian day is longer than its year. It laps completely around the Sun before it can even spin once on its axis. . . .

If we have a bad day, a new and different one will begin in just a few hours. Our weeks, months, seasons, and years also put rhythms into our lives that help us focus and be fruitful. And as faithful as the sunrise, God is faithful in the execution of His promises to us. Though we have trials in the midst of them He delivers, protects, strengthens, and provides. "Weeping may tarry for the night, but joy comes with the morning" (Psalm 30:5 ESV).

KEVIN HARTNETT

The Heavens

The heavens declare the glory of God,
and the sky above proclaims his handiwork.
Day to day pours out speech,
and night to night reveals knowledge.
There is no speech, nor are there words,
whose voice is not heard.

PSALM 19:1 3 ESV

But this I call to mind,
and therefore I have hope:
The steadfast love of the LORD never ceases;
his mercies never come to an end;
they are new every morning;
great is your faithfulness.

LAMENTATIONS 3:21—23 ESV

Sing praise to the LORD, you saints of His,
And give thanks at the remembrance of His holy name.
For His anger is but for a moment,
His favor is for life;
Weeping may endure for a night,
But joy comes in the morning.

PSALM 30:4—5

Morning

. . . .

Thank You— and Yes!

[Dag Hammarskjöld, who served as United Nations Secretary General from 1953 to 1961,] wrote this line to God:

For everything that has been, thank you, and for everything that will be, yes! . . .

Hammarskjöld cultivated the twin habits of thankfulness and joyful submission to God's agenda—whatever that agenda might entail.

Could we do the same thing? As we long for Paradise while living in this broken world, could we, like Dag Hammarskjöld, give thanks to God for what He already has done even as we make up our minds to joyfully accept whatever He brings next? I don't claim it's easy. Although Hammarskjöld had no way of knowing it, he said yes to the plane crash that ultimately took his life. If you could interview him now, would he still say yes? Having read much of what he wrote about his spiritual journey, I believe he would. He trusted not in *what* he might be saying yes to, but rather he trusted the One to whom he said yes!

SHEILA WALSH

God Loves Broken People

Evening

. . . .

[Jesus] knelt down and prayed, saying, "Father, if it is
Your will, take this cup away from Me; nevertheless
not My will, but Yours, be done." Then an angel
appeared to Him from heaven, strengthening Him.

LUKE 22:41—43

As for God, His way is perfect;
The word of the LORD is proven;
He is a shield to all who trust in Him.
For who is God, except the LORD?
And who is a rock, except our God?

PSALM 18:30—31

In God is my salvation and my glory;
The rock of my strength,
And my refuge, is in God.
Trust in Him at all times, you people;
Pour out your heart before Him;
God is a refuge for us.

PSALM 62:7—8

673

Morning

. . . .

A Lesson in Trust

English sparrows. They're worth barely a penny, Jesus said so. Yet of the world's nine thousand bird species, Jesus singled out the least-noticed and most insignificant of birds to make a point.

If God takes time to keep tabs on every sparrow—who it is, where it's going, whether or not its needs are being met—then surely He keeps special tabs on you. Intimately. Personally. And with every detail in mind.

The Bible may point to eagles to underscore courage and power, and it may talk about doves as symbols of peace and contentment. But God's Word reserves sparrows to teach a lesson about trust. Just as God tenderly cares for a tiny bird, even making note of when it is harmed, or when it falls to the ground, He gently reminds you that He is worthy of your greatest trust, your deepest confidence.

JONI EARECKSON TADA

Diamonds in the Dust

"Are not two sparrows sold for a copper coin? And not one of them falls to the ground apart from your Father's will."

MATTHEW 10:29

[Cast] all your care upon Him, for He cares for you.

1 PETER 5:7

Bless the LORD, O my soul,
And forget not all His benefits:
Who forgives all your iniquities,
Who heals all your diseases,
Who redeems your life from destruction,
Who crowns you with lovingkindness
and tender mercies.

PSALM 103:2—4

Morning

. . . .

Remember the Bad

Mom taught me that Thanksgiving is about remembering to focus on good things, even in the presence of bad things. This gospel tutorial on thanksgiving goes a step further. It illustrates how remembering bad things can actually bring divine goodness and mercy into sharper focus. In the context of being *lost*, being *found* is more wondrous. In the context of being *persecuted*, finding *acceptance* is more precious. In the context of being *sick*, being *healed* is more miraculous. So I don't want to forget all the mistake chapters in my story, such as when I ran away from my senses and into the arms of a young man who only wanted one thing from me, and it certainly wasn't my undying love. Or when I stopped praying for my stepfather to come to faith in Christ, because he could be so difficult that I wasn't sure grace was big enough to include him. Apart from Jesus, I'm a faithless prodigal waiting to happen. But I'm learning that the roots of gratitude grow deepest in the sober soil of remembering how hopeless my life is without God.

LISA HARPER

Stumbling into Grace

Evening

. . . .

Remember, O LORD, Your tender mercies
and Your lovingkindnesses,
For they are from of old.
Do not remember the sins of my youth, nor my transgressions;
According to Your mercy remember me,
For Your goodness' sake, O LORD.

PSALM 25:6—7

Oh, give thanks to the LORD!
Call upon His name;
Make known His deeds among the peoples!
Sing to Him, sing psalms to Him;
Talk of all His wondrous works!

1 CHRONICLES 16:8—9

"The father said to his servants, 'Bring out the best
robe and put it on him, and put a ring on his hand
and sandals on his feet. And bring the fatted calf
here and kill it, and let us eat and be merry; for
this my son was dead and is alive again; he was
lost and is found.' And they began to be merry."

LUKE 15:22—24

677

Morning

. . . .

Learning to Be Content

Contentment is a stranger to most of us. Like octopi we spend ourselves gathering goods, scrambling after promotions, and juggling to include one more handful. Eventually, we collapse with full hands and empty hearts.

The wealthiest man, King Solomon, probably wrote, "Better one handful with tranquility than two handfuls with toil and chasing after the wind" (Ecclesiastes 4:6 NIV). Perhaps we would do well to listen.

What could you do with one free hand?

A content heart keeps a free hand.

JAN CARLBERG
The Hungry Heart

Evening

Now godliness with contentment is great gain.
For we brought nothing into this world, and it is
certain we can carry nothing out. And having food
and clothing, with these we shall be content.

1 TIMOTHY 6:6—8

"Do not worry, saying, 'What shall we eat?' or 'What
shall we drink?' or 'What shall we wear?' For after
all these things the Gentiles seek. For your heavenly
Father knows that you need all these things. But seek
first the kingdom of God and His righteousness,
and all these things shall be added to you."

MATTHEW 6:31—33

I observed all the work and ambition
motivated by envy. What a waste! Smoke.
And spitting into the wind. . . .
One handful of peaceful repose
Is better than two fistfuls of worried work—
More spitting into the wind.

ECCLESIASTES 4:4, 6 MSG

Morning

· · · · · · · · ·

Proof of God's Love

God's love is not squeamish. It voluntarily handles the least presentable parts of our lives. The last thing we want God to see in us is the first thing He kneels down to touch with His strong healing hands.

The most convincing proof of God's love toward us is found in His cleansing, not in His gifting. Jesus showed His love for the Twelve not by giving them gifts or increasing their abilities or endowing them with more authority but by washing them clean.

We need look no further than our own dirty feet and cleansed hearts to begin each morning confident of God's love for us!

ALICIA BRITT CHOLE

Sitting in God's Sunshine

Then great multitudes came to [Jesus], having with
them the lame, blind, mute, maimed, and many
others; and they laid them down at Jesus' feet,
and He healed them. So the multitude marveled
when they saw the mute speaking, the maimed
made whole, the lame walking, and the blind
seeing; and they glorified the God of Israel.

MATTHEW 15:30–31

Show me Your ways, O LORD;
Teach me Your paths.
Lead me in Your truth and teach me,
For You are the God of my salvation;
On You I wait all the day.

PSALM 25:4–5

Delight yourself in the LORD.

ISAIAH 58:14

Every day I will bless You,
And I will praise Your name forever and ever.

PSALM 145:2

Our Good God

The sea, the sand, the rocks, the birds, the fish, the waves—God made every detail. Every molecule, every grain, every crevice, feather, and gill—He made the entire scene you're taking in [when you are at the beach]. And then, He went even further: He gave us His Son, who provided a way for us to live forever. . . .

Yes, God may have provided for the way for us to have eternal life, but what about the groceries we need for this week? the unexpected bill? . . . day to-day details that nag and aggravate and weigh us down? How would He have time to deal with that and—better yet—why would He care?

He who loves us with a steadfast love is as into the details of our lives as He was when He created the details of bringing together the water and the sandy shores.

So have you given your details to God to figure out? . . . When we hand them over to Him, something wonderful happens. . . . He's got this plan. . . . And we'll see that it . . . is good.

MIRIAM DRENNAN
Devotions for the Beach

Thus says the LORD,
Who created the heavens,
Who is God,
Who formed the earth and made it,
Who has established it,
Who did not create it in vain,
Who formed it to be inhabited:
"I am the LORD, and there is no other."

ISAIAH 45:18

Be anxious for nothing, but in everything by
prayer and supplication, with thanksgiving,
let your requests be made known to God.

PHILIPPIANS 4:6

The hand of our God is upon all
those for good who seek Him.

EZRA 8:22

Morning

· · · · · · · · ·

Following the Golden Rule

The benefit of following Jesus' golden rule isn't that we will automatically be rewarded for our efforts, but that we come to see and understand and appreciate the way Christ first loved us. It is almost too much to comprehend when we are living for ourselves; but if we choose to obey Christ's command in doing unto others, we begin to walk in step with Him and His thoughts become our own.

Do you desire a life free from the expectation that you'll always be treated well or get the outcome you think you deserve? Are your thoughts sometimes consumed by life's unfairness? Focus on treating others as Jesus would. Your reward will be a newfound, heartfelt appreciation for how much He loves you.

A Jane Austen Devotional

"Whatever you want men to do to you, do also to
them, for this is the Law and the Prophets."

MATTHEW 7:12

Who shall separate us from the love of
Christ? Shall tribulation, or distress, or persecution,
or famine, or nakedness, or peril, or sword? . . . I
am persuaded that neither death nor life, nor angels
nor principalities nor powers, nor things present
nor things to come, nor height nor depth, nor any
other created thing, shall be able to separate us from
the love of God which is in Christ Jesus our Lord.

ROMANS 8:35, 38—39

"If you were of the world, the world would love
its own. Yet because you are not of the world, but
I chose you out of the world, therefore the world
hates you. Remember the word that I said to you,
'A servant is not greater than his master.' If they
persecuted Me, they will also persecute you."

JOHN 15:19—20

God's Plan for the Whole World

I think God's hope and plan for us is pretty simple to figure out. For those who resonate with formulas, here it is: add your whole life, your loves, your passions, and your interests together with what God said He wants us to be about, and that's your answer. If you want to know the answer to the bigger question—what's God's plan for the whole world?—buckle up: it's us.

We're God's plan, and we always have been. We aren't just supposed to be observers, listeners, or have a bunch of opinions. . . . Tell me about the God you love; tell me about what He has inspired uniquely in you; tell me about what you're going to do about it, and a plan for your life will be pretty easy to figure out from there. I guess what I'm saying is that most of us don't get an audible plan for our lives. It's better than that. We get to be God's plan for the whole world by pointing people toward Him.

BOB GOFF

Love Does

Evening

. . . .

"A new commandment I give to you, that you love one another; as I have loved you, that you also love one another. By this all will know that you are My disciples, if you have love for one another."

JOHN 13:34—35

In this is love, not that we loved God, but that He loved us and sent His Son to be the propitiation for our sins. Beloved, if God so loved us, we also ought to love one another. No one has seen God at any time. If we love one another, God abides in us, and His love has been perfected in us.

1 JOHN 4:10—12

[The believers] continued steadfastly in the apostles' doctrine and fellowship, in the breaking of bread, and in prayers. . . . All who believed were together, and had all things in common, and sold their possessions and goods, and divided them among all, as anyone had need.

ACTS 2:42, 44—45

Morning

Your Perfect Mission

Are you willing to do whatever God asks of you?

I love the story about a little boy and his grandfather walking along the beach after a storm. Hundreds of starfish had washed up on the shore and the little boy was busy picking them up and throwing them back into the water. The grandfather asked the little boy why he was doing this because he could not possibly save them all. The little boy looked at the starfish in his hand and replied, "No, but I can make a difference in the life of this one." You'll never know what kind of difference you can make until you surrender your desires for your life to the perfect mission God has for you.

In order to get a clear vision of your mission, you must understand three important biblical truths. You are a new *creation* of God, who has been *chosen* by God, to fulfill a *calling* from God. God has uniquely equipped you to answer the calling of your mission.

LYSA TERKEURST

Living Life on Purpose

This commandment we have from Him: that he
who loves God must love his brother also.

1 JOHN 4:21

"If anyone serves Me, let him follow Me; and
where I am, there My servant will be also.
If anyone serves Me, him My Father will honor."

JOHN 12:26

Since we are receiving a kingdom which cannot be
shaken, let us have grace, by which we may serve
God acceptably with reverence and godly fear.

HEBREWS 12:28

December

Behold, I bring you good tidings of great joy which will be to all people. For there is born to you this day in the city of David a Savior, who is Christ the Lord.

LUKE 2:10–11

Morning

. . . .

The Joy of God's Word

Food makes me happy. Some of my favorite food memories include . . .

- Dipping Oreo cookies in milk at midnight with Daddy.
- Mom and I stuffing ourselves with Senora Martinez's tacos in Progresso, Mexico.
- Eating approximately 972 Shanghai dumplings in Shanghai, China, with my husband.
- Crisp mornings of fresh scrambled eggs (lots of salt) with my son.

For me, good company enriches any meal. And Jeremiah felt the same way. His favorite food was God's Word in the company of . . . God Himself!

What an incredible banquet God gives us through His Word. . . . Food may make us happy for a moment. God's Word gives us joy for a lifetime!

ALICIA BRITT CHOLE

Pure Joy

Evening

. . . .

Your words were found, and I ate them, And
Your word was to me the joy and rejoicing of my heart;
For I am called by Your name, O LORD God of hosts.

JEREMIAH 15:16

And I will delight myself in Your commandments,
Which I love.

PSALM 119:47

How sweet are Your words to my taste,
Sweeter than honey to my mouth!

PSALM 119:103

DECEMBER 2

Children Are a Blessing

Flip through prime time's sitcoms, and it won't take you long to absorb what our culture thinks about children: they drain your love life, your wallet, your independence, your patience, and your sanity. If there's one message you probably won't get, it's the one God wants you to hear: children are a blessing.

At the very heart of God is relationship. Father, Son, and Holy Spirit have eternally and blissfully enjoyed togetherness. Perfect relationship overflows with love. And at the beginning of time, love overflowed in creation. God created man in His image. He created us to be like Him.

When God gives us children, He gives us some of His best gifts. He gives us the gift of relationship. He gives us the opportunity to know one of life's deepest joys: serving another with selfless love. And He gives us a taste of the delight there is in creation, of the delight there is in seeing another made in one's image.

CATHERINE CLAIRE LARSON

Waiting in Wonder

Like arrows in the hand of a warrior,
So are the children of one's youth.
Happy is the man who has his quiver full of them.

PSALM 127:4—5

Hear, O Israel: The LORD our God, the LORD is one! You
shall love the LORD your God with all your heart,
with all your soul, and with all your strength.
And these words which I command you today shall
be in your heart. You shall teach them diligently
to your children, and shall talk of them when
you sit in your house, when you walk by the way,
when you lie down, and when you rise up.

DEUTERONOMY 6:4—7

Jesus called them to Him and said, "Let the
little children come to Me, and do not forbid them;
for of such is the kingdom of God. Assuredly, I say
to you, whoever does not receive the kingdom of
God as a little child will by no means enter it."

LUKE 18:16—17

The Most Important Thing

I would like to believe that I have a heart like Mary's. One that stops to listen to God whenever the opportunity arises. I am afraid, though, that I probably come much closer to being like Martha. Hurrying about, planning, preparing, fixing, organizing, making lists, and worrying. Will it all get done? "It" can be my grocery shopping, the laundry, the meal for the potluck supper later on, the Bible study lesson, my latest craft project, etc., etc., etc.

These thoughts can overtake me during church, while having my devotions, in the midst of prayer— almost anywhere, the still, small voice of the Lord can get drowned out. . . .

I still believe that the planning, preparing, fixing, and organizing is important. I believe it is important to God. After all, I am trying to be faithful to do well the tasks He has set before me. I need to remember, though, that by far the most important thing I can do is to take the time to sit at Jesus' feet and really listen.

MARY HAMPTON

Tea and Inspiration

Evening

· · · · · · · · ·

Now it happened as [Jesus and His disciples] went
that He entered a certain village; and a certain woman
named Martha welcomed Him into her house. And
she had a sister called Mary, who also sat at Jesus' feet
and heard His word. But Martha was distracted with
much serving, and she approached Him and said,
"Lord, do You not care that my sister has left me to
serve alone? Therefore tell her to help me."
And Jesus answered and said to her, "Martha, Martha,
you are worried and troubled about many things.
But one thing is needed, and Mary has chosen that
good part, which will not be taken away from her."

LUKE 10:38—42

The LORD passed by [Elijah], and a great and
strong wind tore into the mountains and
broke the rocks in pieces before the LORD,
but the LORD was not in the wind; and after
the wind an earthquake, but the LORD was not
in the earthquake; and after the earthquake
a fire, but the LORD was not in the fire;
and after the fire a still small voice.

1 KINGS 19:11—12

Taking Action

Faith is trust that's put to the test. It acts on what it believes to be true. If you have faith that your best friend can keep a secret, you'll risk being honest about your biggest mistakes and regrets. If you have faith that God really loves you, you'll risk making a decision you believe will honor Him, even if it promises not to be easy.

Faith grows the more you use it, the more you try it on for size. Give God the chance to grow yours. Act on what He's asked you to do. Risk moving out of your comfort level. Do more than believe with your heart. Move forward in faith, wherever He's leading you to go.

Living God's Way

Evening

· · · · · · · · · ·

What does it profit, my brethren, if someone says he
has faith but does not have works? Can faith save him?

JAMES 2:14

By faith Abraham obeyed when he was called to
go out to the place which he would receive as an
inheritance. And he went out, not knowing where
he was going. By faith he dwelt in the land of
promise as in a foreign country, dwelling in tents
with Isaac and Jacob, the heirs with him of the
same promise; for he waited for the city which has
foundations, whose builder and maker is God.

HEBREWS 11:8—10

We walk by faith, not by sight.

2 CORINTHIANS 5:7

Morning

. . . .

Clinging to Our Unchanging God

Christmas dinner had long since ended and we were still visiting around the table.

"Why don't we go sit in the living room?" I suggested.

My sister-in-law quipped, "Because we fear change!"

We erupted in laughter over such a dramatic answer to my simple question. But there was a bit of truth in her humor.

Most of us feel a tinge of reluctance when it comes to change, because it means we must take a risk and release some of our control. . . .

We wrap ourselves around what we know and love and are reluctant to release. But if we cling to God's Word, then we are more willing to take risks in this life because we realize that we're made for adventure.

JENNIFER ROTHSCHILD

Lessons I Learned in the Dark

Evening

· · · · · · · · ·

Jesus Christ is the same yesterday, today, and forever.

HEBREWS 13:8

Every good gift and every perfect gift is from above,
and comes down from the Father of lights, with
whom there is no variation or shadow of turning.

JAMES 1:17

He is the living God,
And steadfast forever;
His kingdom is the one which shall not be destroyed,
And His dominion shall endure to the end.
He delivers and rescues,
And He works signs and wonders
In heaven and on earth,
Who has delivered Daniel from the power of the lions.

DANIEL 6:26—27

On a Dark Winter's Night . . .

If we are afraid, we should turn on the light. . . .

Turn on the light of God's Word. "For God has not given us a spirit of fear, but of power and of love and of a sound mind" (2 Timothy 1:7).

Turn on the light of faith. And risk taking the next step out of your self-imposed limitations. What do you have to lose? Fear? Go for it.

Turn on the light of your mind by believing what you can't see, which is that God holds you safely in His care no matter where you are and that He is unfolding His plan for your life. You can't travel outside His presence.

Turn on the light of friendship. Let others know when you are uneasy and then allow them to stand with you. It will comfort you, strengthen you, and keep you humble. We weren't meant to go this life alone.

PATSY CLAIRMONT

I Second That Emotion

More to be desired are [the Lord's law
and His judgments] than gold,
Yea, than much fine gold;
Sweeter also than honey and the honeycomb.
Moreover by them Your servant is warned,
And in keeping them there is great reward.

PSALM 19:10–11

"I am the light of the world. He who follows Me shall
not walk in darkness, but have the light of life."

JOHN 8:12

You were once darkness, but now you are light in the
Lord. Walk as children of light (for the fruit of the
Spirit is in all goodness, righteousness, and truth).

EPHESIANS 5:8—9

Morning

. . . .

Something You Need

Sabbath. I love the way the word sounds. It resonates deep within me, and it's something I know I need.

Sabbath is the time set aside for my soul to breathe. Really breathe. So much of my daily life is inhaling, inhaling, inhaling—taking so much in and holding my breath hoping I can manage it all. But we can't just inhale. We must also exhale—letting it all out before God and establishing a healthier rhythm by which to live.

Even though I'm not very good at it, I love that God wants us to rest. I love that He's not just interested in what we do but also in making sure we don't get burned out. God reminds us to Sabbath so we'll have new rhythm in our everday. . . .

When I'm coming unglued, I feel like I've lost my joy. So, anything that will help me find joy, especially soul-resonating "joy in the LORD," sounds so good. My soul exhales with one long "Yes!"

LYSA TERKEURST

Unglued

Remember the Sabbath day, to keep it holy. Six days
you shall labor and do all your work, but the seventh
day is the Sabbath of the LORD your God. In it you shall
do no work: you, nor your son, nor your daughter,
nor your male servant, nor your female servant,
nor your cattle, nor your stranger who is within
your gates. For in six days the LORD made the
heavens and the earth, the sea, and all that is in
them, and rested the seventh day. Therefore
the LORD blessed the Sabbath day and hallowed it.

EXODUS 20:8–11

"If you turn away your foot from the Sabbath,
From doing your pleasure on My holy day,
And call the Sabbath a delight,
The holy day of the LORD honorable,
And shall honor Him, not doing your own ways,
Nor finding your own pleasure,
Nor speaking your own words,
Then you shall delight yourself in the LORD."

ISAIAH 58:13–14

Morning

. . . .

A Messy Life

It would be great if life went along in a smooth, neat, and orderly kind of way. That would mean that the rules were the same for everyone, that kindness was the order of the day, and that promises were always kept. Of course, it isn't like that!

Life makes us jump right into the mud and the chaos. With no warning we're up to our knees in the trenches. We wonder if we'll get out of the muck or if we can wade out on our own. The answer is we need help, God's help. Only He can truly clean up the messes.

God has an exquisite clean-up crew. He's ready to come in and give you a new heart and mind and renew a right and bright spirit within you.

Your Promises from God Today

Evening

· · · · · · · · ·

Many are the afflictions of the righteous,
But the Lord delivers him out of them all.
He guards all his bones;
Not one of them is broken.

PSALM 34:19—20

And be renewed in the spirit of your mind, and that
you put on the new man which was created according
to God, in true righteousness and holiness.

EPHESIANS 4:23–24

And we know that all things work together
for good to those who love God, to those who
are the called according to His purpose.

ROMANS 8:28

707

Morning

· · · · · · · · ·

DECEMBER 9

The Perfect Gift

Are you on a quest for that perfect gift for someone you love? If so, you are undoubtedly considering personality, likes, dislikes—and your budget. You may be spending hours, if not days, going from website to website, store to store, sale to sale, trying to find exactly what you're looking for. Why ? Because you love that person. Because of the joy you'll experience when you give the gift!

God already has the perfect gift for you, and it is . . . grace. It is a perfect fit. No exchanges are necessary. And it is unique: it comes only from Him through Jesus. In His grace, God accepts you not for who you are or what you have or haven't done, but because of who He is and what He allowed Jesus to do on the cross on your behalf. Yes, it's the perfect gift.

JACK COUNTRYMAN

The Hope of Christmas

By grace you have been saved through faith,
and that not of yourselves; it is the gift of God,
not of works, lest anyone should boast. For
we are His workmanship, created in Christ
Jesus for good works, which God prepared
beforehand that we should walk in them.

EPHESIANS 2:8—10

For the LORD God is a sun and shield;
The LORD will give grace and glory;
No good thing will He withhold
From those who walk uprightly.
O LORD of hosts,
Blessed is the man who trusts in You!

PSALM 84:11—12

Let each one give as he purposes in his
heart, not grudgingly or of necessity;
for God loves a cheerful giver.

2 CORINTHIANS 9:7

Morning

. . . .

Marvel!

Think how many . . . countless moments [of wonder] there must have been among the people of Nazareth and Judea who were witnesses to the first Christmas: A virgin conceiving a child? Angels in the sky? The Messiah born in a stable, sleeping in a manger? Royal officials from the east appearing and worshiping this baby? Prophets in the temple declaring that Jesus was the Messiah, never having seen Him before? King Herod killing scores of male babies? What did it all mean?

What would you and I have thought if we had been living there when the first Christmas took place? How many nights would we have sat up late talking about these events? . . . I can assure you we would have exhibited far more wonder than we do today. . . .

Spend some time reflecting on the wonders of the true Christmas story. Raise the questions, study the Scriptures, give thanks for what you know, and pray about what you don't.

Wonder and marvel at what God has done.

DAVID JEREMIAH

The 12 Ways of Christmas

Evening

. . . .

Suddenly there was with the angel a multitude
of the heavenly host praising God and saying:
"Glory to God in the highest,
And on earth peace, goodwill toward men!"
So it was, when the angels had gone away from
them into heaven, that the shepherds said
to one another, "Let us now go to Bethlehem
and see this thing that has come to pass,
which the Lord has made known to us."

LUKE 2:13–15

Now when [the shepherds] had seen [the Christ
child], they made widely known the saying which
was told them concerning this Child. And all those
who heard it marveled at those things which were
told them by the shepherds. But Mary kept all
these things and pondered them in her heart.

LUKE 2:17–19

Uncommon Faith

From all appearances, Mary was an ordinary girl living in a one-stoplight town—when an amazing moment revealed both her extraordinary character and her uncommon faith in her unseen and ever-faithful God. Believing the angel's outrageous claim that she would give birth to God's Son and completely trusting that the Almighty would enable her to walk that path, Mary yielded her life—her very body—to her Creator. Despite the cost to her, despite the public shame and her derailed dreams, Mary was a model of humble and willing submission to the Lord's plans. . . .

Mary was upset by the angel's sudden and glorious appearance, so after he greeted her, Gabriel said, "Do not be afraid" (Luke 1:30). Somewhat reassured, Mary listened, asked a few questions, and then set an example of godly submission and trust: "I am the Lord's servant. May it be to me as you have said" (v. 38).

May we follow the example of this one chosen by God.

JACK COUNTRYMAN
The Hope of Christmas

Evening

. . . .

Now in the sixth month the angel Gabriel was
sent by God to a city of Galilee named Nazareth,
to a virgin betrothed to a man whose name was
Joseph, of the house of David. The virgin's name
was Mary. And having come in, the angel said
to her, "Rejoice, highly favored one, the LORD is
with you; blessed are you among women!"
But when she saw him, she was troubled at his
saying, and considered what manner of greeting
this was. Then the angel said to her, "Do not be
afraid, Mary, for you have found favor with God.
And behold, you will conceive in your womb and
bring forth a son, and shall call His name JESUS."

LUKE 1:26–31

When Elizabeth heard the greeting of [her
cousin] Mary, the baby leaped in her womb. And
Elizabeth was filled with the Holy Spirit, and she
exclaimed with a loud cry, "Blessed are you among
women, and blessed is the fruit of your womb!"

LUKE 1:41–42 ESV

DECEMBER 12

Needing One Another

Women can understand and affirm each other on a feminine level, which can strengthen and encourage us. Think of the strength Jesus' mother, Mary, and her cousin, Elizabeth, brought to each other during their pregnancies and the births of Jesus and John the Baptist. God gave each of them a task that neither of them could fully comprehend. He gave them wonderful, supportive husbands, but He also gave them each other. They must have giggled with delight behind closed doors as they shared each other's joy and marveled over God choosing them to take part in the most wonderful miracle of all time. They must have also encouraged each other's faith. . . .

That's what we women do for each other, and that is why we need each other.

GAYLE HAGGARD

A Life Embraced

Two are better than one,
Because they have a good reward for their labor.
For if they fall, one will lift up his companion.
But woe to him who is alone when he falls,
For he has no one to help him up.

ECCLESIASTES 4:9–10

"Whoever does the will of My Father in heaven
is My brother and sister and mother."

MATTHEW 12:50

For as the body is one and has many members,
but all the members of that one body, being
many, are one body, so also is Christ. For by one
Spirit we were all baptized into one body.

1 CORINTHIANS 12:12–13

DECEMBER 13

The Ultimate Gift

When we open our gifts at Christmas, we might be thrilled . . . or mildly pleased . . . or even, on occasion, disappointed, but at the end of the day, we're the same person we were before the gifts. Such is not the case when we receive God's Gift. . . .

- We are forgiven. . . . Your sins are paid for. . . . You have the receipt in your hand, written in the very blood of the One who paid the price. . . .
- We are adopted into [Jesus'] family and given citizenship in His kingdom. . . . with all the privileges.
- We receive the Gift of [Jesus'] Holy Spirit to live with us. . . . He will guide and counsel and protect and empower us.
- We are given God's peace. Because of our sin, we were enemies of God. . . . Christ died to take enemies and make them friends.

Jesus is the ultimate Gift ever given because of His effect on us!

LANCE WUBBELS

Jesus, the Ultimate Gift

The wages of sin is death, but the gift of
God is eternal life in Christ Jesus our Lord.

ROMANS 6:23

When the fullness of the time had come, God sent
forth His Son, born of a woman, born under the
law, to redeem those who were under the law, that
we might receive the adoption as sons. And because
you are sons, God has sent forth the Spirit of His
Son into your hearts, crying out, "Abba, Father!"

GALATIANS 4:4–6

Having been justified by faith, we have peace
with God through our Lord Jesus Christ.

ROMANS 5:1

Morning

. . . .

Let Them Know You Care

The blessings that come from reaching out to others cannot be overestimated. I learn this anew every year around Christmas. We usually have several dozen families who have lost a loved one during the year, either from AIDS, suicide, or some other tragedy. So over the years I have started around December 14 . . . and I set aside everything else and start telephoning the families who have experienced a loss.

Usually when I get them on the phone it takes a minute for them to connect *me* with the person who writes the books and sends them newsletters. Then they call another person to the phone, and soon every phone in the house has a family member talking. They appreciate that someone cared enough to remember their loss at holiday time. Their reaction proves the truth of that adage:

People don't care how much you know.

They just need to know you *care*.

BARBARA JOHNSON

I'm So Glad You Told Me What I Didn't Wanna Hear

Evening

· · · · · · · · · ·

"A new commandment I give to you, that you love
one another; as I have loved you, that you also love
one another. By this all will know that you are
My disciples, if you have love for one another."

JOHN 13:34—35

"Whoever desires to be first among you, let
him be your slave—just as the Son of Man
did not come to be served, but to serve, and
to give His life a ransom for many."

MATTHEW 20:27—28

You, brethren, have been called to liberty; only
do not use liberty as an opportunity for the
flesh, but through love serve one another.

GALATIANS 5:13

719

Letting Go of Worry

Worry can be a real waste of precious time. It does nothing but deplete our energy and steal moments that we can never recover or reclaim.

Furthermore, time spent worrying is time *not* spent trusting God. We would be putting our energy to much better use if we chose to pray! The Bible tells us, "Don't worry about anything; instead, pray about everything" (Philippians 4:6 NLT).

So the next time you are burdened by worry, choose to give those anxious thoughts to God. Let Him carry that burden. He longs to do so. You simply need to ask Him—as Holocaust survivor Corrie ten Boom knew: "Any concern too small to be turned into a prayer is too small to be made into a burden."

A Jane Austen Devotional

Evening

. . . .

"Do not worry about your life, what you will eat
or what you will drink; nor about your body,
what you will put on. Is not life more than food
and the body more than clothing? Look at the
birds of the air, for they neither sow nor reap nor
gather into barns; yet your heavenly Father feeds
them. Are you not of more value than they?"

MATTHEW 6:25—26

"Can all your worries add a single moment to your
life? And why worry about your clothing? Look at
the lilies of the field and how they grow. They don't
work or make their clothing, yet Solomon in all his
glory was not dressed as beautifully as they are."

MATTHEW 6:27—29 NLT

The Happiest People on Earth

Joy is found in Christ's presence.

At the Feast of Passover, after giving commandments to His disciples, Jesus said, "These things I have spoken to you, that My joy may remain in you, and that your joy may be full" (John 15:11). The Bible tells us that in "[God's] presence is fullness of joy" (Psalm 16:11). God's Word also instructs us to worship Him joyfully: "Make a joyful shout to God, all the earth!" (Psalm 66:1) and "Break forth in song, rejoice, and sing praises" (Psalm 98:4).

Our worship does not always have to be solemn or solitary. Sometimes it is right to sing, shout, laugh, and praise God. Jesus said that when the Word of God is in our hearts, we receive it with joy (Luke 8:13). God our Father is the Creator of happiness, so delight yourself in Him. As Christians, we should be the happiest people on Earth! Joy is good for us. Laugh, fill your heart with gladness, rejoice in the Lord, and be happy.

A Charles Dickens Devotional

A merry heart does good, like medicine.

PROVERBS 17:22

Rejoice in the Lord always. Again I will say, rejoice!

PHILIPPIANS 4:4

Give unto the LORD the glory due to His name;
Worship the LORD in the beauty of holiness.

PSALM 29:2

Rejoice always, pray without ceasing, in
everything give thanks; for this is the
will of God in Christ Jesus for you.

1 THESSALONIANS 5:16—18

Morning

. . . .

Resting on the Sabbath

So the week has been overwhelming? You want a sanitized house. Your family deserves nutritious meals. Your job is demanding (whether you are an office slave or a house-hold servant!). You would like to take an art course, write a poem, create a garden, maybe take a trip. . . .

"I can't do it all!" you screamed above the hiss of the shower over and over when you were alone half a blissful moment.

Of course, you can't. Don't you think God knew that? That's why He created Sundays. Now the helter-skelter existence will commence anew on Monday. But maybe you can face life a day at a time if you use Sunday wisely—breathing in God in big, big doses.

JUNE MASTERS BACHER

The Quiet Heart

Then God blessed the seventh day and
sanctified it, because in it He rested from all
His work which God had created and made.

GENESIS 2:3

For so the LORD said to me,
"I will take My rest,
And I will look from My dwelling place
Like clear heat in sunshine,
Like a cloud of dew in the heat of harvest."

ISAIAH 18:4

And remember that you were a slave in the
land of Egypt, and the LORD your God brought
you out from there by a mighty hand and by an
outstretched arm; therefore the LORD your God
commanded you to keep the Sabbath day.

DEUTERONOMY 5:15

Morning

. . . .

Listen for Your Name

Stars are first mentioned in the Bible in Genesis. Genesis 1:16 tells us that God created the stars. When God made His covenant with Abram, He told Abram to look up at the stars. He said, "Count the stars if you are able to number them. . . . So shall your descendants be" (15:5). The best-known star in the Bible is the star that appeared at Christ's birth: "Wise men from the East came to Jerusalem, saying, 'Where is He who has been born King of the Jews? For we have seen His star . . . and have come to worship Him'" (Matthew 2:1-2). "They departed; and behold, the star . . . went before them, till it came and stood over where the young Child was. When they saw the star, they rejoiced with exceedingly great joy" (vv. 9-10).

Today we gaze at stars and wonder what lies beyond them. . . . We can only wonder. Scientists estimate there are more than ten billion trillion stars; yet, there is a God who calls each one by name (Psalm 147:4). That same God loves you and calls you by name.

A Charles Dickens Devotional

[The LORD] counts the number of the stars;
He calls them all by name.

PSALM 147:4

"Are not five sparrows sold for two copper coins? And
not one of them is forgotten before God. But the very
hairs of your head are all numbered. Do not fear
therefore; you are of more value than many sparrows."

LUKE 12:6—7

"The sheep hear [the good shepherd's] voice;
and he calls his own sheep by name and leads
them out. And when he brings out his own
sheep, he goes before them; and the sheep
follow him, for they know his voice."

JOHN 10:3—4

Morning

. . . .

Mary's Example

Mary was not a feeble girl, weak and without spunk, imagination, or initiative. Subsequent action proves that. But she was meek. Never confuse weak with meek. She was meek as Moses was meek—strong enough and holy enough to recognize her place under God. Thoughts of what people would say, what Joseph her fiancé would say, or how she would ever convince them that she had not been unfaithful were instantly set aside. "Here I am, the Lord's handmaid," she said. "I will accept whatever He gives me." . . .

The angel left her, the account says. Back he flies, past Mars, Jupiter, Saturn, Uranus, beyond the Southern Cross and the Milky Way. . . .

Gabriel, too, had obeyed. He delivered the message. He brought back a message: on that planet, in Galilee, in a town called Nazareth, in the house to which God had sent him, the girl named Mary had said yes.

ELISABETH ELLIOT
On Asking God Why

Evening

· · · · · · · · ·

And he came and dwelt in a city called Nazareth,
that it might be fulfilled which was spoken by
the prophets, "He shall be called a Nazarene."

MATTHEW 2:23

[Mary's cousin Elizabeth] spoke out with a
loud voice and said, "Blessed are you among
women, and blessed is the fruit of your
womb! But why is this granted to me, that the
mother of my Lord should come to me?"

LUKE 1:42—43

My soul magnifies the Lord,
And my spirit has rejoiced in God my Savior.
For He has regarded the lowly state of His maidservant;
For behold, henceforth all generations will call me blessed.
For He who is mighty has done great things for me.

LUKE 1:46—49

Morning

. . . .

God Hears; God Acts

We are used to hearing promises that are too good to be true. But we aren't at all used to promises being delivered by an angel of the Lord. Neither was Mary.

This young girl was going about her daily duties when suddenly the angel Gabriel came calling. As if his appearance weren't surprising enough, his announcement made his remarkable presence pale in comparison. *She* was blessed among women? She, who had never been with a man, would conceive a son? And had Gabriel really said to call this miracle baby "the Son of God"?

The answer to these questions was yes, and Gabriel sealed his announcement with this black-and-white, matter-of-fact statement: "With God nothing will be impossible" (Luke 1:37).

What situation in your life seems impossible? What physical circumstances, what state of the heart, what relationship seems beyond repair and even beyond hope?

Keep calling out to the One for whom nothing is impossible.

Evening

Did you know that your cousin Elizabeth
conceived a son, old as she is? Everyone called
her barren, and here she is six months pregnant!
Nothing, you see, is impossible with God.

LUKE 1:36—37 MSG

While [Joseph] was trying to figure a way out [of
his engagement to Mary that would not disgrace
her], he had a dream. God's angel spoke in the
dream: "Joseph, son of David, don't hesitate to get
married. Mary's pregnancy is Spirit-conceived.
God's Holy Spirit has made her pregnant. She
will bring a son to birth, and when she does,
you, Joseph, will name him Jesus—'God saves'—
because he will save his people from their sins."

MATTHEW 1:20—21 MSG

Give ear, O LORD, to my prayer;
And attend to the voice of my supplications.
In the day of my trouble I will call upon You,
For You will answer me.

PSALM 86:6—7

731

Morning

· · · · · · · · ·

A Holy Interruption

Here comes Gabriel to us, interrupting our common labors. . . .

And this to our hearing hearts is what he says:

"Your Savior is born. Your Savior is here and very near. Nevermore shall you be ignorant of God and Gods' deep love for you, because I will give you signs for finding that love. Look, he is a baby, wrapped in plain baby clothing, lying in the humblest of homes, a manger. . . . Glory to God in the highest of heavens! And peace to the people with whom he is pleased!"

And who are these people? With whom does the good Lord choose to take his pleasures?

The shepherds.

The plain and nameless—whose every name the Lord knows very well.

You.

And me.

Merry Christmas.

WALTER WANGERIN JR.

Preparing for Jesus

There were sheepherders camping in the neighborhood. They had set night watches over their sheep. Suddenly, God's angel stood among them and God's glory blazed around them. They were terrified. The angel said, "Don't be afraid. I'm here to announce a great and joyful event that is meant for everybody, worldwide: A Savior has just been born in David's town, a Savior who is Messiah and Master. This is what you're to look for: a baby wrapped in a blanket and lying in a manger."

LUKE 2:8—12 MSG

"For God so loved the world that He gave His only begotten Son, that whoever believes in Him should not perish but have everlasting life."

JOHN 3:16

We speak the wisdom of God in a mystery, the hidden wisdom which God ordained before the ages for our glory, which none of the rulers of this age knew; for had they known, they would not have crucified the Lord of glory.

1 CORINTHIANS 2:7—8

A Gift for Every Day of the Year

Every day we witness miracles that we know no human could perform—miracles like being able to breathe, walk, talk, move, see, think, taste, and touch. Evidence of God's presence and power is all around us in the universe—the sun, the stars, the birth of each new day. And yet, like Jesus' disciples of old, we continue to search for peace outside of Him, even when He is with us moment by moment on our journey. We sometimes ask the same question the disciples did: "Who is this?" (Mark 4:41 NIV).

Well, let's unwrap the gift He is to us.

He's someone we can pray to.
He knows what we need before we ask.
He keeps His promises.
He's our example.
He understands our tears.
He's always near.

THELMA WELLS
Extravagant Grace

Evening

· · · · · · · · ·

"When you pray, do not use vain repetitions as the heathen do. For they think that they will be heard for their many words. Therefore do not be like them. For your Father knows the things you have need of before you ask Him."

MATTHEW 6:7—8

So when [Jesus] had washed [His disciples'] feet, taken His garments, and sat down again, He said to them, "Do you know what I have done to you? You call me Teacher and Lord, and you say well, for so I am. If I then, your Lord and Teacher, have washed your feet, you also ought to wash one another's feet. For I have given you an example, that you should do as I have done to you."

JOHN 13:12—15

You number my wanderings;
Put my tears into Your bottle;
Are they not in Your book?
When I cry out to You,
Then my enemies will turn back;
This I know, because God is for me.

PSALM 56:8—9

735

Morning

. . . .

The Gift of Jesus

No one has ever come close to defining the fullness of what the gift of Jesus Christ means. All of the Church's most thoughtful scholars and theologians have never been able to unfold to us "the mystery of godliness," which the apostle Paul states is "great" (1 Timothy 3:16). How does one possibly put into words what it means for a living man to be able to state, "I and my Father are one" (John 10:30)?

Ignatius of Antioch, an early Church Father, wrote to the church at Ephesus and said this of Jesus:

VERY FLESH, YET SPIRIT TOO:

UNCREATED, AND YET BORN;

GOD AND MAN IN ONE AGREED,

VERY LIFE-IN-DEATH INDEED.

FRUIT OF GOD AND MARY'S SEED.

AT ONCE IMPASSIBLE AND TORN

BY PAIN AND SUFFERING HERE BELOW;

JESUS CHRIST, WHOM AS OUR LORD WE KNOW.

LANCE WUBBELS

Jesus, the Ultimate Gift

Evening

. . . .

Beloved, let us love one another, for love is of God; and everyone who loves is born of God and knows God. . . . In this is love, not that we loved God, but that He loved us and sent His Son to be the propitiation for our sins. Beloved, if God so loved us, we also ought to love one another. . . . And we have seen and testify that the Father has sent the Son as Savior of the world. Whoever confesses that Jesus is the Son of God, God abides in him, and he in God.

1 JOHN 4:7, 10—11, 14—15

The angel answered [Mary] and said to her, "The Holy Spirit will come upon you, and the power of the Highest will overshadow you; therefore, also, that Holy One who is to be born will be called the Son of God."

LUKE 1:35

"God with Us"

Three simple words contain the fullness of the Christmas story:

God with us.

Yet who would be so brazen as to claim he or she comprehends the meaning of those words? Who can explain this miracle that transcends all other miracles? How does the infinite omnipotent, self-existent One, co-equal with God the Father and the Holy Spirit, join Himself with our human nature? How does the uncreated Creator of the heavens and earth become a part of His very own creation?

In Christmas, we celebrate the astonishing, phenomenal generosity and love of God—the marvel and mystery of God loving us so much that He chose to become one of us. Into the midst of the world's problems and pain, the invisible and transcendent God came near in the touchable form of His only Son. The Eternal One stepped into time!

LANCE WUBBELS

Jesus, the Ultimate Gift

Evening

· · · · · · · · ·

Christ Jesus, who, being in the form of God, did not consider it robbery to be equal with God, but made Himself of no reputation, taking the form of a bondservant, and coming in the likeness of men. And being found in appearance as a man, He humbled Himself and became obedient to the point of death, even the death of the cross. Therefore God also has highly exalted Him and given Him the name which is above every name, that at the name of Jesus every knee should bow, of those in heaven, and of those on earth, and of those under the earth, and that every tongue should confess that Jesus Christ is Lord, to the glory of God the Father.

PHILIPPIANS 2:5–11

Pondering Christmas

The best Christmas moments are the quiet ones, and the best reflection of Christmas takes place in the mirror of our own hearts.

One verse in the Bible tells us exactly how to celebrate Christmas, and who better than Mary herself to set the example? Luke 2:19 says, "But Mary kept all these things and pondered them in her heart."

Pondering is a word worth pondering. According to the dictionary, it means "to weigh in the mind, to think about, to reflect on." This describes a biblical pattern, for the psalmist wrote: "Reflect in your heart and be still. . . . I will reflect on all You have done and meditate on Your actions. . . . I reflect on the work of Your hands" (Psalm 4:4; 77:12; 143:5 HCSB).

"Sober reflection is good for the heart," says Ecclesiastes 7:3 (NET). . . .

How wonderful to reflect on the timeless story of Jesus, keeping it in mind and pondering these things in your heart.

DAVID JEREMIAH
The 12 Ways of Christmas

Evening

· · · · · · · · ·

So they ran into town, and eventually they found Mary
and Joseph and the baby lying in the feeding trough.
After they saw the baby, they spread the story of what
they had experienced and what had been said to them
about this child. Everyone who heard their story
couldn't stop thinking about its meaning.
Mary, too, pondered all of these events,
treasuring each memory in her heart.
The shepherds returned to their flocks, praising God
for all they had seen and heard, and they glorified
God for the way the experience had unfolded just
as the heavenly messenger had predicted.

LUKE 2:16—20 THE VOICE

I will remember the works of the LORD;
Surely I will remember Your wonders of old.
I will also meditate on all Your work,
And talk of Your deeds.
Your way, O God, is in the sanctuary;
Who is so great a God as our God?
You are the God who does wonders.

PSALM 77:11—14

Morning

. . . .

The Savior Has Come!

The verb *Epiphainein* means in Greek "to show forth, display." . . .

Epiphany celebrates the "manifestation" in this human child of His deep divinity. It shines forth like a flood of light, and "all flesh . . . sees it together!" . . .

Jesus, wholly human; Jesus, God among *us*, this place and this day—Jesus *is* the light of our lives and of the world.

No longer need we pray, *Come.*

He has come. . . .

Upon us the favor of God, the same favor God shed upon Mary, rests and increases. . . .

Jesus is in us now. Therefore:

> The strength and the wisdom of God,
> The grace and the joy of our Lord Jesus Christ,
> The life and the light of His salvation
> Be with you all
> Now and forever.
> Amen.

WALTER WANGERIN JR.

Preparing for Jesus

Evening

. . . .

The people who walked in darkness
Have seen a great light;
Those who dwelt in the land of the shadow of death,
Upon them a light has shined. . . .
For unto us a Child is born,
Unto us a Son is given;
And the government will be upon His shoulder.
And His name will be called
Wonderful, Counselor, Mighty God,
Everlasting Father, Prince of Peace.

ISAIAH 9:2, 6

"I am the light of the world. He who follows Me shall
not walk in darkness, but have the light of life."

JOHN 8:12

Devoted—and Blessed

Anna was a blessed woman indeed. She had the unique honor of being in the presence of the infant Jesus and knowing who He was and why He had come into the world. But it was no accident that Anna was chosen by God to be introduced to His only Son.

After Anna's husband died only seven years after their marriage . . . Anna devoted herself to God and never left the temple. She had no life apart from Him. She fasted and prayed without ceasing and prayed over those who came into the temple. (There are some things that only happen with fasting and praying.) Anna set herself apart with her steadfast faith that God would show up in that place, and He did literally! . . . She [had] asked that God would let her live long enough to see the Savior come into the world! God heard her prayer, saw her heart for Him, and gave her what her heart desired.

When we surrender our lives to God, He will reveal Himself by bringing us face-to-face with His Son, Jesus.

MICHELLE CLARK JENKINS

She Speaks

Evening

. . . .

Now there was one, Anna, a prophetess, the daughter
of Phanuel, of the tribe of Asher. She was of a great
age, and had lived with a husband seven years from
her virginity; and this woman was a widow of about
eighty-four years, who did not depart from the
temple, but served God with fastings and prayers
night and day. And coming in that instant she
gave thanks to the Lord, and spoke of Him to all
those who looked for redemption in Jerusalem.

LUKE 2:36—38

Hear, O LORD, when I cry with my voice!
Have mercy also upon me, and answer me.
When You said, "Seek My face,"
My heart said to You, "Your face, LORD, I will seek."

PSALM 27:7—8

"Blessed are the eyes which see the things you
see; for I tell you that many prophets and kings have
desired to see what you see, and have not seen it, and
to hear what you hear, and have not heard it."

LUKE 10:23—24

745

His Grace Is Sufficient

Whether I choose to believe it or not, if I am [God's] child, the Truth is that "His grace is sufficient for me." His grace is sufficient for every moment, every circumstance, every detail, every need, and every failure of my life.

When I'm exhausted . . . *His grace is sufficient for me.* . . .

When I don't know which direction to go . . . *His grace is sufficient for me.*

When my heart is breaking . . . *His grace is sufficient for me.*

What do you need God's grace for? Wayward children? Aching body? No money in the bank? . . . Church going through a split? Desperately lonely? . . .

Fill in the blank. Whatever your story, whatever your situation, right now, *His grace is sufficient for me.* His divine resources are available to meet your need—no matter how great. That's the Truth. And the Truth will set you free. . . .

Your heavenly Father will never lead you anywhere that His grace will not sustain you.

NANCY LEIGH DEMOSS

Lies Women Believe

Evening

I [Paul] pleaded with the Lord three times that
[this thorn in my flesh] might depart from me.
And He said to me, "My grace is sufficient for you,
for My strength is made perfect in weakness."

2 CORINTHIANS 12:8—9

"If you abide in My word, you are My disciples
indeed. And you shall know the truth,
and the truth shall make you free."
[The Jews who heard Jesus say this] answered
Him, "We are Abraham's descendants,
and have never been in bondage to anyone.
How can You say, 'You will be made free'?"
Jesus answered them, "Most assuredly, I say to
you, whoever commits sin is a slave of sin. And
a slave does not abide in the house forever, but a
son abides forever. Therefore if the Son
makes you free, you shall be free indeed."

JOHN 8:31—36

"I am with you always, even to the end of the age."

MATTHEW 28:20

Morning

. . . .

I Believe . . .

I believe with all my heart that God is both loving and sovereign. . . .

I believe that God's fiery love for us is so overpowering that He willingly allowed His own Son to walk the hardest mile of all, in human shoes, to pay for our sin.

I believe that Christ chose to endure the most devastating agony and death any man or woman will ever face so that you and I can be forgiven.

I believe that when we weep, God catches every tear.

I believe that no pain is wasted, and that even out of the greatest tragedies, God has promised He will bring good.

I believe that you have never lived an unloved moment in your life.

I believe He has been there too. You are not alone! You were not alone then, you are not alone now, and He will never, *ever* leave you.

SHEILA WALSH

God Loves Broken People

"Teacher, I brought You my son, who has a
mute spirit. And wherever it seizes him, it
throws him down; he foams at the mouth,
gnashes his teeth, and becomes rigid." . . .
[Jesus] asked his father, "How long has
this been happening to him?"
And he said, "From childhood. And often he has
thrown him both into the fire and into the water
to destroy him. But if You can do anything, have
compassion on us and help us."
Jesus said to him, "If you can believe, all
things are possible to him who believes."
Immediately the father of the child cried out and said
with tears, "Lord, I believe; help my unbelief!"

MARK 9:17—18, 21—24

"Thomas, because you have seen Me, you
have believed. Blessed are those who have
not seen and yet have believed."

JOHN 20:29

Glorify God in the Mundane

In a million unique ways—as we change diapers, eat dinner, return e-mails, pay the bills—we are to be evidence of God. Jesus factored in the mundane. . . . Embrace the common: a Sunday afternoon watching sports, Starbucks with a friend, cooking dinner for a neighbor, taking the dog for a walk, heading to a job that is making you more humble and needy because it is so unfulfilling. . . .

Do your everyday and your ordinary. Godliness is found and formed in those places. No man or woman greatly used by God has escaped them. Great men and women of God have transformed the mundane, turning neighborhoods into mission fields, parenting into launching the next generation of God's voices, legal work into loving those most hurting, waiting tables into serving and loving in such a way that people see our God.

Jesus says the way we glorify God . . . is by accomplishing the work God gives us to do. Jesus glorified His Father on earth by doing that very thing.

JENNIE ALLEN

Anything

Evening

. . . .

As the elect of God, holy and beloved, put on
tender mercies, kindness, humility, meekness,
longsuffering; bearing with one another, and
forgiving one another, if anyone has a complaint
against another; even as Christ forgave you, so you
also must do. But above all these things put on love,
which is the bond of perfection. . . . And whatever
you do in word or deed, do all in the name of the Lord
Jesus, giving thanks to God the Father through Him.

COLOSSIANS 3:12—14, 17

Teach me Your way, O LORD;
I will walk in Your truth;
Unite my heart to fear Your name.

PSALM 86:11

We all, with unveiled face, beholding as in
a mirror the glory of the Lord, are being
transformed into the same image from glory
to glory, just as by the Spirit of the Lord.

2 CORINTHIANS 3:18

751

Christ Our Hope

Authentic hope is not dependent on what we hope for but on the One we hope in. Circumstances always change, but Christ alone is unchanging. When He is the object of our hope, we will not be shaken; but when we rely on people or events to secure our hope, we will continually find ourselves walking on shifting, sinking sand. The Scripture says that hope does not disappoint; therefore, we can confidently trust Christ, our hope and the anchor for our souls—sure and steadfast.

HEATHER MERCER
Women of Faith Devotional Bible

Evening

. . . .

Let us hold fast the confession of our hope without
wavering, for He who promised is faithful.

HEBREWS 10:23

Hope does not disappoint, because the love
of God has been poured out in our hearts
by the Holy Spirit who was given to us.

ROMANS 5:5

This hope [in God's promises] we have as an
anchor of the soul, both sure and steadfast.

HEBREWS 6:19

Acknowledgments

Grateful acknowledgment is made to the following authors and publishers for permission to reprint copyrighted material.

100 Favorite Bible Verses. Thomas Nelson, 2011.

Allen, Jennie. *Anything: The Prayer That Unlocked My God and My Soul*. Thomas Nelson, 2012.

Allen, Jennie. *Stuck: The Places We Get Stuck & the God Who Sets Us Free*. Thomas Nelson, 2011.

Babbitt, Kathy. *Habits of the Heart: Self-Discipline for the Not-So-Disciplined*. Wolgemuth & Hyatt, 1990.

Bacher, June Masters. *The Quiet Heart: Daily Devotionals for Women*. Harvest House, 1988.

Bacher, June Masters. *Quiet Moments for Women*. Harvest House, 1979.

Barnhill, Julie Ann. *Exquisite Hope*. Tyndale, 2005.

Barnhill, Julie Ann. *Scandalous Grace*. Tyndale, 2003.

Bateman, Lana, Lynda Hunter Bjorklund, Dee Brestin, Cynthia Heald, Nicole Johnson, Denise Jones, Babbie Mason, Heather Mercer, Sara Trollinger, Luci Swindoll. *Women of Faith Devotional Bible: A Message of Grace & Hope for Every Day*. Thomas Nelson, 2003.

Bishop, Jenna Lucado (with Max Lucado). *Redefining Beautiful: What God Sees When God Sees You*. Thomas Nelson, 2009.

Boom, Corrie Ten. *Messages of God's Abundance*. Zondervan, 2003.

Briscoe, Jill. *Heartstrings: Finding a Song When You've Lost Your Joy*. Tyndale, 1998.

Briscoe, Jill. *Here Am I, Lord . . . Send Somebody Else*. Thomas Nelson, 2004.

Briscoe, Jill. *Quiet Times with God*. Tyndale, 1997.

Burroughs, Esther. *Splash the Living Water: Turning Daily Interruptions into Life-Giving Encounters*. Thomas Nelson, 1999.

Carlberg, Jan. *The Hungry Heart: Daily Devotions from the Old Testament*. Hendrickson, 2005.

A Charles Dickens Devotional (Devotional Classics Series). Thomas Nelson, 2012.

Chole, Alicia Britt. *Pure Joy*. Thomas Nelson, 2003. www.aliciachole.com.

Chole, Alicia Britt. *Sitting in God's Sunshine: Resting in His Love*. Thomas Nelson, 2005. www.aliciachole.com.

Clairmont, Patsy. *All Cracked Up: Experiencing God in the Broken Places*. Thomas Nelson, 2006.

Clairmont, Patsy. *Contagious Joy*. Thomas Nelson, 2006.

Clairmont, Patsy. *I Second That Emotion: Untangling Our Zany Feelings*. Thomas Nelson, 2008.

Clairmont, Patsy. *Stained Glass Hearts: Seeing Life from a Broken Perspective*. Thomas Nelson, 2011.

Cloninger, Claire. *When God Shines Through*. W Pub Group, 1994.

Countryman, Jack. *The Hope of Christmas*. Thomas Nelson, 2012.

Davis, Ken. *Fully Alive: A Journey That Will Change Your Life*. Thomas Nelson, 2012.

Davis, Ken. *Lighten Up!: Great Stories from One of America's Favorite Storytellers*. Zondervan, 2000.

Davis, Verdell. *Riches Stored in Secret Places*. W Pub Group, 1994.

Dawn, Marva. *Morning by Morning: Daily Meditations from the Writings of Marva J. Dawn*. William B. Eerdmans Publishing Company, 2001.

Dawn, Marva. *To Walk and Not Faint: A Month of Meditations on Isaiah 40*. William B. Eerdmans Publishing Company, 1997.

Demoss, Nancy Leigh. *Lies Women Believe: And the Truth that Sets Them Free*. Moody Publishers, 2006.

Drennan, Miriam. *Devotions for the Beach . . . and Days You Wish You Were There*. Thomas Nelson, 2012.

Elliot, Elisabeth. *Keep a Quiet Heart*. Revell, 2004. elisabethelliot.org.

Elliot, Elisabeth. *On Asking God Why: And Other Reflections on Trusting God in a Twisted World*. Revell, 2006.

Elliot, Elisabeth. *A Path Through Suffering: Discovering the Relationship Between God's Mercy and Our Pain*. Regal, 2003. elisabethelliot.org.

Elliot, Elisabeth. *The Shaping of a Christian Family: How My Parents Nurtured My Faith*. Revell, 2005. elisabethelliot.org.

Gaither, Gloria. *Decisions: A Christian's Approach to Making Right Choices*. Word Books, 1982. Copyright © 1982 Gloria Gaither. All rights reserved. Used by permission.

George, Denise. *Cultivating a Forgiving Heart: Forgiveness Frees Us to Flourish*. Zondervan, 2005.

Goff, Bob. *Love Does: Discover a Secretly Incredible Life in an Ordinary World*. Thomas Nelson, 2012.

Haggard, Gayle. *A Life Embraced: A Hopeful Guide for the Pastor's Wife*. WaterBrook, 2005.

Hale, Mandy. *The Single Woman: Life, Love, and a Dash of Sass*. Thomas Nelson, 2013.

Hampton, Mary. *Tea and Inspiration: A Collection of Tea Celebrations to Share with Your Lord and Your Loved Ones*. Thomas Nelson, 1995.

Harper, Lisa. *Stumbling into Grace: Confessions of a Sometimes Spiritually Clumsy Woman*. Thomas Nelson, 2011.

Hartnett, Kevin. *The Heavens: Intimate Moments with Your Majestic God*. Thomas Nelson, 2011.

Higgs, Liz Curtis. *Only Angels Can Wing It: The Rest of Us Have to Practice*. Thomas Nelson, 1995.

Jackson, Denise. *It's All About Him: Finding the Love of My Life*. Thomas Nelson, 2007.

Jackson, Denise. *The Road Home: Footsteps of Faith, Hope, and Love*. Thomas Nelson, 2008.

A Jane Austen Devotional (Devotional Classics Series). Thomas Nelson, 2012.

Jenkins, Barbara. *Wit and Wisdom for Women: A Book of Quotations*. Dover Publications, 2000.

Jenkins, Michelle Clark. *She Speaks: Wisdom from the Women of the Bible for Modern Black Women*. Thomas Nelson, 2013

Jeremiah, David. *The 12 Ways of Christmas*. Thomas Nelson, 2008.

Johnson, Barbara, Luci Swindoll, and Thelma Wells (Women of Faith). *Boundless Love*. Zondervan, 2001.

Johnson, Barbara, Luci Swindoll, and Thelma Wells. *Extravagant Grace*. Zondervan, 2000.

Johnson, Barbara. *I'm So Glad You Told Me What I Didn't Wanna Hear*. Thomas Nelson, 2006.

Johnson, Barbara. *Mama, Get the Hammer! There's a Fly on Papa's Head!* Thomas Nelson, 1994.

Johnson, Barbara. *Stick a Geranium in Your Hat and Be Happy*. Word, 1987.

Kent, Carol. *Secret Longings of the Heart*. Copyright © 1991. Used by permission of NavPress, All Rights Reserved. www.navpress.com (1-800-366-7788).

Lanier, Laura Lewis. *All Things Bright and Beautiful*. C. R. Gibson Co., 1993.

Larson, Catherine Claire. *Waiting in Wonder: Growing in Faith While You're Expecting*. Thomas Nelson, 2013.

Little Seeds of Hope. Thomas Nelson, 2013.

Living God's Way: Inspirational Insights for the Path Ahead. Thomas Nelson, 2007.

Lotz, Anne Graham. *I Saw the Lord*. Zondervan, 2007.

MacDonald, Gail. *High Call, High Privilege: A Pastor's Wife Speaks to Every Woman in a Place of Responsibility*. Hendrickson Publishers, 1998.

Marshall, Catherine. *A Closer Walk*. Revell, 1986.

More Than a Bucket List. Thomas Nelson, 2012.

Omartian, Stormie. *The Power of a Praying Wife*. Harvest House, 2007.

Omartian, Stormie. *Praying God's Will for Your Life*. Thomas Nelson, 2001.

Omartian, Stormie. *Seven Prayers That Will Change Your Life Forever*. Thomas Nelson, 2006.

Ortlund, Anne. *Disciplines of the Heart*. W Publishing, 1989.

Ortlund, Anne. *Fix Your Eyes on Jesus*. Royal Publishers, 1994.

Parsons, Marian (Miss Mustard Seed). *Inspired You: Breathing New Life into Your Heart and Home*. Thomas Nelson, 2012.

Patty, Sandi. *Layers: Uncovering and Celebrating God's Original Idea of Me*. Thomas Nelson, 2008.

Pearcey, Nancy. *Total Truth: Liberating Christianity from Its Cultural Captivity*. © 2004. Used by permission of Crossway, a publishing ministry of Good News Publishers, Wheaton, IL 60187, www.crossway.org.

Renfroe, Anita. *The Purse-Driven Life: It Really Is All About Me*. Copyright © 2005. Used by permission of NavPress, All Rights Reserved. www.navpress.com (1-800-366-7788).

Rinehart, Paula. *Strong Women, Soft Hearts*. Thomas Nelson, 2001.

Rothschild, Jennifer. *Lessons I Learned in the Dark: Steps to Walking by Faith, Not by Sight*. Multnomah, 2002.

Schaeffer, Edith. *The Tapestry*. Word, 1981.

Silvious, Jan. *Big Girls Don't Whine: Getting On with the Great Life God Intends*. Thomas Nelson, 2003.

Silvious, Jan. *Look at It This Way: Straightforward Wisdom to Put Life in Perspective*. Thomas Nelson, 2004.

Silvious, Jan. *Moving Beyond the Myths*. Moody, 2001.

Skoglund, Elizabeth. *Safety Zones*. Word, 1986.

Swindoll, Luci. *You Bring the Confetti, God Brings the Joy*. Thomas Nelson, 1997.

Tada, Joni Eareckson. *Diamonds in the Dust: 366 Sparkling Devotions*. Zondervan, 1993.

Tada, Joni Eareckson. *Seeking God: My Journey of Prayer and Praise*. Wolgemuth & Hyatt, 1991.

TerKeurst, Lysa. *Becoming More Than a Good Bible Study Girl*. Zondervan, 2009.

TerKeurst, Lysa. *Living Life on Purpose: Discovering God's Best for Your Life*. Moody, 2000.

TerKeurst, Lysa. *Radically Obedient, Radically Blessed*. Harvest House, 2003.

TerKeurst, Lysa. *Unglued: Making Wise Choices in the Midst of Raw Emotions*. Zondervan, 2012.

Thomas, Angela. *My Single Mom Life: Stories and Practical Lessons for Your Journey*. Thomas Nelson, 2008.

Trobisch, Ingrid. *The Hidden Strength: Rooted in the Security of God's Love*. Thomas Nelson, 1988.

Walsh, Sheila. *The Best Devotions of Sheila Walsh*. Zondervan, 2001.

Walsh, Sheila. *God Loves Broken People: And Those Who Pretend They're Not.* Thomas Nelson, 2012.

Walsh, Sheila. *The Shelter of God's Promises.* Thomas Nelson, 2011.

Wangerin, Walter, Jr. *Preparing for Jesus: Meditations on the Coming of Christ, Advent, Christmas and the Kingdom.* Zondervan, 1999.

Wells, Thelma. *Listen Up, Honey: Good News for Your Soul.* Thomas Nelson, 2006.

Whelchel, Mary. *How to Thrive from 9 to 5.* Word, 1995.

Williams, Leslie. *Night Wrestling.* Thomas Nelson, 2008.

Williams, Leslie. *Seduction of the Lesser Gods.* Thomas Nelson, 1998.

Wood, Christine. *Character Witness: How Our Lives Can Make a Difference in Evangelism.* IVP Books, 2003.

Wright, Bryant. *Right from the Heart.* Thomas Nelson, 2011.

Wubbels, Lance. *Jesus, the Ultimate Gift.* Thomas Nelson, 2011.

Yates, Susan Alexander. *A House Full of Friends: How to Like the Ones You Love.* Focus on the Family, 1995.

Your Promises from God Today. Thomas Nelson, 2013.